WARRIORS AND CHURCHMEN
IN THE HIGH MIDDLE AGES

WARRIORS AND
CHURCHMEN IN THE
HIGH MIDDLE AGES

ESSAYS PRESENTED TO KARL LEYSER

EDITED BY

TIMOTHY REUTER

THE HAMBLEDON PRESS
LONDON AND RIO GRANDE

Published by The Hambledon Press, 1992

102 Gloucester Avenue, London NW1 8HX (U.K.)

P.O. Box 162, Rio Grande, Ohio 45672 (U.S.A.)

ISBN 1 85285 063 9

A description of this book is available from
The British Library and The Library of Congress

Printed on acid-free paper and bound
in Great Britain by Cambridge University Press

Contents

Preface

Most of the forty years of Karl Leyser's academic career have been spent as a teacher at Magdalen. Although within Oxford he soon acquired a reputation as an inspiring if formidable teacher, and though his early articles and reviews already showed the power and originality of his work, it was not really until the publication of *Rule and Conflict in an Early Medieval Society* in 1979 that a wider audience became aware of his scholarship. Honours and recognition then accumulated rapidly: Chichele Professor of History at Oxford; Fellow of the British Academy; member of the advisory boards of German historical institutions in Göttingen, London and Munich; corresponding member of the Monumenta Germaniae Historica; visiting professor at Harvard and at Berkeley. Inplanning a Festschrift to mark his seventieth birthday we decided to restrict participation to those medievalists who had been taught extensively by Karl, either as undergraduates or as graduates. This circle is not a vast one; though Karl has taught great numbers of undergraduates, he has not had many research students (probably because his main field of interest, medieval German history, has seemed too distant to most aspiring medievalists) and he has certainly founded no school. I hope that the quality, range and approach of the contributions will nevertheless be felt to be an adequate tribute to a scholar who, despite being inimitable in both his working methods and his originality, has still been among the most influential medievalists in Britain since the war.

The present volume contains, with only minor editorial changes, the essays as they were presented to Karl at a dinner in Worcester College on 27 October 1990. Editing a Festschrift at a distance of several hundred miles has not been easy for editor or edited. I should like here to thank the contributors for their patience and Martin Sheppard for helping to keep the show on the road. My thanks also go to James Campbell, Gerald Harriss and Peter Lewis, who got the show on the road in the first place, and to Henrietta Leyser for her encouragement and her help with the bibliography.

Timothy Reuter   Munich, April 1992

Karl Leyser. *Drawing by Peter Greenham 1991.*

Karl Leyser as a Teacher

Gerald Harriss

Although these essays are a tribute to Karl Leyser as a scholar, all the contributors have been his pupils, as undergraduates or graduates, and owe their emergence as historians in no small degree to Karl's teaching.[1] It is therefore proper to recall, however imperfectly, what impressed and influenced us in the hours we spent in his rooms in the New Buildings at Magdalen. A great part of Karl's life has been spent there: from Michaelmas term 1948, when he became a fellow, until Hilary term 1984, when he moved to All Souls. Throughout those years he fulfilled, term by term, the duties of a tutorial fellow and university lecturer. The relentless routine of those duties is worth insisting on, because only someone who was highly professional in his teaching but whose teaching was never merely professional could have continued to nurture successive generations of scholars.

Karl Leyser has been a remarkable teacher in many ways. In the first place he has taught over an impressive range. For most of us it was Karl's teaching of 'Historical Geography' and 'Einhard' in the old History Prelim which first fired our enthusiasm for the middle ages. Thereafter whichever paper in European history we took, from the age of the Visigoths to that of Luther, we came under his jurisdiction, as did many for the first paper in English history up to the accession of Edward III. For as long as 'Stubbs' Select Charters' remained the required discipline for all medievalists he guided strong and weak alike through the technical problems of Anglo-Saxon laws and Henry II's assizes with all the minutiae of scholarly controversy about them; then, as the first small breeze of syllabus change was felt, he was much sought after for teaching on the new and highly popular 'Crusades' further subject; finally, when the 'Carolingian Renaissance' entered the syllabus, he taught and lectured on the texts, vividly conveying the wealth and symbolism of Charlemagne's palace and church at Aachen. His teaching for these

---

[1] This account draws on the recollections of a number of pupils.

'further subjects' brought him many pupils from outside Magdalen as, to a lesser degree, did that for special subjects. As an undergraduate he had taken Sir Maurice Powicke's 'Church and State under Edward I', and his very first task as a tutor was to teach this and 'Stubbs' Charters' to those of us whom, a year earlier, he had sat next to in hall at low table. We at least felt assured that the path to a brilliant first was well mapped. Eventually he introduced a special subject reflecting his own interests, on 'Gregory VII and Henry IV', which he taught for the rest of his career as a tutor. Yet another side of his character was engaged by the special subject on 'The History of War', for which he delighted to take pupils through Clausewitz. Finally throughout his years as a tutor he instructed countless undergraduates patiently but with relish in the thought of Aristotle, Hobbes and Rousseau, and shared with a more select group his enthusiasm for Aquinas and Marsiglio. All this required a huge investment in reading, thinking, and preparation, quite apart from the intellectual demands of switching between one and another of these subjects in the course of a morning. In fact it has always been an outstanding quality of Karl's teaching that in his mind, and in his talking, these were not compartmentalised subjects. Quite unselfconsciously he would move from one period to another, making connections, drawing analogies, re-interpreting particular situations and particular characters as they were caught up in the wide sweep of historical comparisons.

The great width of his reading also produced extraordinarily evocative and memorable vignettes. The scene at Canossa, or an encounter between St. Hugh of Lincoln and Henry II, or the meeting of an Amglo-Saxon court would be evoked with an extraordinary sense of situation. Coupled with this was the ability to select a single, often obscure, fact and make it tellingly illustrate a large theme. In this Karl was drawing on his extensive reading in the chronicles and his impressive memory, but it also reflected not only what but how he read. His alertness to what was significant, because unusual and illuminating, meant that his learning could be distilled into the selection of a few telling points. This was a lesson in understanding, not accumulating, detail. As well as fixing a particular truth indelibly in the mind, such *exempla* taught us where to look, how to look, and what to look for. Above all one became aware of the relation between the source and the events: the viewpoint of Thietmar or William of Malmesbury was as important as what they were describing. Thus although historical scenes and figures were vividly recreated they were not romanticised. One remembers searing accounts of the volcanic and impulsive Gregory VII, not merely reprimanding but cursing, or of the brutal standards of sexuality which provided the backdrop to Catharism's paradoxical appeal to women, or of the origins of the Spanish pogroms. In a lighter and more sardonic vein there would be references to the misdemeanours of Charlemagne's unhappy daughters or to the humanists' (whether of the twelfth or fifteenth century) enjoyment of material success: 'with their large and sumptuous book collections, their furs and fat incomes, they were not exactly hermits or ascetics: they started at the bottom and liked what they got'. Nor was the acerbity and the sarcasm just for effect. We were taught insistently to look behind renaissances, spiritual movements, and political events to material circumstances and interests – population pressure, patronage, the uncertainty of harvests, the church's need for land, and the nobility's for plunder. More recent generations of pupils were directed to the works of Evans-Pritchard and other anthropologists for an understanding of the peace in the feud and the reciprocity of gift giving in the earlier centuries.

The width and profundity of Karl's own experience itself led pupils to a deeper insight into human nature and activity. Here his own background was important in at least three respects. First there was his foreignness. To a provincial English schoolboy in the fifties who had never known anyone who did not have four English grandparents, Karl's appearance, verve, and excited (if at times unintelligible) mode of expressing himself all came as a considerable shock. His rich and fluent, but distinctively continental, use of English fascinated and compelled attention. It gave his learning a touch of the exotic, but more important was the sense that beyond the learning and behind the man there stood centuries of European culture which, in an unnerving and enviable way, Karl was part of and most of us were not. Just to listen to Karl was to be invited and required to transcend one's mental horizons. Secondly his personal history made him acutely aware of the disruptive passions in human nature and society. His language was highly charged with phrases which evoked the violence and intensity of the struggles for power and survival within his period: 'profound cleavages', 'terrifying threats', 'urgent need to create a historical past', 'arrogant and harsh ruling class', 'encircling and overwhelming', 'brutal and bloody minded'. Thirdly there were his own experiences in the war, which gave him an insight into the military mind and military practicalities. The reality and importance of military operations was forcefully brought home as he crawled over a map on the floor whilst describing campaigns, or the battlefield of the Lech or of Hastings. To the influence he thus exerted on some of his pupils this volume happily bears witness.

It is evident that much of what we have learnt from Karl has been learnt from the man: from what Karl is, how he talks, and how he unconsciously reveals his own reading, thinking, and experience. But it would be wrong, of course, to give the impression that he never consciously taught. Something must now be said of his methods. Usually he would have an essay read, listening attentively from his big armchair and occasionally interjecting. He was a generous listener, receiving work with a comforting, usually rather elaborate respect. One took to watching his face for the glow of enthusiasm that always greeted a good point, or the gently sardonic smile that heralded a fruitful disagreement, or the grave nodding that accompanied some unexceptionable but unoriginal truth. Very occasionally he would pay the ultimate compliment of reaching to the floor for a pad of paper to jot down a point that seemed worthy of future reference. Sometimes his verdict could be extravagant: 'My goodness, never have I heard such an essay', or the like. Such rhetoric was doubtless not meant to be taken literally, nor was it so received; but the generous spirit in which it was offered, with a desire to encourage and reward effort, evoked a pupil's warm gratitude. But immature attempts to shock or impress by clever perversity evoked disapproval, almost outrage. A scholarship candidate who was maintaining to his interviewers that Luther and Zwingli were politicians without firm religious convictions who would never lose an opportunity for the sake of a doctrine, suddenly found himself confronted by Karl, rising to his feet from behind a pile of books and scripts to declaim: '*Hoc est enim corpus meum*'.

When it came to giving his own views on a problem, his style – at least in the fifties – was assured and crisp, with a recognisable touch of the military about it. Later he was a more thoughtful and pensive interlocutor whose long silences were seen by some pupils as Karl's own unconscious equivalent of the *terror regalis disciplinae*. Often an essay would provoke an expansive discourse, delivered standing at his mantelpiece in front of the gas fire. It would flow around the topics raised, sometimes touching them only obliquely, always enhancing the understanding or sharpening one's vision of the period. It was the startling freshness of what he said or the irreverence with which he said it which commanded attention. 'The Cistercians were almost selfish in their spirituality, closing their doors on the rest of the world'; 'Castile was inward-looking because there was so much to be aggressive against at home: the land, the sheep, the Moslems and Jews, Portugal and Aragon'; 'To maintain their vigorous liturgy the Cluniacs really did need their seventeen ways of preparing fish and their Benedictine. For their task was similar to that of carrying out unceasing choir practice, night and day.' Although there might be little in the way of dialogue, one still felt that one's mind had been addressed and stretched. In no way had one's contribution been discounted; quite the reverse, for Karl brought to his encounters with us the same attentive sympathy and the same selfless dedication with which he listened to the voice of a Thietmar or a Widukind. Finally came the bibliography for the next essay. This was usually extensive: as many as fifty titles, dictated item by item in quick succession and with many pertinent animadversions. Some titles were revealed by later inspection to comprise dozens of volumes. It was not that Karl expected us to read each one, but it was important to be aware that the subject was vast, intricate and had attracted the best minds, and hence was worthy of intellectual effort. The list would range over many languages; indeed one pupil was asked (whether in earnest, jest, or desperation was never clear) if, perchance, he read Czech.

In some subjects written work on the texts had to be handed in, and this would be returned covered in pencilled if barely legible comments in which Karl's vast and recondite learning was fully evident. Those on passages from 'Stubbs' Charters' proved of lasting value when the recipient found himself teaching that venerated text many years later. When it came to formal lectures some of his exuberance and spontaneity was kept under check, though his improvised pursuit of themes and ideas which sprang to mind while talking often proved immensely fruitful. Karl never talked down; much was compressed into the hour, and detail was important to him. Yet he retained his audience, because here, as nowhere else, could one gain a genuine understanding of the problems. As always, he approached these through the texts, by bringing out their nuances, by pointing to what they did not say as much as what they did, and by placing each work within (and using it to reveal) a wider literary and political setting. Nor did he spare us the difficult problems, beginning one lecture by amending his words of the previous week: new analysis of an erasure in the Salzburg Annals had reopened the whole question of dating. To the first-year student this kind of thing was disconcerting, but it also gave a first glimpse of what research was about. Those postgraduates whom Karl supervised quickly became his friends. He was ever solicitous about their emotional and financial well-being, extending to them the warmth of his family life and lending great support and sympathy at times of discouragement. From the first he treated a research pupil as a fellow historian on an equal footing with himself. If at times this meant perhaps undue reluctance to challenge a researcher's different approach or interpretation, it could also do much to build up self-confidence and

develop self-criticism. Karl usually confined his criticism to detail, or to
pointing to what had been missed or misinterpreted in a particular source;
often one had to listen carefully to realise that what seemed like a gentle
warning was in fact a fundamental criticism. His deep involvement with
the sources enabled him to point to an aspect overlooked, a misplaced
emphasis, or a fruitful line of enquiry. He did not press for written work
at appointed times but was content to let it mature. When it came he
read it with painstaking diligence, checking every reference and bringing
to bear on what one had written the full critical acumen with which he
confronted a historical text.

Karl's intellectual generosity to his pupils involved massive demands
on his own time. Two-hour tutorials were common; they could flow on past
the appointed hour for dinner and pupils would find themselves being
taken to eat in the town, where his animation and erudition never flagged.
He greatly enjoyed entertaining. There were regular end of term parties
for all pupils and also particular occasions as when, on the evening before
Prelims, he invited Bruce McFarlane and three undergraduates to dinner
in his room – almost prejudicing (though perhaps ensuring) the excellent
results attained in next morning's exam. These individual memories of
many different types of encounters in Karl's rooms all have one thing in
common: the room itself. Its magnificent eighteenth-century proportions
were a fit setting for the sophistication of the furniture and carpets and
the many books. These were double-stacked on the shelves and piled
on tables and the floor. The floor itself was strewn with notes and files
in Karl's handwriting, half-written reviews, half-read books, half-eaten
slippers, old newspapers and theatre programmes. It made an enormous
impression on undergraduates, who were only surprised that there was
so little change in these piles in the course of the term. We were naive
enough to imagine that tutors had time to do research in term time.

Karl loved teaching and had a flair for it. He has been a highly individual,
even idiosyncratic teacher, but disciplined and effective. He attracted
pupils to the parts of the syllabus he taught and they got good results
on these papers in Schools. But the strong influence he has exerted was
not through the originality of his character or even the extent of his
erudition, but because he invested what he taught with significance: he
made it matter. This was firstly because he lived the past, and recreated its
experience, with the freshness and insights of a fine historical sensitivity.
Secondly, for him being a historian is not just an enjoyable activity but
essential to his identity. He sees history as a discipline more demanding
(because more complex) than others and concerned with truths about

human society and personality. It has been a vocation; perhaps ultimately a philosophy of living. Even if we only sensed rather than fully grasped this, it compelled attention and respect, and invited a similar dedication. Of course the high seriousness of the subject did not mean that it should not be enjoyed. Karl's discourse was full of humour and light irony. Nor did it depersonalise relations with his pupils – on the contrary it enriched and fed them. All this has made his teaching fruitful – for himself as for others. At times in these years it seemed that he had become immersed in teaching to the exclusion of writing. Happily that eventually proved not to be so. And when his work began to appear in print, and much that we had been privileged to hear *ex ora* became the property of other scholars, it became clear that writing was just another dimension of that varied intellectual discourse and capacious mind of which our tutorials had given us a glimpse.

Bibliography of the Publications of Karl Leyser
(including longer reviews)

1 'Germany, History: The Tenth and Eleventh Centuries to 1056; The Conflict between Empire and Papacy; Germany and the Hohenstaufen', *Encyclopaedia Britannica* (Toronto, 1964), vol. 10, pp. 238–41, 241–42, 242–44.

2 'A Recent View of the German College of Electors', *Medium Aevum* 23 (1954), pp. 76–87 [Review article of C.C. Bayley, *The Formation of the German College of Electors in the Mid-Thirteenth Century*, (Toronto, 1949)].

3 'England and the Empire in the Early Twelfth Century', *Transactions of the Royal Historical Society,* fifth series 10 (1960), pp. 61–83; reprinted in no. 28, pp. 191–214.

4 Review: *Regesta Regum Anglo-Normannorum, 2: Regesta Henrici Primi 1100–1135*, edited by C. Johnson and H.A. Cronne (Oxford, 1956), *Medium Aevum* 29 (1960), pp. 211–15.

5 Review: *The Murder of Charles the Good by Galbert of Bruges*, translated with an introduction and notes by J.B. Ross (New York, 1960) *Medium Aevum* 32 (1963), pp. 52–53.

6 The Battle at the Lech, 955. A Study in Tenth-Century Warfare', *History* 50 (1965), pp. 1–25; reprinted in no. 28, pp. 43–67.

7 'The Polemics of the Papal Revolution', *Trends in Medieval Political Thought*, ed. B. Smalley (Oxford, 1965), pp. 42–64; reprinted in no. 28, pp. 138–60.

8 'Henry I and the Beginnings of the Saxon Empire', *EHR* 83 (1968), pp. 1–32; reprinted in no. 28, pp. 11–42.

9 'The German Aristocracy from the Ninth to the Early Twelfth Century. A Historical and Cultural Sketch', *Past and Present* 41 (1968), pp. 25–53; reprinted in no. 28, pp. 161–90.

10 Review: *Elenchus Fontium Historiae urbanae*, vol. 1, ed. B. Diestel-kamp, M. Martens, C. Van de Kieft and B. Fritz (Leiden, 1967), *Economic History Review,* second series 21 (1968), pp. 425–26.

11 'Maternal Kin in Early Medieval Germany', *Past and Present* 49 (1970), pp. 126–34.

12 Review: J. Fleckenstein, *Die Hofkapelle der deutschen Könige, ii: Die Hofkapelle im Rahmen der ottonisch-salischen Reichskirche* (Schriften der MGH 16/2, Stuttgart, 1966), *EHR* 85 (1970), pp. 113–18.

13 'The Tenth Century in Byzantine-Western Relationships', *Relations between East and West in the Middle Ages*, ed. D. Baker (Edinburgh, 1973), pp. 29–63; reprinted in no. 28, pp. 103–37.

14 'The Emperor Frederick II', *The Listener* August 16, 1973, reprinted in no. 28, pp. 269–76 [Review article of T.C. Van Cleve, *The Emperor Frederick II of Hohenstaufen* (Oxford, 1972)].

15 Review: W. Kienast, *Der Herzogstitel in Frankreich und Deutschland (9. bis 12. Jahrhundert)* (Munich, 1968), *EHR* 88 (1973), pp. 584–88.

16 Review: P.E. Schramm, *Kaiser, Könige und Päpste. Gesammelte Aufsätze*, vols. III, IV/1, IV/2 (Stuttgart, 1968–69), *EHR* 90 (1975), pp. 121–24.

17 'Frederick Barbarossa, Henry II and the Hand of St James', *EHR* 90 (1975), pp. 481–506; reprinted in no. 28, pp. 215–40.

18 'Bruce McFarlane, 1903–1966', *Proceedings of the British Academy* 62 (1976), pp. 485–507.

19 Review: W. Kienast, *Deutschland und Frankreich in der Kaiserzeit (900–1270)* (Monographien zur Geschichte des Mittelalters 9/1–3, Stutgart, 1974–75), *EHR* 93 (1978), pp. 846–51.

20 Review: W. Urban, *The Baltic Crusade* (De Kalb, 1975), *Times Literary Supplement*, no. 3995, p. 1254, October 27, 1978.

21 *Rule and Conflict in an Early Medieval Society Ottonian Saxony* (London: Edward Arnold, 1979), pp. x and 190.

22 eview: E. Christiansen, *The Northern Crusade: The Baltic and the Catholic Frontier, 1100–1525* (London, 1980), *Times Literary Supplement*, no. 4046, p. 1174, October 17, 1980.

23 'Ottonian Government', *EHR* 96 (1981), pp. 721–53; reprinted in no. 28, pp. 241–67.

24 The Anglo-Saxons at Home', *Anglo-Saxon Studies in Archaeology and History*, ed. D. Brown, J. Campbell and S.C. Hawkes (British Archaeological Reports, British Series 92, Oxford, 1981), pp. 237–42. [Review article of D. Whitelock *English Historical Documents, 1, c. 500–1042* (London, 2nd., edn., 1979)].

25 Review: *Famille et Parenté dans l'Occident Medieval*, ed. G. Duby and J. Le Goff (Rome, 1977), EHR 96 (1981), pp. 370–74.

26 Review: I.S. Robinson, *Authority and Resistance in the Investiture Contest* (Manchester, 1978), *EHR* 96 (1981), pp. 380–81.

27 Review: K. Jordan, *Heinrich der Löwe: Eine Biographie* (Munich, 1979), *EHR* 96 (1981), pp. 601–603.

28 *Medieval Germany and its Neighbours, 900–1250* (London: Hambledon Press, 1982), pp. xii and 288. [Collected papers with an index and some *additamenta*].

29 'The Tenth-Century Condition', in no. 28, pp. 1–10.

30 'Some Reflections on Twelfth-Century Kings and Kingship', in no. 28, pp. 241–68.

31 Review: *Die Urkunden der Burgundischen Rudolfinger*, ed. T. Schieffer and H.E. Mayer (Munich, 1977), *EHR* 97 (1982), pp. 113–16.

32 'Die Ottonen und Wessex', *Frühmittelalterliche Studien* 17 (1983), pp. 73–97.

33 'The Crisis of Medieval Germany', *Proceedings of the British Academy* 69 (1983), pp. 409–43.

34 Review: R. Hodges and D. Whitehouse, *Mohammed, Charlemagne and the Origins of Europe: Archaeology and the Pirenne Thesis* (London, 1983), *The Times Literary Supplement*, no. 4240, p. 758, July 6 1984.

35 'Early Medieval Canon Law and the Beginnings of Knighthood', *Institutionen, Kultur und Gesellschaft im Mittelalter: Festschrift für Josef Fleckenstein zu seinem 65. Geburtstag*, ed. L. Fenske, W. Rösener and T. Zotz (Sigmaringen, 1984), pp. 549–66.

36 *Herrschaft und Könflikt: König und Adel im Ottonischen Sachsen*
    (Veröffentlichungen des Max-Planck-Instituts für Geschichte 76,
    Göttingen, 1984), pp. 210 [German translation of no. 21].

37 'Liudprand of Cremona, Preacher and Homilist', *The Bible in the
    Medieval World: Essays in Memory of Beryl Smalley*, ed. K. Walsh
    and D. Wood (Studies in Church History, Subsidia 4, Oxford, 1985),
    pp. 43–60.

38 Review: M. Burleigh, *Prussian Society and the German Order: An
    Aristocratic Corporation in Crisis, c. 1410–1466* (Cambridge, 1984),
    Times Literary Supplement no. 4273, p. 206, February 22, 1985.

39 Review: F.J. Felten, *Abte und Laienäbte im Frankenreich: Studien
    zum Verhältnis von Staat und Kirche im früheren Mittelalter*
    (Monographien zur Geschichte des Mittelalters 20, Stuttgart, 1980),
    EHR 99 (1985), pp. 338–39.

40 *The Ascent of Latin Europe: An Inaugural Lecture Delivered before
    the University of Oxford on 7 November 1984* (Oxford: Clarendon
    Press, 1986), pp. 28.

41 Review: H. Fichtenau, *Lebensordnungen im 10. Jahrhundert* (Mono-
    graphien zur Geschichte des Mittelalters 30, Stuttgart, 1984),
    Francia 14 (1986) 708–10.

42 'John Michael Wallace-Hadrill (1916–85)', *EHR* 100 (1986),
    pp. 561–63; see also 'John Michael Wallace-Hadrill', in *Dictionary of
    National Biography, 1981–85*, ed. R. Blake and C.S. Nicholls (Oxford,
    1990), pp. 403–4.

43 'The Angevin Kings and the Holy Man', *St Hugh of Lincoln,* ed.
    H. Mayr-Harting (Oxford, 1987), pp. 49–73.

44 'Ends and Means in Liudprand of Cremona', *Byzantium and the
    West c. 850–c. 1200: Proceedings of the XVIII Spring Symposium
    of Byzantine Studies, Oxford 30th March–1st April 1984*, ed. J.D.
    Howard-Johnston (Amsterdam, 1988), pp. 119–43.

45 'Frederick Barbarossa and the Hohenstaufen Polity', *Viator* 19
    (1988), pp. 153–76.

46 Review: H. Zimmermann (ed.), *Papsturkunden, 896–1046,* 2 vols.
    (Vienna 1984–5), *Journal of Ecclesiastical History* 39 (1988) pp. 246–
    48.

47   Review: D. Abulafia, *Frederick II.* (Harmondsworth, 1988), *Times Literary Supplement*, January 6, 1989.

48   Review: *Die Urkunden Friedrichs I., 1168–1180*, ed. H. Appelt (MGH Die Urkunden der deutschen Könige und Kaiser 10/3, Hanover, 1985), *EHR* 105 (1990), pp. 394–96.

49   Review: M.J. Enright, *Iona, Tara and Soissons: The Origins of Royal Anointing* (Arbeiten zur Frühmittelalterforschung 17, Berlin 1985), *Speculum* 65 (1990) 149–50.

50   Review: M. Borgolte, *Die Grafen Alemanniens in merowingischer und karolingischer Zeit: eine Prosopographie* (Sigmaringen, 1986), *American Historical Review* 95 (1990), p. 1516.

51   'The Anglo-Norman Succession, 1120–25', *Anglo-Norman Studies* 13 (1991), pp. 225–41.

Abbreviations

AASS	*Acta Sanctorum*
Anglo-Norman Studies	*Proceedings of the Battle Conference on Anglo-Norman Studies* (Woodbridge, 1980–)
Birch	W. de G. Birch, *Cartularium Saxonicum*, 3 vols. (London 1885–99)
D, DD	Diploma(ta); the reference is by convention to the initial of the ruler's name, his number and the edition in the Diplomata series of the MGH; thus D H II 10 is no. 10 in the edition of Henry II's diplomata
DB	Domesday Book
EHR	*The English Historical Review*
MGH	Monumenta Germaniae Historica, with subseries:
SS	*Scriptores in folio*
SRG	*Scriptores rerum Germanicarum in usum scholarum*
Migne, PL	J.-P. Migne, *Patrologiae cursus completus*, 217 vols. (Paris, 1844–55)
Sawyer	P.H. Sawyer, *Anglo-Saxon Charters: An Annotated List and Bibliography* (Royal Historical Society Guides and Handbooks 8, London, 1968)

1

Church, Crown and Community: Public Work and Seigneurial Responsibilities at Rochester Bridge

Nicholas Brooks

The building and repair of bridges was a general public obligation in Anglo-Saxon England. Together with the other 'common burdens' of boroughwork and army-service, the duty to work on bridges was normally specified in royal diplomas as an obligation which took precedence over any immunity that the king might grant to an estate. From the mid eighth century in Mercian charters, from the late eighth in Kent and from the mid ninth century in Wessex, kings were concerned to insist that all land, even bookland, owed bridgework. The English kings of the tenth and eleventh centuries reiterated the threefold duty to serve at borough, bridge and in the army not only in their charters but also in lawcodes, and this *trimoda necessitas* is rightly regarded as one of the foundations of the Anglo-Saxon state.[1] Much debate has been devoted to Anglo-Saxon military obligations, in particular to elucidating the intriguing mixture of

---

[1] W.H. Stevenson, 'Trinoda Necessitas', *EHR* 29 (1914), pp. 689–703; N.P. Brooks, 'The Development of Military Obligations in 8th- and 9th-century England', *England before the Conquest: Studies Presented to D. Whitelock*, ed. P. Clemoes and K. Hughes (Cambridge, 1971), pp. 69–84; H.R. Loyn, *The Governance of Anglo-Saxon England, 500–1087* (London, 1984), pp. 31–34. J. Campbell, 'Was it Infancy in England? Some Questions of Comparison', *England and her Neighbours, 1066–1453: Essays in Honour of Pierre Chaplais*, ed. M. Jones and M. Vale (London, 1989), pp. 1–19.

public or 'national' obligations with private, seigneurial or 'feudal' ones;[2] much has also been learnt from excavation about the changing nature of the burghal defences provided by this system;[3] but almost nothing is known about bridgework, either about how it was levied, or about what bridges were actually built and repaired.

Both in the ninth century and in the reign of Æthelred the Unready it is clear that bridges had a crucial military role in closing rivers to Viking ships.[4] Moreover tenth-century charters often refer to boroughwork and bridgework as a joint service (*pontis arcisve coaedificatione*),[5] which suggests that *brycggeweorc* might be performed at bridges in, or adjacent to, the major English boroughs. Most boroughs were indeed situated on significant rivers, and it seems likely that bridge and borough were conceived as a single military and economic unit. Together they prevented the movement of enemy forces by land or by river; together they channelled men and goods into places where trade could not only be conducted safely but also exploited through the levying of tolls. Post-conquest sources hint at surviving arrangements for the repair of major burghal bridges. Thus Domesday Book tells us that for the repair of the bridge over the Dee at Chester (as of the city wall) one man was summoned from every hide in the shire.[6] The Anglo-Saxon Chronicle informs us that in 1097:

Many shires whose labour was due at London were hard pressed because of the wall that they built around the Tower and because of the bridge that was nearly all carried away by a flood . . . and many a man was oppressed thereby.[7]

[2] C.W. Hollister, *Anglo-Saxon Military Obligations* (Oxford, 1962); R.A. Brown, *Origins of English Feudalism* (London, 1973); R. Abels, *Lordship and Military Obligation in Anglo-Saxon England* (London, 1988).

[3] C.A.R. Radford, 'The Later Pre-Conquest Boroughs and their Defences', *Medieval Archaeology* 14 (1970), pp. 83–103; Idem, 'The Pre-Conquest Boroughs of England, 9th–11th Centuries', *Proceedings of the British Academy* 64 (1978), pp. 131–53; *Anglo-Saxon Towns in Southern England*, ed. J. Haslam (Chichester, 1984); *The Defence of Wessex: The Burghal Hidage and Anglo-Saxon Urbanisation*, ed. D. Hill and A. Rumble (Manchester, forthcoming).

[4] *Anglo-Saxon Chronicle: A Revised Translation*, ed. and trans. D. Whitelock *et al.* (London, 1961), *s.a.* 896A; M. Ashdown, *English and Norse Documents* (Cambridge, 1930), pp. 154–56.

[5] Birch 753, 758, 763, 764, 770, 775, 777, 789, 793 etc. (Sawyer 464, 463, 465, 467, 475, 485, 480, 491, 502).

[6] DB i, f. 262b; R.J. Stewart-Brown, 'Bridgework at Chester', *EHR* 54 (1939), pp. 83–87.

[7] *Anglo-Saxon Chronicle* (as n. 4), *s.a.* 1097.

As late as the fifteenth century the bridges at Huntingdon and at Nottingham were repaired in accordance with custom by 'the commonalty of the whole county' or by levying pontage on the whole shire.[8] Elsewhere, however, as at London between 1170 and 1209 and at Cambridge, probably rather later in the thirteenth century, the need to build an entirely new bridge brought such arrangements to an end. In their place the whole burden of repairing the new bridge was placed on a smaller number of bridge estates specifically designated for the purpose.[9]

There is, however, a single pre-Conquest document which provides details of how the burden of bridgework was in fact distributed among estates in the surrounding district. The early twelfth-century cartulary of the cathedral priory of Rochester, the *Textus Roffensis*, has preserved Old English and Latin versions of a document which assigns responsibility for the repair of each of nine piers and of lengths of the timber superstructure of a bridge over the Medway at Rochester to groups of estates in the vicinity of the city.[10] The factual information contained in the document, that is the estates assigned to the repair of each pier and the number of beams and the amount of planking required from them, are set out in the appendix at the end of this essay. The Latin version of the bridgework list has the same details and is clearly a translation from Old English, perhaps the work of the cartulist himself,[11] but considerable uncertainties have

[8] For Huntingdon, see *Calendar of Patent Rolls, 1441–46* (London, 1900), p. 206; for Nottingham, J.H. Round, 'Burhbot and Brigbot', *Family Origins and Other Studies* (London, 1930), pp. 252–66, at 262.

[9] For successive London bridges, see G. Home, *Old London Bridge* (London, 1931); B. Masters, *To God and the Bridge* (London, 1972); M.B. Honeybourne, 'The Pre-Norman Bridge of London', *Studies in London History Presented to P.E. Jones*, ed. A.J. Hollaender and W. Kellaway (London, 1969), pp. 17–39; T. Dyson, 'London and Southwark in the Seventh Century and Later', *Transactions of the London and Middlesex Archaeological Society* 31 (1980), pp. 83–95. For Cambridge, see *The Victoria County History of Cambridgeshire*, ed. J.P.C. Roach (London, 1959), vol. 3, pp. 2, 114 and the works cited there. For some perceptive remarks on Anglo-Saxon bridgework, see Campbell, 'Infancy?' (as n. 1), p. 4.

[10] Maidstone, Kent County Record Office, DRc/R1, f. 164–67; facsimile in *Textus Roffensis*, part 2, ed. P.H. Sawyer (Early English Manuscripts in Facsimile 11, Copenhagen, 1962). The Old English text is edited by A.J. Robertson, *Anglo-Saxon Charters* (Cambridge, 1939), no. 52; the Latin by W. Lambarde, *Perambulation of Kent* (London, 1576), pp. 419–24 and T. Hearne, *Textus Roffensis* (Rochester, 1720), pp. 379–82.

[11] The notes in Robertson, *Charters*, pp. 351–55 establish that the Latin text is secondary, which (as Mr. P.R. Kitson has kindly pointed out to me) is confirmed by the numerous estate names with weak first elements ending in *-an* or *-a* in the OE version, but in *-a* or *-e* in the Latin. Robertson doubted whether the OE version was the source because

attached to the date and authority of the English text. Like most Old English administrative memoranda it is undated and is simply entitled: *þis is þære bricce geweorc on Hrovecæstre* ('This is [the] work for the bridge at Rochester'). However, the arrangements that it lays down remained in force until the late fourteenth century; whenever it was necessary to determine responsibility for repairs to any part of the bridge, a jury of 'good men' of the county was required to swear to the arrangements defined in the *Textus Roffensis*.[12] The lists of estates assigned to particular piers were therefore subject to revisions to take account of changed circumstances and landholding in subsequent periods. Thus four names have been erased from the estates allocated to the fourth pier, which is said to be 'the king's'. The missing names can, however, be supplied from a version of the document preserved in the early fourteenth-century cartulary from Christ Church, Canterbury (London, British Library, MS Cotton Galba E. IV, f. 20).[13]

More worryingly, the texts of the first halves of both the Latin and the Old English versions of the document in the *Textus Roffensis* are written on replacement leaves, not by the original scribe of *c.* 1120 but in a hand from the end of the twelfth century. It is likely that these leaves were inserted in order to allow adjustments to be made to the estates assigned to one or more of the first four piers. Very probably the changes were to the bishop of Rochester's own piers, that is to pier 1 and pier 3, but we

of its use of the word *per* ('pier'), a loan-word from Latin *pera*, which is not otherwise known until the fourteenth century but which could derive from the Latin text. In the absence of other early documents in English describing bridges, the non-appearance of this word is not, however, of any significance.

[12] See the inquests, commissions etc. into how the bridge should be repaired established in 1277, 1280, 1310/11, 1332, 1343, 1344, 1350, 1354, 1355, 1359, 1360, 1363, 1369, 1377 and 1382: *Calendar of Inquisitions Miscellaneous, 1219–1307* (London, 1916), no. 1066; *Calendar of Patent Rolls, 1272–81* (London, 1901), p. 414; *Calendar of Patent Rolls, 1307–13* (London, 1894), p. 331; *Calendar of Patent Rolls, 1330–34* (London, 1893), p. 348; *Calendar of Inquisitions Miscellaneous, 1307–49* (London, 1916), p. 459–60; *Calendar of Patent Rolls, 1343–45* (London, 1902), p. 425; *Calendar of Patent Rolls, 1348–50* (London, 1905), p. 526; *Calendar of Patent Rolls, 1354–58* (London, 1908), pp. 67, 230; *Calendar of Patent Rolls, 1358–61* (London, 1911), pp. 280, 485; *Calendar of Patent Rolls, 1361–64* (London, 1912), p. 444; *Calendar of Patent Rolls, 1367–70* (London, 1913), p. 343; *Calendar of Patent Rolls, 1377–81* (London, 1895), p. 53; *Calendar of Patent Rolls, 1381–85* (London, 1897), p. 136.

[13] As pointed out by G. Ward, 'The Lathe of Aylesford in 975', *Archaeologia Cantiana* 46 (1934), pp. 7–26; printed by Lambarde, *Perambulation* (as n. 10), pp. 425–26. The four erased estates are those asterisked in the appendix.

cannot tell whether the changes were a matter of erasure, of addition, or of the transfer of estates from one pier to another.[14] Since the text of the document's arrangements for piers 1 to 4 is broadly consistent in form and language with the second half of the document, it seems likely that the changes that necessitated the rewriting of the first half were limited. The fact remains that in the form in which we have it, the Rochester bridgework list is an Old English document, of which the first half is preserved in a text of *c*. 1200 and the second half in one of *c*. 1120.[15]

A document regulating bridgework at Rochester would be unlikely to have been drawn up in English very long after 1066. Indeed there are features of its Old English which enable the composition of the whole document to be placed in the first half of the eleventh century.[16] Scholars have hitherto arrived at a date of 973 × 988 for the bridgework list by comparing the properties assigned to the bishop of Rochester's piers with the known history of the estates of that see.[17] But that is a hazardous exercise. The history of the crucial estates (Fawkham, Snodland and Wouldham) is bedevilled by complex litigation in the late tenth century, so that it is difficult to disentangle exactly when particular properties were in episcopal, royal or lay hands.[18] Moreover several of the texts hitherto used to date Rochester's possession are now known to be forgeries, apparently of the late tenth or early eleventh century.[19] What is more, the

---

[14] The replacement leaf, f. 164, has the Latin text as far as . . . *de dudeslande* . . . (one of the estates assigned to the fourth pier). The replacement leaf, f. 166, has the OE text as far as . . . *þonne is sy fifte per þoes arcebiscope to*.

[15] The dating of the script of the replacement leaves is that of N.R. Ker, *Catalogue of Manuscripts containing Anglo-Saxon* (Oxford, 1957), p. 447. Mr. Kitson points out that the only spellings which might betray the scribe of *c*. 1200 occur under the first pier where the first *n* in *Frinondesbyrig* is a blunder, perhaps reflecting unease with the OE dipthong, and in *Cucclestane*, where the *cc* corresponds to OE *c* + a vowel. Otherwise nothing that he wrote is out of place in Old English of the early eleventh century.

[16] 11th-century forms to which Mr. Kitson draws my attention include the dative plurals in -*an*, never -*um*, weak genitive plurals without the final vowel, and the declension of *per* (nominative singular) with *peran* in the nominative plural. The second half of the document (from pier 5) has more Kentish forms than the first: *sy(o)* against *se(o)*, *ænde*, *dænewaru*.

[17] Robertson, *Charters*, p. 351; Ward, 'Lathe of Aylesford', p. 7.

[18] Robertson, *Charters*, nos. 41, 59; D. Whitelock, *Anglo-Saxon Wills* (Cambridge, 1930), no. 11; Sawyer 1458, 1457, 1511.

[19] For example the supposed grants of Malling by Eadmund and of Bromley by Edgar: A. Campbell (ed.), *Charters of Rochester* (Anglo-Saxon Charters 1, London, 1973), nos. 28, 29; Sawyer 514, 671.

two piers of the bishop are of course precisely those where the extant text was rewritten at the close of the twelfth century.

If we are to understand the Rochester bridgework list correctly, it is therefore wiser to start with the archbishop's piers (nos. 5 and 9), where we at least have the text as it was copied in *c.* 1120. The first two estates assigned to the fifth pier, Wrotham and Maidstone, were indeed major archiepiscopal manors which are likely to have been amongst the earliest possessions of that see.[20] But of the other eleven estates listed, the only Canterbury estate was East Peckham, which in 1066 was a manor of the monks of Christ Church and may have been granted to the cathedral community early in the reign of King Edgar by his grandmother, Eadgifu.[21] The other listed properties, in so far as they can be traced before 1066, were in the hands of lay nobles;[22] by 1086 many of them had come into the hands of Odo of Bayeux. The ninth pier presents a very similar picture. The first named estate, Fleet (that is Northfleet), was indeed an archiepiscopal manor, whilst the second and the seventh (Cliffe and Meopham) belonged to the Canterbury monks.[23] Neither the archbishop nor the monks are known ever to have had any interest in the remaining seven properties. Denton and Snodland, indeed, belonged to the bishop of Rochester.[24] It would seem clear that a pier was assigned to the archbishop, because the major and first-named estate was his. We need not assume that all the estates assigned to the fifth and ninth

[20] DB i, f. 3; N.P. Brooks, *The Early History of the Church of Canterbury* (Leicester, 1984), pp. 105–106.

[21] DB i, f. 4b; the grant of Peckham and other estates attributed to Eadgifu by the twelfth-century Christ Church cartularies (Birch 1065; Sawyer 1212) has no authority, but may derive from the community's commemoration of her anniversary.

[22] All belonged to lay nobles in 1066 according to Domesday Book. Wateringbury and Hadlow had been bequeathed to laymen by Brihtric and his wife, Ælfswith, in their will of 973 × 987 but with arrangements for the payment of two days' food-rent to Rochester cathedral. See Whitelock, *Wills* (as n. 18), no. 11 (Sawyer 1511). Nettlestead had been bequeathed by Ealdorman Ælfred to a layman in 871 × 889 with a similar food-rent to Christ Church. See Harmer, *Select English Historical Documents of the 9th and 10th Centuries* (Cambridge, 1914), no. 9 (Sawyer 1508).

[23] DB i, f. 3, 4b. It was claimed that Cliff had been given to Archbishop Wulfred and the community by the priest Werhard (Birch 402; Sawyer 1414). Meopham was given by King Athelstan to a layman in 939, but bequeathed to Christ Church by Brihtric and Ælfswith in 973 × 987; see Birch 741 (Sawyer 447) and Whitelock, *Wills* (as n. 18), no. 11 (Sawyer 1511).

[24] DB i, f. 5b; for the bequests of Denton and Snodland to Rochester in 973 × 87, see Whitelock, *Wills* (as n. 18), no. 11 (Sawyer 1511).

piers had ever belonged to the cathedral church of Canterbury. Rather it would seem that the archbishop coordinated the work on these two piers from groups of estates belonging to various lords. We may suppose that a reeve or a tenant of the archbishop from the first named manor would have had the task of overseeing the labour.

Very much the same pattern is presented by the fourth pier, which is said to be 'the king's'. The first estate named is the great royal manor of Aylesford, but none of the other nineteen estates originally listed was in the king's hands either in 1066 or in 1086. It seems highly unlikely that they had all been royal properties in the early eleventh century when the bridgework list was compiled, or indeed at any earlier moment in history. No argument about the date of the document can therefore be based upon the fact that one of the estates attributed to the fourth pier, Wouldham, was in the possession of the see of Rochester by 988, or that another, Farleigh, may have been given to Christ Church, Canterbury, in 961 or thereabouts by Eadgifu, the grandmother of King Edgar.[25] The fourth pier was simply one where the king, or rather his agent from Aylesford, organised bridgework as required from the listed lands of various lords.

When, therefore, we find that all the estates assigned to the first pier were properties of the see of Rochester, as were almost all of those assigned to the third pier,[26] we may begin to detect a motive for the alterations to the document. A great lord (or his reeve) would find it convenient to have his entire responsibility for bridgework performed by men from his own estates. Similar pressures in late Anglo-Saxon England led to the designation of the scattered estates of major ecclesiastical and lay lords as private hundreds, no matter how little geographical or administrative sense such territories might make.[27] It seems that we can here detect an incomplete process by which the organisation of bridgework at Rochester, originally territorial, was being altered to suit

[25] Wouldham was recovered for Rochester after prolonged litigation by Archbishop Dunstan (*d.* 988); see Robertson, *Charters* (as n. 10), no. 41. For Eadgifu's supposed grant of Farleigh to Christ Church, see Birch 1065 (Sawyer 1212).

[26] Pinden was held TRE by Alfred who could go to what lord he wished, and in 1086 by Malger from Odo of Bayeux, however: DB i, f. 6.

[27] H.M. Cam, '*Manerium cum hundredo*: The Hundred and the Hundredal Manor', *EHR* 47 (1932), pp. 353–76; idem, 'The Private Hundred in England before the Norman Conquest', in *Studies presented to Sir Hilary Jenkinson*, ed. J. Conway Davies (Oxford, 1957), pp. 50–60. For a dramatic example, see N.P. Brooks, 'The Oldest Document in the College Archives? The Micheldever Forgery', *Winchester College Sixth Centenary Essays*, ed. R. Custance (Oxford, 1982), pp. 189–228.

local patterns of lordship. The attribution of piers 1 and 3 to the bishop, of pier 4 to the king and of piers 5 and 9 to the archbishop represents the stage of the process that had been reached when the Old English text used by the scribe of the *Textus Roffensis* was composed in the early eleventh century. The recording of these arrangements in writing may itself have arrested the process of evolutionary change, except at Rochester cathedral where the cartulary could be emended in the interest of the bishop and community; certainly by the end of the twelfth century the arrangements for the bishop's piers were to be entirely rewritten, perhaps because earlier alterations to the manuscript had become too obvious.

Despite such remaining uncertainties in the text of the bridgework list, the document does enable us to reconstruct the main features of the late Anglo-Saxon bridge at Rochester (Fig.1). We are told that the bridge had nine piers in all, but that those at either end were 'land-piers', with the bishop being responsible for the one on the eastern (Rochester) bank and the archbishop being responsible for the ninth, that is the western (or Strood) pier. Each of the groups of estates assigned to the piers was required to provide three beams (*sylla*) and to board them over with planks (*to pillanne*) in accordance with measurements which are stated in rods (*gyrda*). The only exception is the estate of the people of Hoo (*Howaran lande*) which had to maintain two piers (nos. 7 and 8) and therefore had to provide six beams.[28] The Anglo-Saxon bridge at Rochester therefore seems to have had a simple timber superstructure, comprising a planked roadway resting on three beams which spanned the gaps between the piers. It seems likely that the amount of planking due from each group of communities was sufficient to cover the beams they had to provide. Though we are not told the width of the piers, these measurements therefore indicate a timber roadway across the whole bridge of $26\frac{1}{2}$ rods, that is 437 feet and 3 inches. That may be compared with the modern bridge on the same general site which measures 485 feet and with the late medieval bridge, some 40 yards upstream (where the river is wider), which measured 566 feet.[29]

[28] The figures of beams and planking assigned to the estates of each pier are set out in the appendix, below pp. 18–20.

[29] For the measurements of the bridge completed in 1392, see E. Hasted, *History and Topographical Survey of the County of Kent* II (Canterbury, 1782), pp. 18–19; For the bridge of 1851–56, see *Crossing the Medway: The Story of Rochester Bridge Trust* (Rochester, 1984), p. 9. An official *History of Rochester Bridge*, ed. W.N. Yates is to be published in 1992, the 600th anniversary of the completion of the medieval stone bridge.

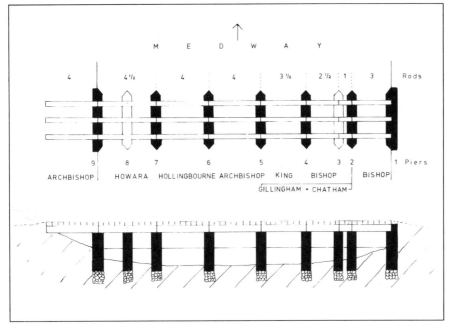

Fig. 1 Piers of Rochester Bridge.

It is noticeable that the document specifies what timber is to be provided for the roadway, but says nothing about wooden piles or other structural timbers being required for the piers. Yet in any river, and particularly in a major tidal estuary like the Medway, the piers bear the brunt of the scouring action of the water. In fact it seems that the piers of the late Anglo-Saxon bridge at Rochester were of stone and were not expected to need significant maintenance. In the fourteenth century, when particular piers of this bridge began to require structural repairs, the sources make clear that it was a job for the most experienced masons in the kingdom;[30] Moreover, when the western pier of the modern cast-iron bridge was being constructed in 1851, the builders came upon one of the massive stone piers of the earlier bridge. This ancient stone pier:

> had to be dug out for a depth of fifteen feet below the bed [*1851*] of the river. It was founded in hard ballast which was eight feet thick overlying the chalk. The 'Roman' piles were shod with iron shoes and penetrated into the ballast.[31]

As the 1851 engineers realised, this form of bridge construction was far beyond the skills of Anglo-Saxon builders. It involved the construction of coffer dams and the removal of the water and of the alluvial mud from within them, so that each pier could be founded on the natural chalk. That method of construction (coffer-dams, rammed ballast, iron-tipped elm or oak piles supporting piers of fine ashlar masonry) was the standard Roman technique for major bridges in northern Europe. Excavations at Trier of the first Roman bridge over the River Mosel have revealed exactly the same details as were recorded in 1851 at Rochester.[32] The second Roman bridge there, built in the mid second century, is still in use and its nine stone piers now carry modern traffic into the city over a river of comparable size to the Medway. The existence of a Roman bridge at

[30] See for example the appointment of Master Henry Yevele, stonemason, to the group of notables supervising the repairs to the bridge in February 1383: *Calendar of Patent Rolls, 1381–5* (London, 1909), p. 221.

[31] G. Payne, 'Researches and Discoveries in Kent, 1908–10', *Archaeologia Cantiana* 29 (1911), pp. lxxiv–lxxv, quoting a paper to the Institute of Civil Engineers of 13 May 1851 by Mr. Hughes.

[32] H. Cuppers, *Die Trierer Römerbrücken* (Rheinisches Landesmuseum Trier, Trierer Grabungen und Forschungen 5, Mainz, 1969), pp. 42–51, Abb. 36; for Roman bridges in Britain, see D.P. Dymond, 'Roman Bridges on Dere Street, Co. Durham', *Archaeological Journal* 118 (1961), pp. 136–64.

Rochester is proved by the name of the Roman town, *Durobrivae*, which means 'the fort by the bridge (s)'.[33] There can therefore be little doubt that the piers of the late Saxon bridge at Rochester were the surviving piers of the Roman bridge of Rochester.

Thus the Rochester bridgework list provides for the construction of a timber superstructure resting upon the piers of the Roman bridge built to take Watling Street across the Medway. We cannot be certain whether the Roman bridge would, as at Trier, have originally had a roadway of timber or whether it would have had stone arches, as has been recently conjectured for the Roman bridges on Hadrian's Wall at Chesters and at Willowford.[34] The Rochester bridgework list may therefore be describing the direct Anglo-Saxon successor of a standard Roman bridge with stone piers and timber superstructure; alternatively it may be describing the arrangements for replacing in timber a roadway whose stone arches had decayed or had been damaged beyond repair. On either interpretation it is clear that at Rochester the Anglo-Saxon 'common burden' of bridgework was directed towards the maintenance of a bridge whose core was Roman. The evidence of royal diplomas shows that that labour was due at bridges in Kent at least from the late eighth or early ninth century,[35] and we may suppose that the Mercian and West Saxon rulers of Kent would have considered the Medway crossing to be the most important bridge in Kent, as it has been in all subsequent periods. The arrangements defined in the bridgework list of the early eleventh century may have been preceded by comparable arrangements in the previous two centuries or more.

It is therefore worthwhile considering how bridgework was actually exacted from the listed estates. Though the document itself is silent, the example of Chester (where the bridge may also have been Roman) or of the arrangements for boroughwork in Wessex would suggest that one man from every hide (or in Kent from every sulung) may have been

---

[33] A.L.F. Rivet and C. Smith, *Place-Names of Roman Britain* (London, 1979), pp. 346–48.

[34] P.T. Bidwell and N. Holbrook, *Hadrian's Wall Bridges* (London, 1989), pp. 34–40, 66–71. The only direct evidence that these bridges were arched is the interpretation of certain stones from the River Tyne at Chesters as belonging to a stone cornice and parapet flanking the carriageway.

[35] Brooks, 'Development of Military Obligations' (as n. 1), pp. 78–80. However, no charter from the Rochester archives mentions bridgework until the mid ninth century. See *Charters of Rochester* (as n. 19), nos. 22, 25 (Sawyer 299, 331).

required to appear for bridgework at Rogationtide every year.[36] Certainly in the fourteenth century when repairs were needed to the bridge at Rochester, it was the practice to share the burden among the estates assigned to that pier according to their assessment in sulungs. Thus the Canterbury version of the bridgework list records the obligation of the men of the estates contributing to the fourth and sixth piers in terms of sulungs: the men of Burham *de sex sull'*, the men of Wouldham *de tribus sull'* etc.[37] The assessments very largely coincide with those of Domesday Book for 1086. In 1340 an inquisition held at Rochester before Roger de Southwyk and John Frere of Strood determined which estates customarily had to repair and maintain the fifth pier and specified for how many sulungs each answered.[38] It is therefore of interest that almost all the estates in the bridgework list are to be found in Domesday Book, and that their assessments (see appendix) help to explain some of the list's apparent anomalies. Thus the men of the Hoo peninsular might seem most heavily burdened of all, with the repair of two piers and $4\frac{1}{2}$ rods of planking; but the Domesday assessment of the manor of Hoo at 50 sulungs suggests that this area of rich arable land was not too harshly treated. There is indeed sufficient relation between the assessments and the quantities of timber that had to be provided to hint that the original allocation of estates to piers may have been calculated to spread the burden equitably, though any pattern will have been disturbed by subsequent beneficial hidation and changes to the listed estates.

It is also possible to define the territory that contributed to Rochester bridge with some precision. Eight of the estates named in the bridgework list have extant royal diplomas which detail their pre-Conquest boundaries.[39] Wherever the bounds can be plausibly identified, they prove to

[36] For Chester, see above n. 6; for boroughwork in Wessex, see the *Burghal Hidage* in Robertson, *Charters* (as n. 10), pp. 246–49; for annual boroughwork in the fortnight after Rogation, see 2 Athelstan 13, printed by F. Liebermann, *Die Gesetze der Angelsachsen*, 3 vols. (Halle, 1903–16), vol. 1, p. 156.

[37] London, British Library, MS Cotton Galba E. IV, f. 20, printed by Lambarde, *Perambulation* (as n. 10), pp. 424–25.

[38] Printed by C.T. Flower, *Public Works in Mediaeval Law* (Selden Society 32, London, 1915), pp. 203–209, who, however, misunderstood *sullyng* in the document as 'shillings' and supposed the inquest to be charging the contributory estates fixed sums of money! See Campbell, 'Infancy?' (as n. 1), p. 4.

[39] *Charters of Rochester* (as n. 19), nos. 3 (Stoke), 12 (Trottiscliffe), 15 (Halling), 27 (Cuxton), 28 (Malling) and 31 (Wouldham) and Birch 741 (Meopham); Sawyer 27, 129, 37, 321, 514, 885 and 447.

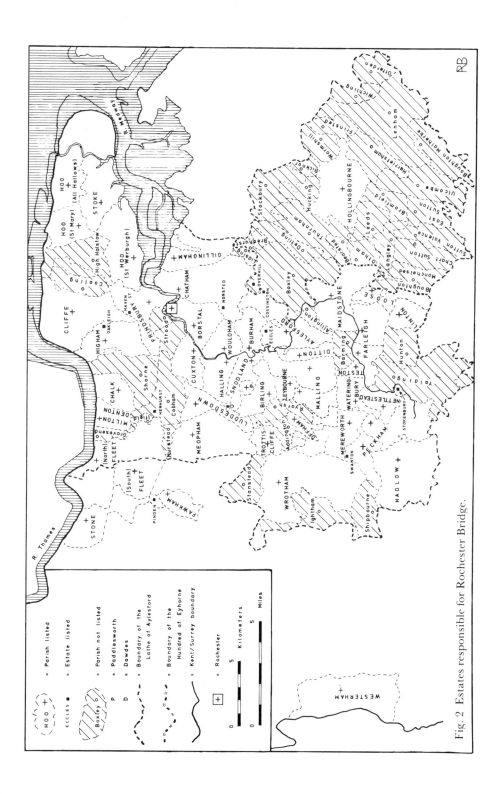

Fig. 2 Estates responsible for Rochester Bridge.

coincide, as is normal, with the bounds of the ancient ecclesiastical parishes first recorded in the mid nineteenth-century Tithe Awards. Since most of the estates named in the bridgework list reappear as parishes, it seems reasonable to follow the example of the Kentish antiquarian, Dr. Gordon Ward, and to map the estates in the list following parish boundaries (Fig. 2). What emerges from the exercise most clearly is that the bridgework estates are almost all located within the division of Kent known in Domesday Book as the lathe of Aylesford. Indeed it seems clear that the estates listed were intended to comprise the whole lathe of Aylesford.

At first sight the map appears to show that almost as many parishes in the lathe were omitted from the bridgework list as were included. A high proportion of the parishes that seem to be absent lie in the south-eastern quarter of the lathe in the vicinity of Hollingbourne. In fact every one of the parishes lying to the east of Aylesford, Maidstone and Loose can be shown to have belonged to the hundred of Eyhorne, and fourteenth-century versions of the bridgework document name all the parishes in this hundred as being responsible for the sixth pier;[40] in the *Textus Roffensis* this pier is simply allocated to 'Hollingbourne and all that lathe'. It seems clear that the 'lathe' of Hollingbourne was the same territory as the Domesday and medieval hundred of Eyhorne; the change of name may have been occasioned by the bequest of Hollingbourne to Christ Church by the ætheling Athelstan in 1014.[41] Other apparent omissions from the list also disappear upon investigation. Thus the parishes of Ryarsh and Addington did not become separate estates until after the Conquest and are therefore not to be found in Domesday Book; in fact the bounds of the adjacent Trottiscliffe establish that they had previously formed part of Birling, which is listed.[42] Similar evidence can be adduced to show that what was to be the parish of Strood was still part of Cuxton,[43] and the absence from Domesday Book of Stansted, Ightham and Shipbourne, of Cobham and Shorne, of Gravesend and of High Halstow suggests that they too had not been separated from their parent manors of Wrotham, Chalk, Milton and Hoo by the early eleventh century. With the exception

[40] See the Canterbury version in London, British Library, MS Cotton Galba E. IV, f. 20; Lambarde, *Perambulation* (as n. 10), pp. 424–25 and the inquisition of 1343 in *Calendar of Inquisitions Miscellaneous, 1307–49* (as n. 12), pp. 459–60.

[41] Whitelock, *Wills* (as n. 18), no. 20; Sawyer 1503.

[42] *Charters of Rochester* (as n. 19), no. 12; Sawyer 129.

[43] *Charters of Rochester* (as n. 19), no. 27; Sawyer 321.

of Cooling, which was an estate in lay hands both in the ninth century and in Domesday, and also of Yalding and Barming which were both in lay hands in 1066,[44] it is clear that the Rochester bridgework document lists every estate in the lathe of Aylesford. Bridgework, then, was essentially a territorial or regional responsibility.

Only five estates outside the lathe were liable to bridgework at Rochester. Four of them – Southfleet, Stone, Pinden and Fawkham – were the last properties in the list assigned to the bishop of Rochester's pier (no. 3) and are adjacent properties, on or close to the north-eastern boundary of the lathe. Since we know that they come from that part of the *Textus Roffensis* that was subject to twelfth-century alterations, they should probably be identified as late additions instituted by the bishop in order to spread the burden of bridgework more evenly over his estates, whether they were in the lathe or not. The only other listed property that was not in the lathe of Aylesford is Westerham, the last-named manor assigned to the fifth pier, that is the archbishop's. Westerham is certainly an anomaly in the scheme. Lying on the western boundary of Kent, it makes a nonsense of the the geographical unity of the scheme. It is therefore of interest that Westerham is the one estate whose inhabitants are known to have objected to being required to provide bridgework. In 1311 the king's bailiff, William Mot, who had distrained a horse and five cows from the tenants of Westerham because they had not contributed to the repair of the fifth pier, was attacked, beaten and forced to release the animals by Richard Trewe and Hamon le Brun of Westerham. In 1340 the Westerham tenants objected once again, but the jurors of Kent determined that the men of the vill *were* obliged to contribute by reason of the tenements which they held in the city of Rochester.[45] We cannot tell whether that was the reason why Westerham had originally been included in the scheme, but the fact that it is the last name recorded for the fifth pier suggests that Westerham may also have been an addition to the scheme.

Thus we may conclude that the Old English version of the Rochester bridgework list in the *Textus Roffensis* preserves an early eleventh-century document in which the simplicity of an original regional obligation was already being modified by tenurial and seigneurial considerations. It is

[44] Birch 326 (Sawyer 163); DB i, f. 9 for Cooling; DB i, f. 6 for Pinden and ff. 8v, 14 for Barming.

[45] *Calendar of Inquisitions Miscellaneous, 1307–49* (as n. 12), p. 26; Flower, *Public Works* (as n. 38), pp. 203–209.

difficult to be certain how ancient the obligation of the 'lathe of Aylesford' to provide bridgework at Rochester may have been. It is not a territory that is likely to have been devised for the sole purpose of providing for the bridge. Many of the contributory estates lie too far south to have had much occasion to use Watling Street; their need for east-west communications would rather have been met by the ancient route that crossed the Medway at Aylesford. But the lathes were certainly very primitive divisions of the early kingdom of Kent, even though there is room for debate about exactly how many early *regiones* there were in the kingdom.[46] However, the Domesday lathe of Aylesford and the Rochester bridgework district may plausibly be identified with the territory of the *Cæsterwara* or *Cæstersæte* ('the people of the chester', i.e. Rochester) that is referred to in royal diplomas of the eighth and ninth centuries;[47] the charters in question certainly all refer to estates that lay within the lathe and had dependent woodlands in the Weald. Such wealden *denns* would of course have been essential sources of the timber required for bridgework.

If the possibility is allowed that the responsibility of the *Cæsterwara* for keeping the Roman bridge at Rochester in repair may go back at least to the early ninth century, when bridgework first appears in Kentish charters, then we must also consider whether it may have been far more ancient than that. In the Roman empire major road bridges had been built by the state, rather than by individuals, but in the late fourth century the burden of their repair was shifted, first in Italy and then throughout the empire, onto the landowners of the locality.[48] In the early fifth century it was emphasised that church estates were not immune from bridgework.[49] The bridge over the Medway at Rochester was one of the largest, possibly the largest, Roman bridge in Britain. From 382 its repair would have been the responsibility of landowners in the territory

[46] N.P. Brooks, 'The Creation and Early Structure of the Kingdom of Kent', *The Origins of Anglo–Saxon Kingdoms* (Leicester, 1989), pp. 69–74.

[47] *Charters of Rochester* (as n. 19), nos. 4, 16 and Birch 199; Sawyer 30, 157, 31.

[48] B. Ward–Perkins, *From Classical Antiquity to the Middle Ages: Urban Public Building in Northern and Central Italy, AD 300–850* (Oxford, 1984), pp. 186–91 citing *Codex Theodosianus* xi. 10. 2 (370), ed. T. Mommsen (Berlin, 1905), for Italy and ibid. xi. 16. 15 (382), xi. 16. 18 (390) for the whole empire.

[49] *Leges Novellae ad Theodosianum Pertinentes*, ed. T. Mommsen and P.M. Meyer (Berlin, 1905), Nov. Val. 10 (441); *Codex Iustinianus* i. 2. 7 (423), ed. P. Krüger (Berlin, 1954).

of the city. Since we know that this bridge survived in use until 1388, the possibility must be conceded that territorial responsibility for its repair had a continuous history from the late fourth century. In other words the late Anglo-Saxon bridgework territory, the lathe of Aylesford, may have been the late Roman *civitas* of Rochester.

We are entering the realms of heady conjecture. Historians have been more willing to allow the possibility that Roman monuments continued in use into the Anglo-Saxon centuries than that there was any real continuity of the administrative structures that supported them. But on any reckoning Rochester bridge provides an astounding example of administrative continuity. For from 1392 when the new medieval bridge was completed and new endowments secured, the Anglo-Saxon contributory parishes continued to have a residual ultimate financial responsibility for the bridge's maintenance. Every year until 1911 the parishes were required to send men to Rochester to elect two bridge wardens responsible for ensuring that the revenues of the bridge properties and from alms were sufficient to maintain it in good condition.[50] Even today Rochester Bridge Trust is still in existence, administering the endowments of the late medieval bridge in order to maintain its modern successors. Though the bridge wardens and their twelve assistants have since 1911 no longer been elected by the parishes of the lathe of Aylesford, they are still predominantly members of the Kentish gentry and nobility. In a very real sense they are the successors of the great lords who had to ensure that men from their manors went to work on the bridge in the eleventh century. They may even be the successors of nameless Romano-British notables of the same territory who assigned their slaves to the same work. The motto of the Bridge Trust, *Publica privatis*, nicely encapsulates that mixture of lordly involvement in public and territorial responsibilities that is so characteristic of the late Anglo-Saxon state. Indeed it may be thought a typically woolly English compromise of opposing concepts that helps to explain the continuity of our institutions and class-system.[51]

---

[50] For the later constitutional arrangements for Rochester bridge, see Hasted, *History of Kent* (as n. 29), vol. 2, pp. 18–22; J. Becker, *Rochester Bridge, 1387–1856* (Oxford, 1928) and the forthcoming *History of Rochester Bridge*, ed. W.N. Yates, where the evidence will be set forth at length.

[51] My attempt to solve the thorny problems of the Rochester bridgework list have been aided by expert advice on matters philological from Mr. P.R. Kitson and on the history of Rochester cathedral priory from Mr. C.R. Flight, though any errors and the conclusions reached are solely mine.

Appendix

Bridgework Estates	Obligation	DB Manor	DB Assessment (1066)

Pier 1 (The Bishop)

Borstal	3 rods of planking + 3 beams	Borstal	2 sulungs
Cuxton		Cuxton	2½ sul.
Frindsbury		Frindsbury	10 sul.
Stoke		Stoke	5 sul.

19½ sul.

Pier 2

Gillingham	1 rod of planking + 3 beams	Gillingham	6 sulungs
Chatham		Chatham	6 sul.

12 sul.

Pier 3 (The Bishop)

Halling	2½ rods of planking + 3 beams	Halling	6 sulungs
Trottiscliffe		Trottiscliffe	3 sul.
Malling		[W] Malling	3 sul.
[South] Fleet		[South] Fleet	6 sul.
Stone		Stone	6 sul.
Pinden		Pinden	½ sul.
Fawkham		Fawkham	2 sul.

26½ sul.

Pier 4 (The King)

Aylesford & all that lathe		Aylesford	1 sulung
Overhill [in Boxley]		[Boxley]	[7 sul.]
Oakleigh		Oakleigh	1 sul.
þam smalanlande			
Cozenton			
Dowdes			
Gisleardesland			
Wouldham	3½ rods of planking + 3 beams	Wouldham	6 sul.
Burham		Burham	6 sul.
Eccles		Eccles	3 yokes
*Stokenbury		Stokenbury	½ sul.
*Loose		Loose	1 sul.
*Linton			
Lichebundesland			
Horsted			
Farleigh		E[+W?]Farleigh	6[+1] sul.
Teston		Teston	1 sul.
Chalk		Chalk	3 sul.
Henhurst		Henhurst	½ sul.
Haven		Haven	1 sul.

27 sul. [35 s.] + 3 yokes

18

Pier 5 (The Archbishop)

Wrotham		Wrotham	8 sulungs
Maidstone		Maidstone	10 sul.
Wateringbury		Wateringbury	2 + 2 sul.
Nettlestead		Nettlestead	3 sul.
The two Peckhams	4 rods of	E & W Peckham	6 + 2 sul.
Hadlow	planking +	Hadlow	6 sul.
Mereworth	3 beams	Mereworth	2 sul.
Leybourne		Leybourne	2 sul.
Swanton			
Offham		Offham	1 + 1 sul.
Ditton		Ditton	1 sul.
Westerham		Westerham	4 sul.

49 sul.

Pier 6

Hollingbourne and	4 rods of	Hollingbourne	6 sulungs
all that lathe	planking +		
	3 beams	[Otham	1 sul. + 1 yk.]
		[Langley	1½ sul.]
		[Leeds	3 sul.
		[Boughton	
		Monchelsea	1 sul.]
		[Chart Sutton	3 sul.]
		[Sutton Valence	4 sul.]
		[East Sutton	1½ sul.]
		[Ulcombe	2½ sul.]
		[Boughton	
		Malherbe	½ sul]
		[Harrietsham	2 sul.]
		[Lenham	5½ sul.]
		[Otterden	½ sul.]
		[Frinsted	1 sul.]
		[Wichling	½ sul.]
		[Stockbury	2 sul.]
		[Wormshill	1 sul.]
		[Harbilton	1 sul.]
		[Fairbourne	1 + 1 sul.]
		[Bowley &	
		Marley	2 sul.]
		[Shelborough	1 yoke]
		[Old & New	
		Shelve	½+3½+½sul.]
		[Thurnham	3 sul.]
		[Allington	3 sul.]
		[Aldington	2 sul.]
		[Broomfield	1 sul.]

55½ sul.

19

Pier 7 & 8

The *Howara* } 4½ rods of planking + 6 beams   Hoo   50 sulungs   50 sul.

Pier9 (TheArchbishop)

[North] fleet		[North] fleet	6 sulungs	
his Cliffe		[Bishops] Cliffe	3½ + ½ sul.	
Higham		Higham	5 sul.	
Denton		Denton	2 sul.	
Milton	4 rods of	Milton	1 sul. + 3 yokes	43 sul.
Luddesdown	planking +	Luddesdown	2½ sul. + ½ yk.	+ 3 yokes
Meopham	3 beams	Meopham	10 sul.	
Snodland		Snodland	6 sul.	
Birling		Birling	6 sul.	
Paddlesworth and all the *Dænewaru*		Paddlesworth	½ sul.	

2

A Context for 'Brunanburh'?

Simon Walker

In an early piece of literary criticism, Henry of Huntingdon remarked that the Old English panegyric on Athelstan's victory at *Brunanburh*, though 'full of strange words and figurative language', allowed the reader to 'learn from the majesty of the language about the majesty of this nation's deeds and courage'.[1] Neither literary scholars nor historians have since advanced much upon this acute but basic perception. Literary scholars have generally accorded 'Brunanburh' a dutiful, if puzzled, respect, categorising it as a highly conventional piece in which 'patriotic emotion and a sense of national identity receive distinguished and memorable expression'.[2] Historians have chiefly used the poem as a quarry for the scanty information it provides about the course of the *Brunanburh* campaign and the location of the (still-undiscovered) battlefield.[3] 'Brunanburh' has more to tell than that: in this essay I shall try to demonstrate what it can reveal, when placed in its correct

[1] Henry of Huntingdon, *Historia Anglorum*, ed. T. Arnold (Rolls Series, London, 1879), pp. 159–60.

[2] C.W. Kennedy, *The Earliest English Poetry* (London, 1971), p. 335; D.W. Frese, 'Poetic Prowess in *Brunanburh* and Maldon: Winning, Losing and Literary Outcome', *Modes of Interpretation in Old English Literature*, ed. P.R. Brown, G.R. Crampton, F.C. Robinson (Toronto, 1986), pp. 83–84, usefully reviews critical judgements on the poem.

[3] M. Wood, '*Brunanburh* Revisited', *Saga Book of the Viking Society* 20/3 (1980), pp. 200–17 is the latest and most plausible example.

historical context, about the efforts of the West Saxon kings to establish and maintain their authority throughout tenth-century England. I shall be chiefly concerned with the provenance of the poem. Since Klaeber described its author as a 'gifted and well-trained publicist' of the West Saxon court,[4] the consensus of those who have addressed themselves to the question has been that the poem most probably originated soon after the battle, in Athelstan's immediate entourage. T.A. Shippey remarks of 'Brunanburh', for instance, that 'clearly someone at the West Saxon court thought this composition of panegyric verse a good idea...', while C.N.L. Brooke suggests, 'No doubt the Battle of Brunanburh was recited before Athelstan in his equivalent of Heorot...'[5] But the 'courtly' origins of 'Brunanburh' have been more frequently asserted than demonstrated.[6] I shall try to show that, though the text of the poem will bear such an assertion, the West Saxon court is not the most likely milieu for the composition of 'Brunanburh'.

Such a study can, quite appropriately, start with the 'Brunanburh' poet's own attempt to provide a context for his subject-matter. In the final section of the poem, he turns from an account of Athelstan and Edmund's joyful home-coming in order to set their triumph in a longer perspective. It is the greatest victory, he concludes 'since the Angles and Saxons came hither from the east, invading Britain over the broad seas, and the proud assailants, warriors eager for glory, overcame the Britons and won a country'. The importance of this passage has often been remarked upon. Prosodically, its four-fold parallel variation brings the poem to a deliberate and formal climax; thematically, the long temporal perspective it asserts decisively resolves the tension some critics have seen between the poem's vivid, almost sympathetic, realisation of the defeated and its detached portrayal of the victors.[7] But the passage also

[4] F. Klaeber, *Anglica: Untersuchungen zur englischen Philologie* (Leipzig, 1925), vol. 2, p. 7.

[5] T.A. Shippey, *Old English Verse* (London, 1972), p. 186; C.N.L. Brooke, *The Saxon and Norman Kings* (London, 1963), p. 132.

[6] E.g. 'The identification of the West Saxon court with poetry is after all, a sufficient reason to explain why such events as the Battle of *Brunanburh* and the coronation of Edgar were recorded in the poems in the *Anglo-Saxon Chronicle*': N.F. Blake, 'The Dating of Old English Poetry', *An English Miscellany Presented to W.E. Mackie*, ed. B.S. Lee (Oxford, 1977), p. 24.

[7]

Engle and Seaxe	*siþþan eastan hider*
ofer brad brimu	*up becoman*
	Brytene sohtan

contains an important indication of the poem's immediate purpose, for, by comparing Athelstan's triumph at *Brunanburh* to the earliest Anglo-Saxon victories over the Britons, its closing lines clearly seek to rank him among the small band of kings, accorded the title *bretwalda*, who held the rule over all the kingdoms of the southern English. The implicit comparison is, indeed, with Northumbrian kings such as Edwin, Oswald and Oswiu, who 'had still greater power and ruled over all the inhabitants of Britain, English and Britons alike'.[8]

This insistence upon Athelstan's position as the heir of the *bretwaldas* is a common theme in contemporary sources. The Latin verse-epistle, *Carta, dirige gressus*, probably written by a clerk in Athelstan's entourage during the king's northern campaign in 927, contains the same emphasis upon an England newly-united under Athelstan exercising authority throughout all Britain (*per totam Bryttanium*).[9] The *drapa* the Norse skald, Egil Skallagrimsson, is said to have composed in praise of Athelstan in the immediate aftermath of *Brunanburh* compares his victories to those of Ælle, the first *bretwalda*, and concludes: 'Athelstan did more'.[10] Athelstan's enemies agreed. To the Welsh author of *Armes Prydein* he was 'the great king' (*mechteyrn*) and his conquests the culmination of the primal theft of Hengest and Horsa;[11] to the Northumbrians, he was the only king of the southern English to whom they had been subject since the first coming of the English to the island of Britain.[12] It

> *wlance wigsmiþas,*   *Wealas ofercoman*
> *eorlas arhwate*   *eard begeatan.*

W.F. Bolton, 'Variation in *The Battle of Brunanburh'*, *Review of English Studies*, new series 19 (1968), p. 367; F.P. Lipp, 'Contrast and Point of View in *Brunanburh'*, *Philological*

[8] *Bede's Ecclesiastical History*, ed. B. Colgrave and R.A.B. Mynors (Oxford, 1969), pp. 148–50; *English Historical Documents, c. 500–1042*, ed. D. Whitelock (London, 2nd. edn., 1979), p. 186 (*s.a.* 829). P. Wormald, 'Bede, the *Bretwaldas* and the Origins of the *Gens Anglorum'*, *Ideal and Reality in Frankish and Anglo-Saxon Society*, ed. P. Wormald (Oxford, 1983), pp. 99–129 is the fullest recent consideration of the *bretwalda* and his status.

[9] M. Lapidge, 'Some Latin Poems as Evidence for the Reign of Athelstan', *Anglo-Saxon England* 9 (1981), pp. 89–93.

[10] *Egils Saga Skalla-Grimssonar*, ed. S. Nordal (Islenzk Fornrit 2, Reyjavik, 1933), p. 146; the comparison would gain added point if Ælle was held to be, as some contemporaries evidently believed, a king of the West Saxons and not, as in fact he was, king of the *South* Saxons. *English Historical Documents, c. 500–1042* (as n. 8), p. 186, n. 3.

[11] *Armes Prydein. The Prophecy of Britain from the Book of Taleisin*, ed. I. Williams (Medieval and Modern Welsh Series 6, Dublin, 1972), p. xvii and lines 8, 31–32, 100.

[12] 'The Chronicle Attributed to John of Wallingford', ed. R. Vaughan, *Camden Miscellany XXI* (Camden Third Series 90, London, 1958), p. 45.

is in order to illustrate and emphasise Athelstan's overlordship of all the English that the 'Brunanburh' poet, in his turn, refers to the participation of the Mercians, as well as the West Saxons, in the victorious army (though it is not clear that the Mercian levies were engaged in the original and decisive encounter *ymbe Brunanburh*[13]) and, by his inclusion of a 'northern warrior' (*guma norþerna*), besides the Scots and Norse, among the defeated, indicates that Athelstan has re-established West Saxon hegemony over the Northumbrians who so willingly allied with his enemies.[14]

The unanimity displayed by both friendly and hostile sources in portraying Athelstan as 'king and ruler of the whole of Britain' was, in part, a recognition of his very considerable military and diplomatic achievements. In 927 he had taken possession of the Norse kingdom of York and received the submission of the kings of Scotland and Strathclyde, as well as of the lord of Bamburgh. Within the next four years he further subordinated the Britons of the south-west to West Saxon rule and successfully demanded tribute from the princes of Wales; their periodic attendance at his court gave some concrete substance to Athelstan's claims to overlordship.[15] To enforce those claims, he invaded the Scottish kingdom in 934 and sent his fleet to ravage the coast as far north as Caithness. But the hegemony over all the peoples of Britain so consistently ascribed to Athelstan in contemporary writings was not a simple tribute to his military abilities; it also, in part, reflects the consistent view of his own position that the king sought, by all the means available to him, to communicate to his willing and unwilling subjects alike. His imperial ambitions were demonstrated as early as 926 by his acquisition of a series of relics – the sword of Constantine, the spear of Charlemagne, the standard of St. Maurice – closely associated with the Carolingian dynasty.[16] The titles accorded Athelstan in his charters elaborate the same theme of overlordship. Whereas the earliest charters of his reign stuck to the usage of his father and grandfather, describing the king as either *Angul Saxonum*

[13] R.I. Page, 'A Tale of Two Cities', *Peritia* 1 (1982), p. 340.

[14] A.P. Smyth, *Scandinavian York and Dublin* (Dublin, 1979), vol. 2, p. 36; Wood, '*Brunanburh* Revisited' (as n. 3), p. 201.

[15] H.P.R. Finberg, 'Sherborne, Glastonbury and the Expansion of Wessex', *Transactions of the Royal Historical Society*, fifth series 3 (1953), pp. 16–18; H. Loyn, 'Wales and England in the Tenth Century: The Context of the Athelstan charters', *Welsh History Review* 10 (1980–81), pp. 283–301.

[16] K.J. Leyser, *Rule and Conflict in an Early Medieval Society* (London, 1979), p. 88.

rex or *rex Anglorum*,[17] by 931 Athelstan was making greater claims for his authority as, most typically, 'rex Anglorum, per omnipatrantis dexteram totius Brytanniae regni solio sublimatus'; his ambitions were still more clearly stated in those charters he subscribed as 'rex totius Brittanniae'.[18] After 935 West Saxon assertions of some form of imperial authority over the whole of Britain became still more insistent; Athelstan's commonest title during this period was 'nodante Dei gratia basileos Anglorum et eque totius Britanniae orbis curagulus' (or some variant upon this) and he habitually subscribes as *rex totius Britanniae*.[19] After 928 the same title was the most common regnal style on Athelstan's coinage as well.[20]

The significance of such 'imperial' epithets as *basileus Anglorum* is a matter of some dispute. While the overlordship they ascribe to Athelstan may never have been very strictly defined, the insistence with which all the sources – literary, administrative, numismatic – most closely connected with the king hark upon the same theme makes it seem unlikely that such a title represents nothing more than an attempt at elegant variation on the part of the scribes who drafted the charters.[21] After 931 the evidence suggests that Athelstan's charters were drafted, often at meetings of the *witan*, under circumstances that allowed direct royal supervision of their content;[22] nor is there any doubt that the moneyers producing Athelstan's coinage were, save in a few exceptional cases, firmly under royal control. The titles accorded Athelstan during the 930s must therefore be taken as a fair indication of the terms in which the king

[17] Sawyer 396, 397, 399, 400, 403, 405.

[18] Sawyer 412, 413, 416–19, 422, 425, 426, 458; Sawyer 421, 423 substitute *Albionis* for *Brytanniae*; see Sawyer 416, 421, 422 for the subscription. H. Kleinschmidt, *Untersuchungen über das Englische Königtum im 10. Jahrhundert* (Göttingen, 1979), pp. 64–88 and 'Die Titulaturen englischer Könige im 10. und 11. Jahrhundert', *Intitulatio III: Lateinische Herrschertitel und Herrschertitulaturen vom 7. bis zum 13. Jahrhundert*, ed. H. Wolfram and A. Schurer (Graz, 1988), pp. 89–120 provide the most recent and detailed discussion of the charter-styles of the English kings from Athelstan to Eadwig.

[19] Sawyer 430, 438, 446, 448; minor variations on this style are Sawyer 411, 431, 447, 449.

[20] C. Blunt, 'The Coinage of Athelstan, 924–939: A Survey', *British Numismatic Journal* 42 (1974), p. 56.

[21] N. Brooks, 'Anglo-Saxon Charters: The Work of the Last Twenty Years', *Anglo-Saxon England* 3 (1974), p. 221, and the references cited in nn. 1–2.

[22] S. Keynes, *The Diplomas of King Aethelred 'the Unready', 978–1016* (Cambridge, 1980), pp. 39–46; but contrast P. Chaplais, 'The Royal Anglo-Saxon "Chancery" of the Tenth Century Revisited', *Studies in Medieval History Presented to R.H.C. Davis*, ed. H. Mayr-Harting and R.I. Moore (London, 1985), pp. 47–49, and Kleinschmidt, 'Die Titulaturen', pp. 79–84.

wished himself to be represented; among those titles, the claim to be king of the whole of Britain – *rex totius Britanniae* – seems the one closest to Athelstan's own heart. That this was, in turn, clearly understood to imply the status of a *bretwalda* is suggested by the contemporary translation of the title 'rex et rector totius hujus Britanniae insule' as 'Ongolsaxna cyning 7 brytaenwalda ealles thyses Iglandes'.[23]

By presenting Athelstan as the heir and equal of the early *bretwaldas*, the 'Brunanburh' poem gives memorable expression to the same theme. Clearly this implies an origin close to the king and the court – produced, perhaps, by a member of the 'intellectual *comitatus*' on whose services Athelstan depended throughout his reign.[24] Cultivation of vernacular poetry was certainly not an unusual activity at the courts of early medieval kings. Charlemagne had the *barbara et antiquissima carmina* of his people gathered together and his English contemporary, Offa, displayed a similar interest in the 'deeds and wars of former kings', just as Alfred was in the habit of learning and reciting *carmina Saxonica*.[25] The crucial question is: how close? While it would be simplest to think of 'Brunanburh' as a nearly-spontaneous celebration of Athelstan's victory over his enemies, an extended vernacular counterpart to the short Latin verse-epistle produced to announce his diplomatic triumph at Eamont in 927, there are difficulties with this view. One such difficulty is presented by the linguistic evidence, for whereas the texts of the Anglo-Saxon Chronicle in which the poem appears generally display standard late West Saxon phonology, the poetic entries among the annals 924–75 present an exception to this rule, preserving a number of apparently dialectal forms. Some of the forms in 'Brunanburh', such as the occurrence of o + nasal consonants and u- for standard o- in inflexional endings, are a feature of tenth-century Mercian texts and might, therefore, be used to point to a Midland origin for the poem, far removed from the usual ambit of the West Saxon court.[26] In

[23] Sawyer 427; Birch 705–6; see E. John, 'The Division of the *Mensa* in Early English Monasteries', *Journal of Ecclesiastical History* 6 (1954), p. 154 n. 4 for the authentic basis of this charter.

[24] M. Wood, 'The Making of King Athelstan's Empire: An English Charlemagne?', *Ideal and Reality in Frankish and Anglo-Saxon Society*, ed. P. Wormald (Oxford, 1983), p. 258.

[25] Einhard, *Vita Caroli*, c. 29, ed. O. Holder-Egger (MGH SRG, Hanover, 6th edn., 1911), p. 33; D. Whitelock, *The Audience of Beowulf* (Oxford, 1951), pp. 58–64; K. Sisam, *Studies in the History of Old English Literature* (Oxford, 1953), p. 137.

[26] *The Anglo-Saxon Chronicle, MS A*, ed. Janet M. Bately (Cambridge, 1986), pp. cxlii–cxlvi; *The Anglo-Saxon Chronicle, MS B*, ed. Simon Taylor (Cambridge, 1983), pp. lxv–lxvi; A. Campbell, *Old English Grammar* (Oxford, 1959), pp. 51–52, 155–56.

the remainder of this essay I shall attempt to show that such a regional origin for 'Brunanburh' can be plausibly argued and, as a corollary, that the poem's composition was neither strictly contemporary with Athelstan nor the product of his immediate court circle.

My starting-point lies in the observation that, although 'Brunanburh' echoes fairly accurately the aspirations to overlordship announced in Athelstan's charter-titles, its language finds a still closer parallel in the 'alliterative' charters issued in the subsequent reigns of Edmund and Eadred. These charters range in date from 939 to 956, stand apart from the main sequence of royal diplomas produced during that period, and, when taken together, constitute a closely-related group.[27] They share a common structure, in which the boundary-clause or anathema often appears after the witness list, a common vocabulary and common formulae, each quite distinct from those in use in the scriptoria responsible for drafting the majority of royal charters during the reigns of Athelstan and his brothers.[28] For our purposes, they display three characteristics immediately relevant to the provenance of 'Brunanburh'. Firstly, the unusually exalted and specific titles these charters grant Athelstan, Edmund and Eadred; the most common of them – 'rex Angulsaxna et Nordhymbra imperator, paganorum gubernator Brittanorumque propugnator' – reflects, in its careful enumeration of those subject to the kings, precisely the same anxiety to assert West Saxon overlordship over all the peoples of Britain that we have identified as one of the principal concerns of the 'Brunanburh' poet. Secondly, their use of an ornamental and rhythmic prose that aspires to the cadences of poetry; this aspiration is best revealed in the free use of alliteration, a technique fundamental to the structure of Old English poetry. Thirdly, the appearance of vernacular words and grammatical forms in these Latin charters; the use of epithets

---

Although these dialectal forms appear chiefly in MS A, they do not appear to be individual scribal peculiarities but to reflect the language of the common exemplar (or exemplars) of the surviving Chronicle manuscripts at this point. *The Battle of Brunanburh*, ed. A. Campbell (London, 1938), pp. 8–13.

[27] Sawyer 392, 479, 484, 520, 544, 548–50, 556–57, 566, 569, 572, 1606; see *English Historical Documents* (as n. 8), pp. 372–73, *Charters of Burton Abbey*, ed. P.H. Sawyer (Anglo-Saxon Charters 2, London, 1979), pp. xlvii–xlviii, for the identification of this group. There are occasional later imitations, e.g. C. Hart, *The Early Charters of Eastern England* (Leicester, 1966), pp. 193–98.

[28] C. Hart, 'Danelaw Charters and the Glastonbury Scriptorium', *Downside Review* 90 (1972), p. 126.

such as *eorl* and *biscop* is relatively common in their witness lists, while the only recorded use of *æpeling* – the vernacular term for a prince of the royal blood – in a Latin context occurs in an 'alliterative' charter of Eadred's reign.[29] From these three features it seems reasonably safe to deduce that the draftsman of the 'alliterative' charter sequence was familiar with the techniques of both Latin and English poetry; that the expression of his thoughts in English came readily to him; and that he was anxious to advance a conception of West Saxon hegemony over the whole *orbis Britanniae* that was the common currency of Athelstan's court.

Since it is these charters that come closest in concern and, occasionally, expression to the subject-matter of 'Brunanburh', their provenance and authorship bears further investigation. Most historians consider them to be the products of the Worcester scriptorium;[30] others would go further and identify their draftsman as Cenwald, bishop of Worcester 929–58.[31] The evidence for this identification is circumstantial but not conclusive; the one royal charter indubitably drafted by Cenwald does not belong to the main alliterative series, though it shares with those charters a characteristic arrangement, displays a free use of the vernacular within the body of the text, and accords Eadred the title *rex et primicerius totius Albionis*.[32] Yet even if Cenwald cannot be identified beyond doubt as the author of the alliterative charters whose titles echo so exactly the claims made on Athelstan's behalf by 'Brunanburh', his career clearly illustrates how the concerns of the 'court' could be carried well beyond the king's own presence. A trusted servant of Athelstan, Cenwald accompanied the king on his northern campaign in 927 and was given the important diplomatic task, in 929, of escorting two of his sisters to the Ottonian court.[33] An inscription in the Gandersheim Gospels, thought to have been entered

[29] D. Dumville, 'The Aetheling: A Study in Anglo-Saxon Constitutional History', *Anglo-Saxon England* 8 (1979), p. 7.

[30] R. Drögereit, 'Kaiseridee und Kaisertitel bei den Angelsachsen', *Zeitschrift der Savigny-Stiftung für Rechtsgeschichte, germanische Abteilung 69* (1952), p. 67; *Charters of Burton Abbey*, p. xlviii; *English Historical Documents*, p. 373. Kleinschmidt, 'Die Titulaturen', pp. 99–103, while accepting a Mercian provenance for the series would, however, tentatively assign its production to Dorchester.

[31] Keynes, *Aethelred* (as n. 22), p. 82; Chaplais, 'Anglo-Saxon "Chancery"' (as n. 22), p. 50.

[32] Sawyer 574.

[33] E.E. Barker, 'Two Lost Documents of King Athelstan', *Anglo-Saxon England* 6 (1977), pp. 139–43; S. Keynes, 'King Athelstan's Books', *Learning and Literature in Anglo-Saxon England*, ed. M. Lapidge and H. Gneuss (Cambridge, 1985), pp. 198–201.

by Cenwald during this German mission, commemorates *apelstan rex angulsaxonum 7 mercianorum*,[34] a strangely redundant form of the West Saxon royal title that nevertheless displays the same anxiety to emphasise Athelstan's overlordship over the Mercians shown by the 'Brunanburh' poet.

By appointing Cenwald, a clerk from his own *familia*, to Worcester, Athelstan clearly hoped to consolidate West Saxon influence over this formerly Mercian see. In this he was largely successful for, long after Cenwald's death, Athelstan and his victory at *Brunanburh* remained strong in the imagination of the Worcester community. A mid eleventh-century forgery from Worcester has Athelstan referring to Olaf Guthfrithsson, his adversary in the battle, as 'the king who tried to deprive me of my life', imparting to their enmity a personal quality quite absent when other scriptoria sought to add a touch of historical plausibility to their forgeries by including a reference to *Brunanburh*.[35] Another Worcester forgery of the same period preserves the memory of Bishop Cenwald's close association with Athelstan, while the tenth-century addition made to Worcester's copy of the Old English *Pastoral Care* seems to imply some connection, at least in the eyes of the community, between Cenwald and this familiar vernacular text.[36] Further, the account of *Brunanburh* given in the *Chronicon ex chronicis* compiled at Worcester early in the twelfth century demonstrates that the community had access to more than one tradition about the events surrounding the battle. Although the chronicle entry clearly draws upon the Old English poem for many of its details, it also, uniquely, preserves the information that Olaf and his fleet landed in England at the mouth of the Humber.[37] While the chronicle entry was being compiled, an unknown hand added the marginal comment – 'Strenuus et gloriosus rex Athelstanus solus per totam Angliam primus regnum Anglorum regnavit',[38] an assertion that

---

[34] P. Chaplais, 'English Diplomatic Documents to the End of Edward III's Reign', *The Study of Medieval Records: Essays in Honour of Kathleen Major*, ed. D.A. Bullough and R.L. Storey (Oxford, 1971), p. 23, n. 1.

[35] Sawyer 406, 439, 433.

[36] Sawyer 401; *The Pastoral Care*, ed. N.R. Ker (Early English Manuscripts in Facsimile, Copenhagen, 1956), p. 24.

[37] *Florentii Wigornensis Monachi Chronicon ex Chronicis*, ed. B. Thorpe (London, 1848), vol. 1, p. 132; cf. M. Brett, 'John of Worcester and his Contemporaries', *The Writing of History in the Middle Ages*, ed. R.H.C. Davis and J.M. Wallace-Hadrill (Oxford, 1981), pp. 101–26.

[38] C. Hart, 'The Early Section of the Worcester Chronicle', *Journal of Medieval History* 9 (1983), p. 308.

demonstrates that the 'imperial' significance of Athelstan's conquests remained well-appreciated at Worcester nearly two hundred years after his death. The particular emphasis upon English dominion throughout Britain that characterises the 'alliterative' charters certainly continued to be a preoccupation of the Worcester scriptorium.[39]

In the light of this continued commemoration of Cenwald, veneration for Athelstan and interest in *Brunanburh*, a Worcester provenance for the poem would, besides explaining the survival of some Mercian dialect forms in its phonology, make good historical sense. The association of religious communities with vernacular epics is well-attested; the Old High German *Ludwigslied* seems most likely to have been composed at the abbey of Saint-Amand, under the patronage of its abbot, Joscelin of Saint-Denis,[40] while it has been suggested that an unreformed English monastery, dominated by secular values, provides the most likely setting for the genesis of *Beowulf*.[41] If it is only 'in Mercia . . . in Alfred's dealings with the see of Worcester' that it is possible to discern the English beginnings of an imperial church on Carolingian lines,[42] then it is the less surprising that Worcester's clerks should retain a particular enthusiasm for Athelstan's imperial ambitions. The poem's emphasis on Mercian participation in the victory at *Brunanburh* would fit a Worcester context, too; while the Welsh author of *Armes Prydein* attached a special importance to the alliance of Mercia and Wessex in the recent successes of the 'Saxons',[43] that alliance always remained a little precarious. The rule of the West Saxon kings in Mercia meant a diminution of Mercian autonomy but not an end to Mercian aspirations for independence, which were to reappear forcefully after Eadred's death.[44] It was important for the security of the newly-united English kingdom, in general, and the see of Worcester – exposed as it was to possible Welsh attack – in particular,

[39] E.g. Sawyer 428 – the grant is to last '. . . tam diu fides Christianae religionis apud Anglos in Britannia permaneat'.

[40] K.F. Werner, 'Gauzlin von Saint-Denis und die westfränkische Reichsteilung von Amiens (März 880)', *Deutsches Archiv für Erforschung des Mittelalters* 35 (1979), pp. 433–7; P.J. Fouracre, 'The Context of the OHG *Ludwigslied*', *Medium Aevum* 54 (1985), p. 98–9.

[41] P. Wormald, 'Bede, Beowulf and the Conversion of the Anglo-Saxon Aristocracy', *Bede and Anglo-Saxon England*, ed. R.T. Farrell (Oxford, 1978), p. 58.

[42] J. Nelson, 'A King Across the Sea: Alfred in Continental Perspective', *Transactions of the Royal Historical Society*, fifth series 36 (1986), p. 66.

[43] *Armes Prydein* (as n. 11), line 109 and pp. 50–51.

[44] A. Williams, '*Princeps Merciorum gentis*: The Family, Career and Connections of Ælfhere, Ealdorman of Mercia, 956–983', *Anglo-Saxon England* 10 (1982), pp. 161–63.

that these aspirations should be contained within peaceful bounds. One means of doing this was to emphasise Mercian participation in what were primarily West Saxon triumphs. Another was to disseminate the 'idea of empire smacking more of confederacy than autocracy, and harking back to an earlier Anglo-Saxon tradition of *ducatus*-leadership of allied peoples'[45] that the Worcester scribes, with their precise enumeration of the allied peoples over whom the West Saxon kings exercised their *imperium*, so clearly sought to publicise. By depicting Athelstan as the heir and equal of the *bretwaldas* 'Brunanburh' does both these things. For Cenwald, *praesul Hwicciorum*,[46] presiding over a diocese roughly co-terminous with the ancient kingdom of the Hwicce but the friend and intimate of the West Saxon kings, such a notion was obviously attractive.

There is, then, a case for arguing that 'Brunanburh' has its origins at Worcester and was produced under the influence of Bishop Cenwald. This leaves open the question of the *date* of the poem's composition for, once removed from the immediate environs of Athelstan's court, the assumption that it was produced as a victory piece immediately after the battle itself becomes less compelling. A close reading of the text of 'Brunanburh' suggests that its composition could be ascribed with as much plausibility to the reign of Edmund (939–46) as to the years 937–39. One reason for this is that, in contrast to all the other sources that bear upon the battle, the 'Brunanburh' poem is almost as much in praise of the ætheling Edmund, Athelstan's younger brother and eventual successor, as of the king himself. The poet distinguishes them by rank, as *cyning and ætheling*, but lays greater emphasis upon the bond of blood that unites them as *afaran Eadwardes*. There are two points to make about this phrase. First, it is a strangely modest epithet for a king who was not afraid to make large claims for his own authority and ascribes to Edmund, a boy of sixteen at the time of the battle who had hitherto played little part in Athelstan's rule, a degree of responsibility for the victory that is entirely lacking in those accounts of the *Brunanburh* campaign that are independent of the poem. Second, it presents an ideal of fraternal concord and co-operation within the West Saxon royal house that was largely illusory. Since there was no system of designated succession to the throne in tenth-century Wessex, the crown usually passed to 'the most credible contender for power and responsibility among eligible members

---

[45] J. Nelson, 'Inauguration Rituals', *Early Medieval Kingship*, ed. P.H. Sawyer and I.N. Wood (Leeds, 1977), p. 69.

[46] Sawyer 1290.

of the royal house';[47] friction between brothers was, in consequence, common. Athelstan himself had initially had to be content, on his father's death, with the kingdom of Mercia, ceding Wessex to his elder brother Ælfweard. Even after Ælfweard's death in August 924 he had been briefly compelled to recognise the claims of another of his brothers, Edwin, by associating him in the kingship before finally sending him into exile in 933.[48] In turn, Edmund had to cope with the claims of his brother, Eadred, by allowing him an exceptionally prominent part in government – a demonstration of unity that has been thought to suggest fear of a challenge.[49] Both Athelstan and Edmund thus had reason to welcome the picture of brotherly amity the 'Brunanburh' poet sought to paint but it was Edmund, whom the phrase *afaran Eadwardes* directly associates with the prestige of his famous father while excluding Eadred from all consideration, who had the most to gain from such an image.

Naturally there are objections to this view. The triumphalist tone of the poem would, at first sight, hardly seem appropriate to the circumstances of the early part of Edmund's reign. Within two months of Athelstan's death, Olaf Guthfrithsson – whose defeat and flight to Dublin, *æwiscmode*, is so resoundingly celebrated by the 'Brunanburh' poet – had gained control of York. By the end of the following year, Edmund had been forced to cede the whole territory between Watling Street and the Humber to the Norse king; it was 'an ignominious surrender'[50] that can have done little for his reputation within his own kingdom. Yet this objection is hardly insuperable. Strict adherence to the facts of the case had never been a characteristic of the West Saxon publicists who compiled the Chronicle in which 'Brunanburh' is to be found;[51] and the crisis of 940–42 is as likely a context for the genesis of the poem as Athelstan's untroubled final years. The Chronicle itself was part of the literary response to the still greater crisis that had threatened Alfred during the 880s and can be read as the 'reflection of an urgent political need – the need, not of a people, but of a dynasty, the House of Wessex'.[52] Born of a similar crisis,

[47] Dumville, 'Aetheling' (as n. 29), p. 2.

[48] Keynes, 'King Athelstan's Books' (as n. 33), p. 187, n. 206; O. Holder-Egger (ed.), *Folcwini diaconi gesta abbatum S. Bertini Sithensium*, MGH SS 13, p. 629.

[49] P. Stafford, 'The King's Wife in Wessex, 800–1066', *Past and Present* 91 (1981), p. 25.

[50] F.M. Stenton, *Anglo-Saxon England* (Oxford, 2nd. edn., 1947), p. 353.

[51] R.H.C. Davis, 'Alfred the Great: Propaganda and Truth', *History* 66 (1971), pp. 170–77 is the clearest statement of the reasons for this belief.

[52] J.M. Wallace-Hadrill, 'The Franks and the English in the Ninth Century: Some Common Historical Interests', *Early Medieval History* (Oxford, 1975), p. 211.

'Brunanburh' reflects that same need; in the poem, the emphasis Alfred had laid upon the dynastic pre-eminence of the West Saxon kings appears once again and Edmund and Athelstan's success in war is presented as a quality innate in their blood – 'swa him geæþele wæs / from cneomægum'. This was another theme common to contemporary praise-poetry. Egil Skallagrimsson hailed Athelstan as 'the kin-famous king', while the Latin panegyric on which William of Malmesbury draws commends him as 'a royal son' of a noble line.[53] Athelstan and Edmund could be justly proud of their ancestry; the powerful but parvenu Ottonians showed themselves anxious enough to associate themselves with the antiquity and nobility of the kin of Cerdic.[54] But there *were* contemporaries to whom Athelstan's lineage, particularly on his mother's side, did not seem beyond question, and it was against these doubts that the poet's assurances were, perhaps, principally directed.[55] Propaganda is no less inherently probable a motive for composition than panegyric and there are indeed signs that the poet wrote for an audience that was aware of the fragility of the West Saxon hegemony he praises and, in praising, does his best to maintain and perpetuate. An obvious instance of this is that, while considerable emphasis is placed upon the heavy enemy casualties ('Hettend crungun/Sceotta leoda and scipflotan/fæge feollan'), no mention is made of West Saxon losses – though one Irish account claims a 'great number' of Saxons died.[56]

The crisis of political control that created a need for such propaganda was at its most acute early in Edmund's reign and continued to exist, in a less threatening manner, until 955. Although Edmund regained control of the East Midlands in 942 and the kingdom of York in 944, the West Saxon hold on the north of England remained precarious. Northumbria submitted to the Norwegian adventurer Eric 'Bloodaxe' in 947 and between 949 and 954 the kingdom of York remained under Norse control. Edmund's brother, Eadred, died in possession of a united English kingdom once again in 955 but he had no illusions about the

---

[53] *Egils Saga* (as n. 10), p. 146; William of Malmesbury, *De Gestis Regum Anglorum*, ed. W. Stubbs (Rolls Series, London, 1887–89), vol. 1, p. 145.

[54] K.J. Leyser, 'Die Ottonen und Wessex', *Frühmittelalterliche Studien* 17 (1983), p. 78.

[55] *Gesta Ottonis*, lines 74–82, *Hrotsvithae Opera*, ed. P. v. Winterfeld (MGH SRG, Berlin, 1902), pp. 206–7.

[56] *Annals of Ulster*, ed. W.M. Hennessy (Dublin, 1887), vol. 1, p. 456; cf. also William of Malmesbury, *De Gestis Regum Anglorum*, vol. 1, p. 151, *De Gestis Pontificum Anglorum*, ed. N.E.S.A. Hamilton (Rolls Series, London, 1870), p. 178 for further English casualties.

permanence of his supremacy, leaving 1600 pounds of silver to his people in his will, lest they should need to buy peace from a heathen army.[57] The political context in which I have sought to place 'Brunanburh', one in which the West Saxon hegemony over the peoples of Britain required all the support it could muster if it was to survive, remained essentially unchanged, therefore, until 955. 'Brunanburh's' date of composition might be plausibly placed at any point within this period, though the prominence the poem accords the *ætheling* Edmund perhaps tilts the balance of probabilities towards the early years of Edmund's reign as king. Certainly, it was then that Edmund was most in need of the kind of panegyric 'Brunanburh' accords him, for he seems to have derived little personal prestige from his rule. The charter evidence suggests that his mother, Eadgifu, took an exceptionally active role in government during Edmund's reign, while almost half his kingdom lay under the effective control of his greatest ealdorman, Athelstan 'Half King' and his family.[58] When, at the end of the tenth century, the chronicler Æthelweard came to record the achievements of his kinsman, he found only two events in Edmund's reign worthy of comment: the expulsion of the Norse from York was one, though this was credited to Archbishop Wulfstan and the ealdorman of Mercia, and the death of Edmund's wife was the other.[59]

To be any more precise about the date of 'Brunanburh''s composition requires a short consideration of the compilation of the Chronicle in which the text of the poem is found, for the textual and palaeographic evidence of the Chronicle manuscripts can advance the question a little further. Palaeographically, the most valuable witness is MS A, in which the whole set of annals 924–55 was entered by a single scribe at, in all probability, a date soon after 955.[60] This would indicate that a copy of 'Brunanburh' was available at Winchester soon after the death of Eadred. Textual considerations seem to confine the date of the poem's composition within rather narrower limits. The scribe of MS A had to change his previous habits of layout in order to accommodate the annals 937–46 in his text and this has been taken to suggest that these annals originally

[57] Sawyer 1515; Birch 912.

[58] P. Stafford, 'King's Wife' (as n. 49), p. 25; C. Hart, 'Athelstan "Half King" and his Family', *Anglo-Saxon England* 2 (1973), p. 123–4.

[59] *The Chronicle of Æthelweard*, ed. A. Campbell (London, 1962), p. 54.

[60] N.R. Ker, *A Catalogue of Manuscripts Containing Anglo-Saxon* (Oxford, 1957), pp. 57–9; M. Parkes, 'The Palaeography of the Parker Manuscript of the Chronicle, Laws and Sedulius', *Anglo–Saxon England* 5 (1976), p. 169.

became available to him as a single unit.[61] The invariable (and distinctive) openings of the annal-entries within the 937–46 group and the identical nature of the annals for these years in MSS A, B and C would seem to support this conjecture, as would the fact that it is precisely at 946 that MS C ceases to use the exemplar of MS B and becomes, from that date, a direct copy of B itself.[62] The annals for 937–46 look, therefore, to have become available as a single group; since Edmund is mentioned in every one of them, either as ætheling or king, and they portray his equivocal achievement in a consistently favourable light, it is difficult not to think that the king, or someone close to him, was involved in their circulation. While this yields no conclusive evidence for the date of 'Brunanburh', it suggests quite strongly that the poem had been composed by 946, since its text was available in more than one scriptorium soon after that date; it also strengthens the earlier arguments that 'Brunanburh' was more closely tied to the interests of Edmund than to his elder brother, Athelstan.

A second objection might be raised: whereas the language of 'Brunanburh' is demonstrably in tune with the 'imperial' aspirations of Athelstan and his court, the poem's continued insistence on the theme of Anglo-Saxon lordship over all the peoples of Britain sets it at one remove from the more muted ethnic nationalism that was the keynote of Edmund and Eadred's reigns. Though Oda, archbishop of Canterbury, was prepared to ascribe to him a *regalis imperium* 'to which all peoples are subject',[63] Edmund himself was more modest. In the charters of Edmund's reign the commonest title accorded the king is 'rex Anglorum ceterarumque gentium in circuitu persistentium' (or some slight variation upon this),[64] a significantly smaller claim than Athelstan's *rex totius Britanniae*. As Edmund's political position improved, so his charters became a little more assertive, adding the doublet *gubernator et rector* to the royal title towards the end of his reign,[65] but although a handful of his charters repeat Athelstan's claims to an overlordship of all the peoples of Britain, the authenticity of most of them is open to serious doubt, while the very variety of their phrasing suggests that, even if genuine, the scribes or

---

[61] Bately, *The Anglo-Saxon Chronicle, MS A*, pp. xlix–l.

[62] Taylor, *The Anglo-Saxon Chronicle, MS B*, pp. xxxvii–l.

[63] *Councils and Synods with Other Documents Relating to the English Church, Part 1 (871–1066)*, ed. D. Whitelock, M. Brett and C.N.L. Brooke (Oxford 1981) vol. 1, p. 67.

[64] Sawyer 465, 467, 471, 474, 475, 482, 483, 486, 487–9, 491–2, 502, 510, 512.

[65] Sawyer 493, 494, 496–97, 499, 500, 504, 506–507, 513.

draftsmen were here acting on their own initiative.[66] Eadred, in his turn, generally continued to use the style he inherited from his brother, invariably subscribing such charters as *rex Anglorum*,[67] though his diplomas show greater variety in the royal titles they employ. One group, apparently connected with the abbeys of Abingdon and Glastonbury, looks back to Athelstan's ambitions, hailing the king as *rex et primicerius totius Albionis*.[68] Another looks forward to the simpler form that was eventually to be adopted by Edgar, *rex Anglorum*[69] – a style designed to emphasise the reality of West Saxon control over the English homeland rather than their cloudier aspirations to a British overlordship. If 'Brunanburh' were a product of the West Saxon court, this would be a major objection to any attempt to locate the origins of the poem in Edmund's reign. It fits well, though, with the view of the poem advanced here, as the product of a provincial scriptorium, less influenced by the current practice of the royal scribes than by the ideals of the diocesan bishop, a former clerk of Athelstan's household who remained steeped in the aspirations of his reign, still loyal to the receding vision of the separate peoples of Britain united under the rule of a single king.

I conclude this discussion of the context of 'Brunanburh', therefore, with the suggestion that the poem is likely to have been a product of the Worcester scriptorium and is perhaps best dated to the early years of the reign of Edmund, Athelstan's brother and successor. But this suggestion remains, in the end, no more than a conjecture. The exact place and date of the poem's composition is unknown to us and likely, in the present state of knowledge, to remain so. What can be asserted with confidence is that, set within its contemporary context, 'Brunanburh' becomes a more considerable, more artful, achievement than has often been allowed. Much criticism has, in the past, been directed at the poem's alleged lack of originality; it is said to be '. . . only 73 lines of indifferent verse . . . as full of clichés as a B.B.C. cricket commentary'.[70] 'Brunanburh''s vocabulary is, indeed, sometimes archaic, its metrical structure conservative, its

---

[66] E.g. Sawyer 498: *provincie Britonum ruris gubernator*; Sawyer 505: *totiusque Albionis primicerius*; Sawyer 509: *rex et primicerius totius Albionis*; Sawyer 511: *tocius Britanniae rex*.

[67] Sawyer 518, 519, 521, 523, 524–28, 530–31, 533–35, 541–43, 547, 579–80.

[68] Sawyer 560, 561, 563–65, 568, 570–71. N. Banton, 'Monastic Reform and the Unification of Tenth-Century England', *Studies in Church History* 18 (1982), pp. 73–74.

[69] Sawyer 551, 552, 558, 578.

[70] Page, 'A Tale of Two Cities' (as n. 13), p. 336.

imagery highly traditional; at least twenty-one half lines in the poem can be found elsewhere in Old English verse.[71] To criticise the poem on these grounds is to misunderstand its purpose and considerably to underestimate the skill with which it allies medium and message. Faced with the gravest political crisis since Alfred's day the West Saxon kings of the mid tenth century responded, as Alfred had done, with a cultural policy of 'vigorous archaism' inspired by their 'profound sense of dynastic insecurity', seeking to gather and preserve the traditions of the West Saxon royal house in their purest form.[72] 'Brunanburh' should be seen as a part of this policy. Far from being the academic exercise in antiquated metres that critics have described, its conservative structure and language constitute a crucial part of its contemporary appeal and serve to remind the poem's audience of the values and traditions now under attack. 'Brunanburh' takes an important but far from conclusive victory and endows it with the inevitability that only history can impart; in the closing lines, the heroic vistas to which its studied archaisms have been consistently pointing are suddenly revealed. In its stately reiteration of the *bretwalda* theme, as in its emphasis on the fraternal concord between Athelstan and Edmund and the nobility of their ancestry, the poem shows itself to be closely in tune with the views and aspirations of the contemporary West Saxon court. It was highly practical in its concerns, a rallying-cry to the West Saxons to take heart from the achievements of Athelstan. Although the short set of verses on the freeing of the Five Boroughs, entered in the Chronicle under the annal for 942, has been described as 'the first political poem in the English language',[73] the accolade could go, with equal justice, to 'Brunanburh'.

But if the contextualisation of 'Brunanburh' helps towards a better appreciation of its content, a close reading of the poem can, in turn, add something to our knowledge of the historical context. 'Brunanburh' is an important witness to the terms in which contemporaries viewed Athelstan and the image of the king it presents differs radically, in one important respect, from that of later generations. To his descendants, Athelstan's reputation was that of a *rex pius*, an assiduous collector of relics and a great benefactor to the churches of his kingdom. It was therefore natural to associate his great victory at *Brunanburh* closely with his careful

---

[71] *The Battle of Brunanburh*, ed. A. Campbell (London, 1938), pp. 38–41.

[72] Wallace-Hadrill, *Early Medieval Kingship*, p. 213; Parkes, 'Palaeography of the Parker MS', p. 167.

[73] Stenton, *Anglo-Saxon England*, p. 354.

cultivation of divine favour. Ælfric, abbot of Eynsham, specifically makes the connection in one of his homilies when, to illustrate his contention that 'kings were often victorious through God,' he chooses the example of 'Athelstan, who fought with Olaf and slew his army and put him himself to flight, and afterwards lived in peace with his people . . .'[74] Similarly, the twelfth-century *Annales Domitiani* ascribe Athelstan's victory to Christ's help, while William of Malmesbury and Simeon of Durham give the credit to the intervention of St. Aldhelm and St. Cuthbert respectively.[75] Yet there is no support for such an interpretation in 'Brunanburh', although it is the text closest in time to Athelstan himself. Besides the single, if striking, kenning for the sun – *Godes condel beorht* – early in the poem, the text carries no suggestion of divine aid or intervention on the king's behalf. If the victory at *Brunanburh* is ascribed to anything other than Athelstan's own valour, it is to the accumulated and inherited *virtus* of his kindred.

Although Athelstan was eager to adopt many of the imperial claims and attitudes of the Carolingians, his contemporary reputation was considerably more secular than theirs. Whereas the Old High German *Ludwigslied*, written to celebrate Louis III's victory over the Vikings at Saucourt in 881,[76] continually insists upon God's favour and protection for Louis, as well as upon the God-given nature of Louis' victory,[77] the Old English poem on Athelstan's triumph at *Brunanburh* makes no such claim. A further contrast can be drawn with the closely-related poem entered in the same manuscripts of the Chronicle as 'Brunanburh', celebrating Edmund's recapture of the Five Boroughs in 942.[78] There, the king's victory is clearly compared with the saving work of Christ Himself, redeeming the Christian Danes from their bondage under the heathen Norse. If Athelstan's public image was so secular, not only in comparison with the later Carolingians but even with his brother and successor on

---

[74] *The Old English Version of the Heptateuch, Ælfric's Treatise on the Old and New Testament and his Preface to Genesis*, ed. S.J. Crawford (Early English Text Society 160, London, 1922), p. 416.

[75] F.P. Magoun, '*Annales Domitiani Latini*: An Edition', *Medieval Studies* 9 (1947), p. 260; *De Gestis Regum Anglorum*, vol. 1, p. 142; Symeon of Durham, *Historia Ecclesiae Dunhelmensis*, ed. T. Arnold (Rolls Series, London, 1882), vol. 1, p. 76, and cf. *Vita Sancti Odonis*, Migne, PL 133, cols. 937–38.

[76] W. Braune and E.A. Ebbinghaus, *Althochdeutsches Lesebuch* (Tübingen, 15th. edn., 1969), pp. 136–38.

[77] Especially lines 21–23, 39–40, 44–47.

[78] A. Mawer, 'The Redemption of the Five Boroughs', *EHR* 38 (1923), pp. 551–57.

the West Saxon throne, it may be that the largely ecclesiastical nature of the surviving source-material relating to him has over-emphasised one side of his character. The *rex pius* has been allowed to obscure the *rex robustissimus*, a warlord 'kind to his own, but everywhere terrible to his enemies', a man with whom Norse mercenaries could, without incongruity, take service.[79] It is within this ancient but still vital tradition that 'Brunanburh', learned and consciously archaising though it is, successfully places Athelstan.

---

[79] *The Chronicle of Aethelweard*, p. 54; *Historia Ecclesiae Dunelmensis*, vol. 1, p. 76; *Egils Saga*, p. 128.

3

Bishop Gerard of Toul (963–94) and Attitudes to Episcopal Office

John Nightingale

The bishop as both *bellator* and *orator* is a familiar figure in the Ottonian Reich. In considering the relationship between these two roles it is customary to look at sources such as the *Vita Brunonis Archiepiscopi Coloniensis*. Its author, Ruotger, reflected the political and military demands made of the Ottonian episcopate and forged them into a compelling ideal which presented the political and religious roles of a bishop as complementary not contradictory: service for king and *respublica* was necessary and laudable as the means by which *pax* and *justitia* could be achieved.[1] Such accounts have helped shape modern approaches to the episcopate in tenth- and eleventh-century Germany, focusing attention on the political, military and religious links between the bishops and their rulers which lent such an important degree of solidity to the *Reich*.[2] The

---

[1] *Ruotgeri Vita Brunonis*, ed. I. Ott (MGH SRG, nova series 10, Weimar, 1951) with the analysis by F. Lotter, *Die 'Vita Brunonis' des Ruotger* (Bonner Historische Forschungen 9, Bonn, 1958), especially p. 115 ff. For other *vitae* conforming to this ideal see O. Köhler, *Das Bild des geistlichen Fürsten in den Viten des 10, 11, 12 Jahrhunderts* (Abhandlungen zur mittleren und neueren Geschichte 77, Berlin, 1935), pp. 9–45, and A. Vauchez, *La Sainteté en Occident aux derniers siècles du moyen âge* (Bibliothèque des écoles françaises d'Athènes et de Rome 241, Paris, 1981), p. 329 ff.

[2] Amongst the huge literature see especially J. Fleckenstein, *Die Hofkapelle der deutschen Könige* 2 (Schriften der MGH 16/2, Stuttgart, 1966), especially p. 53 ff., L. Auer, 'Der Kriegsdienst des Klerus unter den sächsischen Kaisern', *Mitteilungen des Instituts für österreichische Geschichtsforschung* 79 (1971), pp. 316–407 and 80 (1972),

41

portrayal of the bishop's dual roles as harmoniously entwined is seen as exemplifying not only the contemporary perception but even the very nature of episcopal office until the onset of the 'Gregorian reform' in the second half of the eleventh century.[3]

Yet as Karl Leyser has commented with characteristic perception, there was already a restrained debate on the tasks and responsibilities of episcopal office from the very beginning of the development towards an Ottonian *Reichskirche* which the eleventh-century reformers attacked.[4] Beneath the surface of the *vitae, miracula* and charters of the tenth century it is possible to glimpse a widespread unease with the dual role of bishops, most notably within the monastic milieu to which Ruotger himself belonged. This dissatisfaction is often overlooked, in part because its horizons do not extend to the royal service of bishops on which attention is lavished; instead it is grounded in the daily and (if we follow the sources) more pressing activities of bishops within their dioceses, specifically, in the tensions engendered at this local level by the conflicting demands of a bishop's *oratores* and *milites* upon his ever-insufficient land and *gratia*. Such dissatisfaction is also overlooked because the criticisms, which are rarely direct, are easily missed when the portraits of bishops in *vitae* and *miracula* are read at face value without regard for their hortatory and admonitory functions. But this undercurrent of opposition to the worldly and militaristic roles of bishops, with its origins in the conflict between monasteries and their episcopal lords, needs to be recognised. It helped to shape, and to ensure a ready audience for, the thinking on bishops' responsibilities which came to prominence in the second half of the eleventh century.[5]

pp. 48–70, and G. Althoff, *Adels- und Königsfamilien im Spiegel ihrer Memorialüberlieferung* (Münstersche Mittelalter-Schriften 47, Munich, 1984).

[3] For a recent restatement of this view see J. Fleckenstein, 'Problematik der ottonisch-salischen Reichskirche', *Reich und Kirche vor dem Investiturstreit*, ed. K. Schmid (Sigmaringen, 1985), pp. 83–98.

[4] K.J. Leyser, 'The Polemics of the Papal Revolution', *Medieval Germany and its Neighbours, 900–1250* (London, 1982), p. 138 ff. My debt in this paper to Karl Leyser is by no means confined to this theme; only he can know his patience in guiding my footsteps into the history of this period, but he has taught us all to be more alert to the patterns of thought concealed in texts of the tenth and eleventh centuries.

[5] The importance of Lotharingia as a seedbed for the eleventh-century reform has long been recognised: A. Fliche, *La Réforme Grégorienne* (Louvain, 1924), vol. 1, p. 74 ff. But the extent to which Rather of Liège was no isolated critic and the extent to which the struggles between monasteries and their episcopal lords shaped this thinking are not fully appreciated.

It is with these themes in mind that I have chosen to examine the manner in which a single bishop, Gerard of Toul (963–94), fared in his diocese and was perceived by contemporaries. As a protégé of Archbishop Bruno of Cologne and a loyal servant of the *Reich* on one hand, and a patron of monastic reform and a saint on the other, Gerard appears to conform to Ruotger's model of an Ottonian bishop whose political and religious roles harmoniously coexisted. The principal source for the interpretation of Gerard is the *Vita S. Gerardi Tullensis,* composed at the request of Bishop Bruno of Toul (1019–52) who, after his election as Pope Leo IX, promoted Gerard to the status of a fully-fledged saint. Its author, Wideric, the reform abbot of Saint-Evre, attests to Gerard's loyalty to the Ottonians and his concern for the *res publica* but places his activity firmly within a religious, even quasi-monastic, mould.[6] The resulting portrait is of a bishop without blemish: a bishop who shunned company and conversation unless it was with clerics or monks; a bishop who gave up his nights to prayer and the psalter (which, like the best of reform monks he sometimes read at one go); a bishop who strove to instruct his clergy and people in divine doctrine; a bishop who knew the great religious figures of his age, performing miracles in the company of Majolus of Cluny and Adalbert of Prague.[7]

A more ambiguous picture emerges when we turn from the Gerard of the eleventh-century *Vita* and associated *Miracula* to the Gerard of more contemporary sources. The sources for his episcopate are relatively abundant and diverse: six royal diplomata granted at his request;[8] his own episcopal charters transmitted in six different archives;[9] other

---

[6] *Widerici Vita S. Gerardi* and the subsequent *Miracula* and *Translatio anno 1049,* MGH SS 4, pp. 490–509; the account of the former is well covered by M. Parisse, 'L'Evêque Impérial dans son diocèse', *Institutionen, Kultur und Gesellschaft im Mittelalter: Festschrift für J. Fleckenstein zu seinem 65. Geburtstag,* ed. L. Fenske *et al.* (Sigmaringen, 1984), pp. 192–208; N. Bulst, *Untersuchungen zu dem Klösterreformen Wilhelms von Dijon (962–1033)* (Pariser historische Studien 11, Bonn, 1973) p. 97 n. 102 for the reestablishment of Wideric's authorship of the *Vita* against A. Michel, *Die Akten Gerhards von Toul als Werk Humberts und die Anfänge der päpstlichen Reform,* Bayerische Akademie der Wissenschaften, philosophische-historische Klasse, Sitzungsberichte 1957 (Heft 8); J. Choux, 'St. Gérard fut-il canonisé par Léon IX?', *La Lorraine Chrétienne au Moyen Age* (Metz 1981), pp. 73–79.

[7] *Vita S. Gerardi* cc. 4 and 6, p. 493 ff.

[8] D O I 288–90, D O II 62 and 99, D O III 2.

[9] R-H. Bautier, *Les Origines de l'abbaye de Bouxières-aux-Dames au diocèse de Toul* (Nancy, 1987), no. 26, p. 98 ff.; A. Lesort, *Chronique et chartes de l'abbaye de Saint-Mihiel* (Mettensia 6, Paris, 1909–12), no. 29; G. Chevrier and M. Chaume, *Chartes et documents de Saint-Bénigne de Dijon* (Analecta Burgundica, Dijon, 1943), vol. 2, no. 204; M. Schaeffer, 'Chartes de l'abbaye Saint-Evre de Toul', Thèse 3e cycle, Université Nancy II, 1984, nos

contemporary charters from the church of Toul's dependent abbeys, Saint-Evre and Bouxières-aux-Dames; *miracula* of the patron saints of both Saint-Mansuy and Saint-Evre written during and shortly after Gerard's episcopate;[10] the *Chronicon Mediani Monasterii*, which was composed in the same decades as the *Vita S. Gerardi*.[11] These sources can convey a very different picture, namely of a bishop locked in conflict with the region's nobles, his own *milites*, his church's dependent abbeys, and even the *primicerius* of the cathedral community of canons as he struggled to survive and to preserve his church's position. There is of course nothing exceptional in this: the job of a tenth-century bishop was not easy.[12] But the extent to which these struggles and tensions influenced contemporary perceptions of Gerard and sharpened attitudes to episcopal office is not readily apparent. Only detailed examination reveals the ways in which a source such as the *Miracula S. Apri* was a commentary on its own time as much as a record of past events; it did not merely reflect the environment in which it was written but actively set out to shape and change this environment. In order to establish the background against which such texts were written, I will first sketch Gerard's relations with his *milites* and dependent abbeys on the ground.

The *Vita S. Gerardi* does not acknowledge Gerard's military activities. Where we might expect to hear of the bishop's *milites* we find only *fideles* and *familiares* – terms which conveniently covered a wide range of possibilities. However, Gerard's episcopal charters and their witness lists convey a reality in which Gerard was no exception to the rule that a bishop needed to surround himself with a military retinue and to seek wider support from the region's nobility in order both to survive in his diocese and to safeguard the interests of his church. Just how close the resulting ties

24 and 25 (extracts recorded in Paris Bibliothèque Nationale Latin 11902, f. 236–37); for Gerard's authentic charter of 968 and fabricated charter of 971 for the cathedral canons of Toul see respectively A. Calmet, *Histoire eccliastique et civile de Lorraine* (Nancy, 1728), vol. 1, *preuves*, col. 380 f. and *Gallia Christiana* (Paris, 1874) vol. 13, *instrumenta*, col. 457 ff.; for the seven authentic and purported charters of Gerard transmitted in Saint-Mansuy's archive, see below n. 21.

[10] See below, n. 31 and 34.

[11] *Liber de S. Hildulfi successoribus in Mediani Monasterii, alias Chronicon Mediani Monasterii*, MGH SS 4, pp. 87–92.

[12] I have studied these tensions under Gerard's predecessors and also under another 'patron of monastic reform', Bishop Adalbero of Metz (929–62) in 'Monasteries and their Patrons in the Dioceses of Trier, Metz and Toul', unpublished Oxford D.Phil thesis 1988, p. 101 ff. and 179 ff.

between Gerard and these *milites* could be is brought home by the donation he made in 969 to the monks of Saint-Mansuy, Toul in order to provide
both for a feast on the anniversary of his own ordination and for the
celebration of the obit of 'our most rare and most special *miles* Wolcher,
who was innocently and cruelly killed'.[13] One can also cite the evidence
from the witness list appended to Gerard's purported charters of 982 for
Saint-Mansuy that he made his own brother, Azelin, the count of Toul.[14]

The need to cultivate alliances was constant. The history of Gerard's
relations with two of the region's most powerful nobles, Counts Richard
and Odelric provides a graphic illustration of both his dependence on
military support and the fluid nature of this support. Both of these nobles
witnessed Gerard's charters (Richard in 963–65 and 986, Odelric in 969
and 974) and donated or sold lands to the church of Toul and its dependent
abbey of Saint-Evre.[15] As an example of Gerard's fearlessness, passivity
and readiness for martyrdom in the face of murderous attack, the *Vita
S. Gerardi* records how these two nobles set about usurping the church of
Toul's lands and responded to Gerard's anathema with an attempt on his
life when, against the advice of his followers, he ventured outside Toul.
Although the *Vita* claims that Gerard's followers only used kitchen utensils as weapons, a fierce struggle ensued: many of Gerard's followers were
killed, the house and neighbouring church where they had been resting
were both burnt, and Gerard himself was dragged from the church's altar
and forced at swordpoint to absolve those he had anathematised.[16]

---

[13] Paris Bibliothèque Nationale Baluze 47, f. 50 (a seventeenth-century copy).

[14] A. Calmet, *Histoire* (as n. 9), vol. 1, *preuves*, col. 387 f. and 389 ff.: 'Azelin count of
Toul, brother of the lord Pontiff'; also *Vita S. Gerardi*, c. 10, p. 497 for Gerard's 'glorioso
germanus frater, qui vir summae devotionis, ei assistebat incessanter . . .'; D H I 16 and
J. Schneider, 'Note sur quelques documents', *Revue Historique de la Lorraine 87* (1950),
p. 59 ff. for the church of Toul's aquisition of the Toul *comitatus* in the tenth century.

[15] *Vita S. Gerardi* c. 21, p. 503, and D O I 290 for their transactions with the church
of Toul and Saint-Evre. E. Hlawitschka, *Die Anfänge des Hauses Habsburg-Lothringen*,
(Saarbrücken, 1969), p. 139 ff. and 147 for Richard and his identity (notwithstanding
Wideric's claim that his line failed) as the father of Count Gerard of Metz and of Adelheid,
Conrad II's mother. See n. 13, and Schaeffer, *Saint-Evre* (as n. 9), no. 25 for the charters
witnessed by Odelric; Bautier, *Bouxières* (as n. 9), p. 33 ff., and M. Parisse, *La Noblesse
Lorraine* (Paris, 1976), vol. 1, p. 37 f. for the importance of the *Odelrici* in the region.

[16] *Vita S. Gerardi*, c. 20, p. 501 f.; Wideric may well have told the story as a warning to
the descendants of Richard and Odelric in his own day, but its portrayal of the dangers
for a bishop when he left the safety of his *civitas* closely accords with the attack on
Bishop Wigfried of Verdun (959–84) recorded in the *Gesta Episcoporum Virdunensium,
continuatio* c. 3, MGH SS 4, p. 46; also note D O II 157 for evidence of conflict between
Richard and the nunnery of Bouxières-aux-Dames.

The extent to which Gerard was caught between the conflicting demands of his military and religious followers is well illustrated by his charter of 968 for the canons of the church of Toul. This reveals his unsuccessful attempts to find a compromise between the rival claims of the canons and his own *fidelis* Waltfrid. The canons implored Gerard to restore the *abbatiola* of Saint-Martin on the Meuse which had been fraudulently alienated. Gerard endeavoured to do so 'with much labour and great difficulty' but made little headway until his *fidelis* Waltfrid, who was in possession of the foundation, agreed to regularise his position with a 'worthy and laudable precarial agreement'; a promise which in the event remained unfulfilled.[17]

Gerard's relations with the dependent abbeys of the church of Toul were complex and fraught with tension: patronage and spiritual devotion were inseparable from his struggles to retain control over the abbeys and to satisfy the interests of his military retinue. The treatment of Saint-Martin as little more than a valuable and disputed possession in the above transaction was not untypical. Under Gerard, as under his predecessors, both royal diplomata and narrative sources attest to the central importance of abbeys and their possessions as part of the church of Toul's patrimony.[18] Previous studies have already illustrated these themes with regard to Gerard's pursuit of the church of Toul's contentious claims to four abbeys outside the diocese: Montiérender (Chalons-sur-Marne), Enfonville (Besançon), Poulangy (Langres), and Saint-Gengoul at Varennes-sur-Amance (Langres).[19] The picture is little different when one turns to the abbeys which were most closely linked to the church of Toul: Saint-Evre at Toul, one of the leading centres in the monastic reform movement in Lotharingia, and the nunnery of Bouxières-aux-

[17] Calmet, *Histoire* (as n. 9), vol. 1, *preuves*, col. 380 f. For Waltfrid's importance and subsequent comital position see *Translatio et Miracula S. Firmini Flaviniacensibus* II, MGH SS 15/2, p. 808 and Schaeffer, *Saint-Evre* (as n. 9), no. 24.

[18] D O II 62 (despite interpolations it provides a near-contemporary overview of Gerard's claims), and *Vita S. Gerardi*, c. 21, p. 502 f.; note that the grant of circumscribed rights of free abbatial election by Gerard's predecessor was not at the expense of the church of Toul's claims of lordship. Parisse, *Noblesse* (as n. 15), vol. 1, p. 17 ff. for the church of Toul's constrained patrimony.

[19] M. Bur, *La formation du comté de Champagne* (Nancy, 1977), p. 141, and O. Collin, 'Le Sort des abbayes royales d'Enfonvelle, de Varennes-sur-Amance et de Poulangy après le partage de Meersen (870)', *Bulletin philologique et historique du comité des travaux historiques et scientifiques 1964* (1967), pp. 35–44.

Dames which had been established under Gerard's predecessor, Bishop Gauzelin (922–62). Gerard's generosity to both abbeys was confined to the first years of his episcopate: he restored two churches to Saint-Evre, donated at least seven churches to Bouxières, and secured royal confirmations of both abbeys' possessions in the period May 963 to June 965. In the remaining thirty odd years of his episcopate he appears to have donated only one further church to Saint-Evre and nothing at all to Bouxières. This surely exemplifies the process by which a bishop attempted to secure his lordship during the first uncertain years of his rule; once his position was better established his generosity could dwindle or be directed to new endeavours – it was not only kings who had to buy support in this way on their accession. Certainly the material motives behind his patronage are further underlined by the fact that – in contrast to his predecessors – he does not appear to have sought an association of prayer with the most renowned religious foundation in his diocese, namely the royal nunnery of Remiremont whose *Liber Memorialis* attests to the powerful spiritual attraction which it exerted far beyond the diocese.[20]

The diplomata of Saint-Evre and Saint-Mansuy, the latter's authentic and purported charters, and the *Miracula S. Mansueti*, composed during Gerard's episcopate, concur in presenting Gerard as the moving force behind Saint-Mansuy's transformation from a dependent cell of Saint-Evre to a fully-fledged and independent abbey.[21] The *Miracula* attribute

[20] Bautier, *Bouxières* (as n. 9), no. 26, p. 98 ff.; D O I 288 and 290, and for the later donation to Saint-Evre, D C II 200; but note Gerard's replacement as an intercessor by Duke Frederick (on whose conflicts with Gerard see below) and Bishop Wigfried of Verdun in Bautier, *Bouxières*, nos 33 and 37 (= D O II 157), which suggests he lost control of the nunnery despite his massive donation. *Liber Memorialis Romaricensis*, ed. E. Hlawitschka *et al.* (MGH Libri Memoriales 1, Dublin and Zurich 1970), f. 20v1, p. 42 for Ludelm, 11r28/1 and 20v6, pp. 20 and 43 for Drogo, and 6r6, p. 9 for Gauzelin.

[21] Saint-Mansuy's charters still await a detailed study, but see the *Miracula S. Mansueti*, cc. 8 and 10, MGH SS 4, p. 511, together with D O I 92 and 289 and Gerard's charters of 969 and 986, donating two churches to the abbey, which appear authentic: Paris Bibliothèque Nationale Baluze 47, f. 50 and *Gallia Christiana*, vol. 13, *instrumenta*, col. 460. Gerard's purported charters of 971, 974, 982 (x 2), and 988 for Saint-Mansuy were fabricated or extensively reworked in the eleventh century; the most easily accesible, though inaccurate, editions are, with their dates, Calmet, *Histoire* (as n. 9), vol. 1, *preuves*, col. 383–85 (971), 387 f. (982 A), 389–91 (982 B), 393 (988), and *Gallia Christiana* 13, *instrumenta*, col. 459–60 (974). Also see F. Roze, 'L'Abbaye Saint-Mansuy de Toul aux Xe–XIIe siècles', *Le pays Lorrain* 58 (1977), pp. 75–86, and Bulst, *Wilhelm* (as n. 6), pp. 99–102 (who does not question the authenticity of Gerard's charters for Saint-Mansuy).

Gerard's actions to his having been fired with devotion for St. Mansuy from the moment he entered the saint's oratory on first coming to Toul.[22] We should not, however, overlook the fact that Gerard's promotion of Saint-Mansuy was inevitably at the expense of other communities and other claimants to the bishop's *gratia* and, moreover, was subject to serious constraints and limitations. If the tenacity with which other communities opposed the independence of their dependent cells or abbeys is anything to go by, the monks of Saint-Evre were unlikely to have agreed willingly to cede their possession of Saint-Mansuy which, notably, had been confirmed to Saint-Evre in a royal diploma. It is clear that Gerard did not scruple to reappropriate the lands he had apportioned to Saint-Mansuy. This emerges from Gerard's purported charter of 974 for Saint-Mansuy which records his solemn restitution of the abbey's two most important estates, Aingeray and Malzey. The charter does not appear authentic in its present form: the elaborate and hortatory clauses of anathema, which have no parallel amongst the charters of Gerard transmitted in the archives of Bouxières, Saint-Mihiel and Saint-Bénigne, Dijon, point to its composition in the mid eleventh century along with Saint-Mansuy's other reworked charters.[23] It must, however, have drawn on an earlier source, for its details on Gerard's usurpation of the estates hardly tally with his eleventh-century cult. The narrative relates that Gerard gave both estates to the abbey and had them confirmed by royal precept, but later removed them for his own benefit. Their subsequent restitution is ascribed to the fact that Gerard was struck down by a serious fever; attributing this to the anger of St. Mansuy, he hurried to make amends by restoring the estates and recovered as soon as he did so.[24]

The long term effects of any such change of heart on Gerard's part should not be overestimated. Although the *Miracula S. Mansueti* and Otto I's 965 diplomata for Saint-Mansuy present Gerard's appointment of Abbot Adam as the central plank of Saint-Mansuy's new-found independent status, subsequent charters suggest the abbey quickly fell again under the sway of abbots of other abbeys: Adso of Montiérender in 969; Adalbert of Moyenmoutier (d. 985) in 982; Robert of Saint-Evre in 986;

[22] D O I 92.
[23] Editions cited above, nn. 21 (974) and 10.
[24] Note the echoes with the episode in the *Miracula S. Mansueti*, c. 17, MGH SS 4, p. 513 f., discussed below.

and in the eleventh century, the monastic reformer William of Dijon and then his prior from Saint-Evre, Wideric, who also became abbot of Moyenmoutier.[25] Whether the practice of sharing an abbot is attributable to the perennial shortage of suitably experienced religious experts, the lack of a sufficient endowment for an independent existence, or the desire of the bishops of Toul to retain a tighter control over their abbeys, it is clear that the community wished it to be otherwise: the purported general restoration and confirmation charter of Gerard, which appears wholly contrived in the eleventh century, claims that Gerard appointed Abbot Adam since he had realised the foundation could never be made permanent without its own special pastor.[26] What is true here, namely that such praise of Gerard reveals what the community wanted but failed to get from either Gerard or his successors, may also be the case for the other passages of praise in Saint-Mansuy's reworked charters. Against their claims that Saint-Mansuy held the foremost place in Gerard's prayers we should note that Gerard chose to be buried in the cathedral of Toul, not in Saint-Mansuy.[27]

Gerard's relations with the two great Vosges abbeys of Moyenmoutier and Saint-Dié, situated in the southern extremity of the diocese of Toul, likewise appear centred on the struggle for control of abbeys' possessions – an observation underscored by the evidence that the community of Moyenmoutier preferred the lordship of Duke Frederick (959–78), who had presided over the restoration and reform of both this abbey and Saint-Dié. Gerard's claim to lordship over both abbeys stemmed not from any involvement with monastic reform but rather from a demand for reparation in a property dispute elsewhere. Gerard appealed to Otto I against Frederick who had seized the church of Toul's estates in the vicinity of his newly constructed castle at Bar-le-Duc; to make amends, Frederick was ordered to cede the abbeys of Moyenmoutier and Saint-Dié and the great fisc of Bergheim in exchange. In the event Gerard's establishment of even a limited degree of lordship over these two abbeys was fraught with difficulty. Otto I, Otto II and Otto III granted diplomata in

[25] Editions cited above, n. 21, according to dates (969, 982 A, 986), see also Bulst, *Wilhelm* (as n. 6), pp. 99–102.

[26] Edition cited above, n. 21 (982 B).

[27] *Gesta Episcoporum Tullensium*, c. 34 (1*), in contrast to his predecessor, Bishop Gauzelin (922–62) who was buried in the nunnery of Bouxières-aux-Dames which he established, ibid., c. 31, MGH SS 8, p. 640 f.

support of the church of Toul's claims but, as so often, could not provide the support needed to put the terms of such diplomata into effect, and may well have lacked the will to do so in view of the fact that the rival claimant, Frederick, was married to Otto I's niece Beatrice. The extent to which the issues at stake were skirted around is underlined by the failure of Otto II's diploma restoring Saint-Dié (D O II 99) even to mention Frederick's previous and subsequent rights over the abbey. Beneath the apparent finality of the donations and confirmations recorded in the three surviving diplomata acquired by Gerard (D O II 62 and 99 and D O III 2) one can trace a series of tortuous negotiations, setbacks and compromises.[28]

In all three diplomata the church of Toul's interest in these abbeys is presented as an interest in valuable possessions and incomes. D O II 62 records that Gerard sought Moyenmoutier from Otto I for the augmentation of the church of Toul, not for the restoration of the actual abbey or its community which, notably, is not mentioned. Reference is made to the *prebenda monachorum* at Moyenmoutier and in 984 to the *prebenda canonorum* at Saint-Dié, but only as the first of the incomes reserved to the church of Toul. This context suggests the *prebenda* were being used to serve the wider needs of the church of Toul rather than the needs of the communities themselves. Thus it is hardly surprising that Moyenmoutier's later chronicler did not view Gerard's lordship with affection. He wrote at a time when the cult of Gerard was actively promoted and he acknowledged the bishop's reputation for sanctity, but this did not deter him from criticising the means by which Gerard memorialised his control. In addition to the exaction of oaths from the officers of both Moyenmoutier and Saint-Dié, we are told that Gerard took the croziers of their founding saints, Hildulf and Deodatus, away to his cathedral treasury and, to the disdain of the author, embellished them with precious metals and relics of the two saints. His asset-stripping even extended to Moyenmoutier's great bell; delighted by its sound he had it removed

---

[28] *Liber de S. Hildulfi* (as n. 11), cc. 6, 7 and 10, MGH SS 4, pp. 89–91; Richer, *Historia Senonensis Ecclesiae*, II, 10, MGH SS 25, p. 274 f.; *Chronicon S. Michaelis*, c. 7, MGH SS 4, p. 81; D O II 62 and 99 and D O III 2; note that the latter diploma's terms were not met: E. Boshof, 'Untersuchungen zur Kirchenvogtei in Lothringen im 10. und 11. Jahrhundert', *Zeitschrift der Savigny-Stiftung für Rechtsgeschichte, kanonistische Abteilung* 96–97 (1979–80), p. 68 f., and Bulst, *Wilhelm* (as n. 6), p. 102 ff. For the similar difficulties of the bishops of Toul in securing Bergheim see, J. Choux, 'Une possession des évêques de Toul en Alsace; la cour de Bergheim', *Lorraine* (as n. 6), pp. 131–37.

to Toul. The outrage which this engendered within the community of Moyenmoutier is conveyed by a miraculous sign: whereas twelve pairs of oxen struggled to transport it to Toul, its subsequent restitution to Moyenmoutier by Gerard's successor, Bishop Stephen (994–96) was carried out with ease by only four pairs.[29] Elsewhere memories of Gerard's sanctity might burgeon but at Moyenmoutier the monks still remembered him as a bishop against whom it was necessary to work miracles.

On the surface the *Miracula S. Mansueti* and *Miracula S. Apri* appear to bear out the approach of the *Vita S. Gerardi* to its subject. But the conflicts, tensions and criticisms of Gerard which have emerged in this cursory survey of other sources encourage a more circumspect approach. In considering the aims and import of *miracula* we are at an enormous disadvantage compared with their contemporary audiences. Often addressed to an abbey's temporal lord and designed to be read on the saint's feastdays, *miracula* were written for a well-informed audience which, drawing upon its shared experience, would inevitably note parallels and sense criticisms in the author's interpretation of events; each episode engaged and manipulated a larger set of memories that we can only guess at. Although we will miss many nuances, it is still often possible, by placing the *miracula* alongside other available evidence, to trace how stories set in the distant past had a direct bearing on current concerns. Their effect would have been to touch a raw nerve with certain listeners even when recent events were not described, either because they were so well-known or because they were still too highly charged to be broached directly.[30]

The *Miracula S. Mansueti*, written at Gerard's request, are numbered amongst the works of Adso of Montiérender who, although he made something of a profession out of writing *vitae* and *miracula*, had particular

---

[29] *Liber de S. Hildulfi* (as n. 11), c. 10 and 12, p. 91.

[30] For the audience and the admonitory function of *miracula* see B. de Gaiffier, 'L'Hagiographie et son public au XIe s.', *Subsidia Hagiographica* 43 (1967), pp. 475–507, and L. Zoepf, *Das Heiligen-Leben im 10. Jahrhundert* (Beiträge zur Kulturgeschichte des Mittelalters und der Renaissance 1, Leipzig and Berlin, 1908), pp. 12–30. See M. Wallace-Hadrill, *The Frankish Church* (Oxford, 1983), p. 300 ff. for Hincmar's use of the past in the *Vita S. Remigii* as ammunition in the present. Indirect criticism in other genres has been studied more closely: see for example, H. Beumann, 'Topos und Gedankengefüge bei Einhard', *Archiv für Kulturgeschichte* 33 (1951), pp. 337–50, and P. Godman, *Poets and Emperors* (Oxford, 1987), especially pp. 93–148.

reason to be knowledgeable regarding the affairs of Saint-Mansuy and its saint; he was an erstwhile monk of Saint-Evre and may have presided over Saint-Mansuy itself for a short period.[31] Though following the traditional form of a series of individual stories which display the saint's miraculous power, he sets each episode within the wider picture of Saint-Mansuy's gradual transformation into an abbey with its own monastic community. Gerard is given a central role in this process and praised accordingly. The work culminates with descriptions of how Gerard countered a major drought and a terrible plague by exhuming the body of St. Mansuy and taking it in procession from holy place to holy place.[32] But instead of ending on this triumphant note Adso chooses to conclude the work with a short story which brings into focus the more immediate relevance of the whole work to Gerard and the contemporary audience. It describes how Gerard was struck down by a chronic illness but recovered from this 'heavenly chastisement' when he turned to St. Mansuy. Adso makes it clear that Gerard was chastised for a reason but protests against giving the background – a literary device which no doubt had the effect of making Gerard and the audience recall events all too familiar to them. The details which Adso does divulge, namely that Gerard's *milites* opposed his wish to be taken to Saint-Mansuy, since they feared that he would be converted to the monastic life with the result that they would lose their possessions as well as their lord, suggest that the circumstances were similar to those already glimpsed in the 974 charter: Gerard had removed some of Saint-Mansuy's lands for the benefit of his *milites* but, to the chagrin of the new beneficiaries, restored them when he was struck down by illness.

The story conveyed the warning that a bishop should not listen to his *milites*, whose advice is dictated by their own worldly interests. More generally the story brought home the message of the whole work to Gerard, namely that he should never forget the power of St. Mansuy and should be careful to follow the model of episcopal behaviour set out in the *Miracula*. Here we must recognise the contrast between the congratulatory tone of the dedication to Gerard and the underlying

---

[31] Adso, *Miracula S. Mansueti*, MGH SS 4, pp. 489 n. 24 and 509–14. For Adso see *Miracula S. Bercharii*, cc. 9–11, MGH SS 4, p. 487 ff., and B. de Gaiffier, 'L'Hagiographie dans le marquisat de Flandre et le duché de Basse-Lotharingie au XIe s.', *Subsidia Hagiographica* 43 (1967), p. 426.

[32] *Miracula S. Mansueti*, cc. 10–16, pp. 511–13.

admonitory function of the work.³³

The *Miracula S. Apri*, which lack a dedicatory preface, appear to have been composed by a member of Saint-Evre's community shortly after Gerard's death.³⁴ The central chapters of the work describe the community's tribulations at the hands of Bishops Ludelm (895–906) and Drogo (906–22), the introduction of St. Benedict's Rule by Gauzelin in 936 and, as the culmination of the work, Gerard's rediscovery and exhumation of St. Aper's body in 978. These episodes have consequently provided the conventional history of the abbey.³⁵ But we should be cautious of using them in this way. Consideration of the stories composed around Ludelm and Drogo suggests that their contents should be read for what they tell us about the author's own day. The descriptions of the four bishops' relations with the abbey and its saint constitute a rudimentary treatise on the nature of episcopal office as it was seen and experienced by a dependent abbey of the church of Toul in the late tenth century. We are shown not only how bishops ought to act but also where and why they could and did go wrong. In presenting this critical aspect it was politic and less constraining to tell stories set in the distant past. Their relevance to contemporary circumstances would not have been missed by the audience and indeed on occasion the author explicitly alluded to the parallels. It is in this context that I will consider the author's treatment of each of the four bishops.

In his passage on Ludelm, the author describes Ludelm's failings and contrasts them with correct modes of action, thereby depicting both the antithesis and the model of a good bishop. Ludelm is accorded the traditional external qualities of a successful bishop but, by directly coupling

³³ Ibid., c. 17, p. 513 f. Compare with the *Vita Johannis Gorziensis*, praefatio and cc. 95–100 and 110–114, MGH SS 4, pp. 338 and 364 ff. – a work which was dedicated to Bishop Dietrich of Metz (965–84) but recorded a series of *miracula* chronicling land disputes with his esteemed predecessor, Bishop Adalbero.

³⁴ *Miracula S. Apri*, MGH SS 4, pp. 515–20 (AASS Sept V, pp. 70–79 for a full edition); MGH SS 4 p. 489, W. Wattenbach and R. Holtzmann, *Deutschlands Geschichtsquellen im Mittelalter* 1.1 (Cologne and Graz, 1967), p. 188, and Bulst, *Wilhelm* (as n. 6), p. 91 for their dating. The *inventio-elevatio* of 978 appears to have been the immediate stimulus for the work but the terms of c. 31 (see below) suggest Gerard was no longer alive; no reference is made to any subsequent bishop of Toul nor to any event after 978.

³⁵ *Miracula S. Apri*, cc. 20–31, pp. 516–20; see the references of E. Lesné, *Histoire de la propriété ecclésiastique en France*), 2.3 (Lille, 1928), pp. 62 and 101 and E. Sackur, *Die Cluniacenser* (Darmstadt, 1965), vol. 1, pp. 122 and 158.

these with his spiritual failings, it is made clear that such attributes alone could not make a good bishop. He was outstanding on account of his worldly nobility and enjoyed temporal domination and power, but he was less devoted to spiritual matters. With a skilful play on the traditional *topos* we are told that he did not assist monastic communities as a *pius consul* and *patronus* but rather ruled them as a *rigidus gubernator*; he did not hesitate to remove and distribute their possessions even though these had been given to secure the salvation of the donors. From these general contrasts the author then turns to the episode in which St. Aper caught up with Ludelm when the bishop was struck down with a septic arm. The cause of the illness was revealed to a local priest through a vision in which St. Aper appeared in person and furiously berated and battered Ludelm for taking the produce of the monks' meadow, which was meant to provide for the saint's horses, not the bishop's. Though told of the vision, Ludelm delayed carrying out the recommended restoration of alienated possessions with the consequence that his illness worsened and he died soon afterwards. Here the author concludes the episode with the visible proof of the gulf between saint and bishop: whereas all his predecessors were buried in Saint-Evre, Ludelm chose to be buried in Toul. To ensure the audience was left in no doubt as to the significance of this, the author adds a gloss interpreting the bishop's burial in Toul as a punishment for an enemy of the saint's *famuli*: such a choice was not something to be desired but rather to be feared by evil doers.[36]

This story was set in the distant past and can be verified in some, though by no means all, of its details.[37] Yet to confine attention to the narrative content of this story is to overlook the extent to which it was also about the author's own experience of bishops and their failings. We have already seen how Gerard was similarly afflicted with a near fatal illness after removing two of Saint-Mansuy's estates. Just as conflict between

---

[36] *Miracula S. Apri*, c. 20, p. 516 f.

[37] *Gesta Episcoporum Tullensium*, c. 29, MGH SS 8, p. 639, for Ludelm's burial in the cathedral, which he rebuilt. But the *primicerius* Bernefrid, who figures prominently in this and the subsequent story which the *Miracula* set in Drogo's episcopate, appears to have been drawn from an earlier period: a party to an 886 charter preserved at Saint-Mihiel (Lesort, *Chartes* [as n. 10], no. 17), Bernefrid was succeeded by the *primicerius* Rotland, who witnesses two Saint-Evre charters of 916: Schaeffer, *Saint-Evre* (as n. 9), nos. 13 and 14 (= *Gallia Christiana* 13, *instrumenta*, col. 452–53 and J. Mabillon, *Annales Ordinis Sancti Benedicti 3* [Paris, 1706], p. 697 [no 43]).

Gerard's military and monastic interests looms large in the Saint-Mansuy episode so here the references to horses indicate that military pressures were again at the heart of the dispute. The saint's words to Ludelm: 'This place was given to me by God and only committed to you', clearly still needed saying; drumming home the limitations of the rights of the bishop of Toul as the abbey's lord, they made it clear that he could not remove lands at will. Contemporaries were given little chance to miss the parallels: the author's condemnation of the cathedral as a burial place would have signified an unmistakable criticism of Gerard to an audience aware that Gerard had likewise chosen to be buried in the cathedral.[38] At first sight such criticism of Gerard may appear astonishing and directly at odds with the praise of him later in the *Miracula*. It can be more readily understood when considered within the framework of the well-rehearsed convention by which authors only criticised the powerful obliquely. A similarly indirect but pointed approach can be traced in the episode which follows: the well-known story of how the monks outwitted the attempts of Bishop Drogo to liquidate Saint-Evre's possessions and keep St. Aper's relics within Toul.[39]

The scene is set by describing how fear of the Magyar invasions forced the monks to take refuge within the walls of Toul. They brought the body of St. Aper with them and placed it in the church of St. John the Baptist, notwithstanding a clear sign that the saint did not wish to enter the town: his coffin took on such a weight that it could scarcely be carried by any number of the monks. Attention then moves to Bishop Drogo, in whose episcopate these events are placed. Drogo himself is praised: his noble birth and the effortless ability with which he carried out both public and spiritual functions won him universal respect. But he came perilously close to damnation on account of his heeding a 'degenerate' named Bulso, with whom he was accustomed to share his secrets. Here the author, heightening the dramatic effect through the adoption of the first person, recounts a long tirade in which Bulso belittled Saint-Evre's monks as *simulatores* and *seductores* and put forward a barrage of reasons why Drogo should take the abbey's possessions. This would not be a confiscation of alien land since they belonged to the bishop in the first place. It was justified by present necessity and by the fact that the monks

[38] Above, n. 27.
[39] *Miracula S. Apri*, cc. 24–29, p. 518 f.

did not help the bishop in royal expeditions, nor in the fortification of the town. Such a move was advisable because it would be for the good of the *militia patria*, and, more important, because the bishop lacked money. The abbey's possessions would be better deployed by being divided amongst the bishop's needy supporters. Moreover, lest the monks attempt to use their saint to reclaim their lands, the saint's relics should be detained in Toul, where they could be venerated by the populace in the cathedral; placed there they would better protect the bishop and serve the city.

The details of how the monks forestalled this conspiracy by hiding St. Aper's relics are a prerequisite for the author's subsequent account of their rediscovery in 978.[40] But this was not the only purpose of this episode. The opening references to the church of St. John the Baptist as the saint's enforced resting place and to the saint's antipathy to entering the town would have evoked an immediate parallel with Gerard's actions. For, if we follow the *Vita S. Gerardi*, Gerard had the relics of both St. Mansuy and St. Aper brought into the town and placed in this very church while he was seriously ill.[41] Wideric, writing with the benefit of hindsight, saw this as praiseworthy. At the time the monks of Saint-Evre may have been more resentful and suspicious of their bishop's intentions.

The great speech attributed to Bulso also articulates the kind of charges which the author and audience knew or feared were levelled against the community in their own day. Indeed, as one would expect, the arguments attributed to Bulso are in some respects more applicable to the author's time than to the early tenth century. The central thrust of Bulso's tirade, namely that Saint-Evre provided no military support to the hard-pressed bishop, reflected the legal situation in Gerard's episcopate but not that of Drogo: it was not until the reform of Saint-Evre by Gauzelin in the mid 930s that the community was relieved of all military *servitium*.[42] Bulso's argument that St. Aper would better serve

[40] *Miracula S. Apri*, cc. 32–33, p. 520.

[41] *Vita S. Gerardi*, c. 18, p. 500 f. See J. Choux, 'La cathédrale de Toul avant le XIIIe s.', in his *Lorraine* (as n. 6), p. 272 ff., for the church of St. John the Baptist and its use as the bishop's seat during the reconstruction of the cathedral. Note that the time-honoured convention by which St. Aper was held to have resisted removal to Toul was applied directly against Gerard vis-à-vis Moyenmoutier's bell.

[42] See D Charles III 125 and D Louis the Child 49, against Gauzelin's restoration charter, Schaeffer, *Saint-Evre* (as n. 9), no. 15 (= Calmet, *Histoire* [as n. 9], vol. 1, *preuves*, col. 342), and D O I 92; note how Gauzelin and Otto anticipate the possibility that subsequent bishops might try to reimpose a *servitium*.

the city and its populace if his body was relocated at the cathedral within Toul would have reminded the audience of Gerard's similar and, for the Saint-Evre community, equally disturbing priorities. Gerard's overriding concern for his cathedral, which he rebuilt, is well-attested by the *Vita S. Gerardi*.[43] We have already seen how his desire to adorn the cathedral with relics and splendid ornaments led him to remove some of the most important relics and treasures of Moyenmoutier and Saint-Dié. On purchasing the relics of St. Aper's sister St. Apronia from Troyes, he did not place them alongside St. Aper in Saint-Evre, as one might expect, but rather in the new foundation of Saint-Gengoul, which he had established within Toul. In recording this, Wideric echoes Bulso's argument in his attribution of this act to Gerard's desire to establish protection for the populace within the walls of the city.[44] In the light of such an explanation is it far-fetched to assume that at some point Gerard may have wished to act likewise with St. Aper and that Apronia was something of a second best – or at least that the monks of Saint-Evre may have feared as much? A parallel could be drawn with the evidence that Gerard established the nunnery of Saint-Gengoul at Toul in order to attempt to transplant the spiritual *locus* and thus the endowment of Saint-Gengoul at Varennes-sur-Amance (which was claimed by both the bishops of Toul and Langres), but then dissolved its community when this attempt failed. Clearly the kind of dissolution or liquidation urged by Bulso was not foreign to the contemporary audience's experience.[45]

Such parallels leave little doubt that the substance of Bulso's speech was designed by the author to evoke and provide a critical comment on far more recent threats by the bishop and his entourage to the community of Saint-Evre. Indeed an indication that the author knew that the speech

[43] *Vita S Gerardi*, cc. 5 and 12, pp. 494 and 498. See also his donation charter to the cathedral canons (above, n. 17), and *Gallia Christiana*, vol. 13, *instrumenta*, col. 457–59, for the further donations ascribed to Gerard in his purported charter of 971, which was already used by Wideric, *Vita S. Gerardi*, c. 21, pp. 502 f.

[44] *Vita S. Gerardi*, c. 5, p. 495. The continuing nature of such threats is underlined by the subsequent translation of the body of St. Arno from Saint-Mansuy to the cathedral by Bishop Hermann of Toul (1019–26): *Gesta Episcoporum Tullensium*, c. 37, MGH SS 8, p. 643.

[45] Collin, *Abbayes* (as n. 19), p. 38 ff. Such acts should be seen within the context of the urban growth in the Rhineland and Moselle from the mid tenth century onwards which led bishops to promote religious foundations more actively within their towns.

would embarrass and anger some of his audience may be seen in the remarks with which he concluded this passage on the conspiracy and the terrible retribution it brought upon its instigator, Bulso. Directly addressing his readers and listeners he stressed that he represented nothing falsely and that therefore no one should be angry that he wrote such things. Then after recounting how the monks forestalled the conspiracy, he concluded with an explicit reminder that such dangers were not confined to the past. As proof of the miraculous nature of the community's retention of St. Aper, the author contrasts it with what was 'known to nearly everyone', namely that the monks had been robbed of the precious body of the martyr, Eliphius, and other relics of the saints. No clearer sign could be given to the audience that they should consider the whole episode's relevance to their own day. For we know from the *Vita S. Gerardi* that Gerard had himself given the *maiora ossa* of St. Eliphius to Archbishop Bruno; the freedom with which Gerard donated as well as acquired relics might have seemed praiseworthy in hindsight but those who stood the loss saw it very differently.[46]

What does the story tell us about the attitudes of the author and his milieu to the nature of episcopal office? First, the author's praise of Drogo, despite his part in the conspiracy, reminds us that (as with attitudes to kings) it was not the bishops themselves who were held to be at fault, but rather the people in whom they confided; they surrounded themselves with the wrong people, sharing their secrets with *milites* rather than monks. Second, the episode provides graphic testimony to the level of the tension between a bishop's religious and military roles. The speech attributed to Bulso gives us a rare opportunity to hear the persuasive arguments which bishops' *milites* used to defend and further their claims to episcopal possessions; it provides the other side to the arguments put forward in countless *vitae, miracula* and *arengae* in favour of the claims of religious communities and their saints.[47] Third, in contrast to Ruotger's acceptance of a bishop's military and religious roles as complementary, the author's handling of this episode provides an indication of the very

[46] *Vita S Gerardi*, c. 5, p. 495, and the references of Ruotger, *Vita Brunonis* (as n. 1), c. 31 and 49, pp. 32 and 54.

[47] Similar if less detailed justifications of the claims of *milites* on episcopal possessions can be found in *gesta episcoporum*, for example, Anselm of Liège, *Gesta Episcoporum Leodiensium* II c. 29, MGH SS 7, p. 206.

different attitudes which were also current within the milieu of the leading reform monasteries in Lotharingia. At the same time we should note that the bishop's involvement with *milites* was opposed not on theoretical grounds so much as because in practice it was at the expense of the monks' possessions.

In Ludelm we have seen a portrait of a bishop beyond redemption and in Drogo a portrait of a bishop who came perilously close to damnation. In Gauzelin and Gerard we have their respective foils: an ideal bishop and a bishop who had to mix in the world but did not succumb to its dangers. Although Gerard presided over the exhumation which forms the culmination of the *Miracula*, it is Gauzelin who receives the mantle of the ideal bishop *par excellence*. The introduction of St. Benedict's Rule at Saint-Evre is dealt with in just a couple of sentences but the author builds up to this summit of Gauzelin's achievements with an elaborate set-piece on Gauzelin's qualities. Laden with superlatives and unfettered by mention of worldly activity, Gauzelin is lifted out of time to conform to a religious ideal. His noble birth was accompanied (in contrast to Ludelm's) by spiritual qualities in equal measure. Ever vigilant and intent on salvation, deeply committed to St. Aper, and devoted in the cultivation of monastic religion and the restoration of sacred places, Gauzelin never left the path of righteousness and sought to win all men over, not by commanding but by helping them; here the earlier play on this *topos* in connection with Ludelm is recalled.[48]

The author's protestation that such superlatives were the truth and not the stuff of panegyric conforms to the traditions of such set-pieces. It may also reflect his awareness that this portrait was not easily tallied with the kind of bishop his audience knew. For when he turns to Gerard, it is clear that the fresher memories of his audience did not allow him simply to gloss over the tensions between such ideals and the realities of episcopal office. In contrast to the language of love, goodness and happiness, which permeates the chapter on Gauzelin, Gerard is introduced (in the same way as Drogo) with an image which immediately summons up the harsh environment in which he struggled: God ordained Gerard to rule lest his flock, cut adrift without a ruler amidst worldly tempests, should suffer from the incursions of enemies and the loss of lands. Gerard is given the attributes of sanctity – a childhood presage of his future destiny, devotion

---

[48] *Miracula S. Apri*, c. 30, p. 519.

to prayer and chastity, and a constant preoccupation with the places, bodies and relics of the saints. Yet the tone is defensive and apologetic: 'though he was forced to mingle with the world – for no one was able to act otherwise in such an office and so perverse a time – yet with his soul he still showed his wish to live for Christ'. That here the author was actively engaging with an audience which might remember Gerard in a less favourable light is brought home in the striking passage with which he concludes the chapter:

> If, however, he was seen in human eyes to rule less rightfully, he was forced into this for a while by the spectre of the disturbed kingdom. If there is anyone who says this does not please him, he should reflect upon the great perversity of the time, the proximity of this place (Toul) to enemies, and the power of those within the diocese (*facultas subjectarum personarum*), and then perchance he will realise he would have to act in the same way.[49]

Though we can never be a party to the memories which the author felt it so necessary to respond to here, the episodes on Ludelm and Drogo, when read in conjunction with other sources, give some idea of what they may have been. This passage leaves in no doubt the contemporary awareness of the intrinsic tensions between the actual requirements of episcopal office and the ideals of religious life.

The approach of the *Vita S. Gerardi* to its subject betrays little of this complexity. Its Gerard has been sanctified by time, transformed into a bishop without blemish.[50] Although Moyenmoutier might still preserve memories of Gerard which were far from complimentary, Wideric does not appear to have felt any need to defend his hero or engage with the more ambiguous memories of Gerard that can still be glimpsed in

[49] Ibid., c. 31, p. 519. Note the parallels with the similarly defensive tone of Ruotger, *Vita Brunonis*, especially cc. 20, 22, 23 and 38, pp. 19 ff. and 40 f., discussed by Lotter, *Ruotger* (as n. 1), p. 115 ff. Also see *Vita S. Gerardi*, cc. 14 and 15, AASS Sept V, p. 73 (omitted from the MGH edition) for a land dispute with a bishop who, uncharacteristically, is not named; this and the very cautious tone of the criticism gives the episode a contemporary ring.

[50] *Vita S Gerardi*, c. 4, p. 493 f. The way the memory of a bishop could be sanctified by time has been nicely demonstrated by P. Fouracre, 'Merovingian History and Merovingian Hagiography', *Past and Present* 127 (1990), pp. 3–38, especially 11 ff.

the *Miracula*. There are plenty of individual touches – for example how Gerard invoked the nocturnal protection of certain saints by placing books of their lives beside his bed in such a way that they were turned over whenever he turned in his sleep. But the critical undercurrents of the *Miracula* have gone: in the *Vita*, the details of how Gerard turned to St. Mansuy in illness, brought the relics of Saints Mansuy and Aper into Toul, and donated the relics of St. Eliphius to Bruno of Cologne become mere examples of Gerard's devotion to the saints.[51]

However, by presenting such an idealised picture, the *Vita S. Gerardi* formed a further contribution to the active debate on the nature of episcopal office. To tell the militaristic Bishop Bruno of Toul, to whom the *Vita* was dedicated, that his saintly predecessor's retinue only defended Gerard with kitchen utensils was to make a powerful and pointed statement about how a bishop and his retinue should behave and act.[52] Although Wideric records Gerard's close links with the Ottonian rulers and his concern for the *res publica*, the portrait is primarily of a bishop appropriated to the religious and spiritual sphere. If Gerard gave military service to the Ottonians we do not hear of it; his presence in Italy in 983 is explained as a pilgrimage to Rome, though in reality it may have had more in common with the journeys of Wigfried of Verdun (958–84) and Dietrich of Metz (965–84) who combined military service with relic hunting. As presented to us, the moral of Gerard's reactions to the 984 succession crisis is that bishops should be excused from military involvement; they should pray but not fight for the rightful party.[53] It is a pacific and unworldly ideal which can be contrasted with the kind of exaltation of bishops as leaders that is found in Sigebert of Gembloux's life of Gerard's contemporary, Dietrich of Metz.[54] But if we follow the evidence of other sources on Gerard, this difference is to be attributed not so much to a difference between the two bishops as to a divergence

[51] *Vita S. Gerardi*, cc. 18 and 5, pp. 500–1 and 495.

[52] Ibid., *praefatio* and c. 20, pp. 490 and 502 f. For Bruno's military reputation see Wibert, *Vita Leonis IX*, cc. 5–10, ed. J. Watterich, *Pontificum Romanorum ... Vitae* (Leipzig, 1862), vol. 1, p. 131 ff.

[53] *Vita S. Gerardi*, cc. 2, 6, 11 and 16, pp. 492, 495, 498 and 500.

[54] For Dietrich and his *Vita* by Sigebert of Gembloux (MGH SS 4, pp. 462–83) see M. Parisse, 'Thierry Ier, évêque de Metz (965–84)', *Les Cahiers Lorrains* 17 (1965), pp. 110–18, and R. Folz, 'Un évêque ottonien, Thierry I de Metz', *Media in Francia. Mélanges offerts à K-F. Werner* (Maulévrier, 1989), pp. 139–56.

in opinions as to how bishops should act and behave.[55]

To recognise that the *Vita* is part of this dialogue is to understand at least part of how and why Gerard became a saint: Gerard the bishop was refashioned to provide an example to his successors – a process already apparent in the *Miracula S. Mansueti* and *Miracula S. Apri*. In view of Wideric's own violent clashes while he was the prior of Saint-Evre with Bishop Hermann of Toul (1019–26), there is every reason to believe he felt as much dissatisfaction with bishops as these other monastic authors.[56] He describes Gerard's concern with educating the people and the clergy, but in composing the *Vita*, he himself was turning to the urgent task of educating bishops in their tasks and responsibilities.

From the contemporary narrative sources, and from the charters we have seen how Gerard, like other bishops, was compelled to associate with *milites*. The *Miracula* allow us to glimpse the great strain which this imposed on Gerard's relationship with his church's dependent abbeys; beneath the harmonious surface lies an undercurrent of conflict in which the dual roles of a bishop are presented as irreconcilable. The *Vita S. Gerardi*, on the other hand, loses sight of Gerard's military concerns but in so doing puts forward an uncompromising ideal of a bishop as an *orator* which was clearly at odds with the bishops of the author's own day. In both *Miracula* and *Vita* we are thus seeing an ideal strengthened by reaction to practical conflicts on the ground; the opposition to the bishop's role as a *bellator* arose from the fact that there were not enough lands and *gratia* to satisfy the demands upon them. It is to such tensions between the rival claims of a bishop's *bellatores* and *oratores* that we should look in considering what shaped the eleventh-century reform ideology on episcopal office and ensured it a ready audience.

[55] Wideric's account in *Vita S. Gerardi*, c. 17, p. 500 of how Gerard's contemporaries criticised his predecessor Gauzelin for being led astray by secular concerns may perhaps give an idea of how Wideric's own contemporaries were arguing about the character of Gerard and his successors.

[56] *Vita Willelmi Abbatis Divionensis*, c. 11, ed. N. Bulst, *Rodulfus Glaber Opera* (Oxford, 1989), p. 284, and *Vita Leonis IX* (as n. 49), c. 6, p. 133.

4

Episcopal Authority Authenticated and Fabricated: Form and Function in Medieval German Bishops' Catalogues

Benjamin Arnold

In medieval Europe there were few governing elites so firmly entrenched in their power as the bishops of the *regnum Teutonicorum*. Their spiritual authority was, of course, common to all who held episcopal office,[1] so the more formidable standing of German bishops was based upon other considerations: upon their political proximity to the imperial court;[2] upon their social and familial connexions with the secular aristocracy of Germany;[3] and upon their vast material resources consisting of towns, tolls, manors, fortresses, forests, monasteries, and armed retinues.[4] Although

---

[1] K. Pennington *et al.*, 'Bischof', *Lexikon des Mitt Mittelalters*, ed. R.-H. Bautier *et al.* (Munich, 1983), vol. 2, cols. 228–38; F. Merzbacher, 'Bischof', *Handwörterbuch zur deutschen Rechtsgeschichte*, ed. A. Erler and E. Kaufmann (Berlin, 1971), vol. 1, cols. 439–46; F. Prinz (ed.), *Herrschaft und Kirche: Beiträge zur Entstehung und Wirkungsweise episkopaler und monastischer Organisationsformen* (Monographien zur Geschichte des Mittelalters 33, Stuttgart, 1988), pp. 1–108.

[2] See now the account by H. Zielinski, *Der Reichsepiskopat in spätottonischer und salischer Zeit, 1002–1125* (Stuttgart, 1984).

[3] E.g. C. Brühl, 'Die Sozialstruktur des deutschen Episkopats im 11. und 12. Jahrhundert', *Aus Mittelalter und Diplomatik: Gesammelte Aufsätze 1, Studien zur Verfassungsgeschichte und Stadttopographie* (Hildesheim, 1989), vol. 1, pp. 336–50.

[4] On German bishops active in warfare, see F. Prinz, *Klerus und Krieg im früheren Mittelalter: Untersuchungen zur Rolle der Kirche beim Aufbau der Königsherrschaft* (Monographien zur Geschichte des Mittelalters 2, Stuttgart, 1971); L. Auer, 'Der Kriegsdienst des Klerus unter den sächsischen Kaisern', *Mitteilungen des Instituts für österreichische Geschichtsforschung* 79 (1971), pp. 316–407 and 80 (1972), pp. 48–70;

churchmen were forbidden in canon law to exercise jurisdictions which carried the death sentence,[5] the German bishops nevertheless possessed powerful secular jurisdictions, such as counties and duchies, under which it was customary to delegate the infliction of ultimate penalties to secular representatives. In the eleventh century, for example, Adam of Bremen reported that the bishops of Würzburg held all the counties of their diocese in their hands,[6] and in 1168 Bishop Herold of Würzburg was commissioned by Emperor Frederick Barbarossa as *episcopus et dux* in eastern Franconia, with very extensive juridical authority there.[7] In addition to these advanced powers in the military, political and jurisdictional spheres, the bishops also dominated one of the institutions highly cherished by the aristocracy of medieval Germany, the election of kings and emperors.[8] With all this to show, it is not surprising that Caesarius of Heisterbach could claim that 'Nearly all the bishops of Germany carry a double-edged sword . . .', which advanced their secular authority, however perilous this may have been to the salvation of their souls.[9] But in spite of this extraordinary investment of time and energy in their temporal interest, the German bishops were not behind as saints and missionaries, reformers and ecclesiastical administrators either.[10]

We possess enormously rich resources for the study of the medieval German bishops in the form of their charters, letters, biographies, land registers, custumals, cartularies, books of fiefs, synodal statutes, coins and seals, necrological records, chronicles of their reigns, liturgical

K.F. Werner, 'Heeresorganisation und Kriegführung im deutschen Königreich des 10. und 11. Jahrhunderts', *Ordinamenti militari in Occidente nell'alto Medioevo* (Settimane di Studio del Centro italiano di Studi sull'alto Medioevo 15, Spoleto, 1968), pp. 791–843.

[5] A. Erler, 'Ecclesia non sitit sanguinem', *Handwörterbuch* (as n. 1), vol. 1, cols. 795–98.

[6] B. Schmeidler (ed.), *Adam von Bremen, Hamburgische Kirchengeschichte* (MGH SRG, 3rd edn., Hanover, 1917), pp. 188–89.

[7] D F I 546.

[8] L. Weiland (ed.), *Constitutiones et acta publica imperatorum et regum* (MGH Legum, section 4, Hanover, 1893), vol. 1, no. 167, p. 233 (1158): . . . 'electionis primam vocem Maguntino archiepiscopo, regalem unctionem Coloniensi . . .'.

[9] A. Hilka (ed.), *Die Wundergeschichten des Caesarius von Heisterbach* (Publikationen der Gesellschaft für rheinische Geschichte 43, Bonn, 1933), vol. 1, p. 127: 'Duplicem habent gladium pene omnes episcopi Alemannie, unde et magnus eis timor incumbit.' See the essay by T. Reuter in this volume.

[10] From the enormous literature I can only cite here H. Kallfelz (ed.), *Lebensbeschreibungen einiger Bischöfe des 10.–12. Jahrhunderts* (Ausgewählte Quellen zur deutschen Geschichte des Mittelalters. Freiherr vom Stein-Gedächtnisausgabe 32, Darmstadt, 1973).

memorials, records of their courts and visitations, and yet further source categories, including episcopal lists which often include no more than an unadorned succession of personal names.[11] A practice well established in antiquity, the registration of proper names recorded the status of the powerful and the obligations of their subjects as well as preserving the identity of the deceased for commemorative purposes. Accurate knowledge in genealogy and chronology depended to some degree upon raw lists of personal names,[12] and the relative efficiency and simplicity of such written catalogues as a preservative technique ensured their continued use in the church when secular literacy began to die out of the western Roman world in the fifth and sixth centuries.[13] In medieval Germany the construction of lists of bishops and abbots served several purposes, one of them paralleled by the genealogical records of secular lineages;[14] to attest the legitimate transmission of authority and material resources from the office holders of one generation to the next. This common motive was advertised more explicitly in those lists which ran the names of lay founders or patrons in conjunction with the ecclesiastical incumbents of certain sees and monasteries. Such a dual list was appended in the twelfth century to a copy of Rufinus of Aquileia's continuation of Eusebius' *History of the Church* owned by the monastery of St. James at Mainz, the monk completing his computation of the regnal years of the archbishops of Mainz and of the Frankish and German kings and emperors since Pepin the Short (741–68) and St. Boniface (722–754) in the following manner:

Henry, the third of this name, reigned for sixteen years. Bishop Siegfried sat twenty-four years. The fourth Henry reigned for fifty-one years. Bishop

---

[11] The most convenient collection was edited by G. Waitz and O. Holder-Egger: *Catalogi Episcoporum, Abbatum*, MGH SS 13, pp. 272–392.

[12] Discussion of examples by W. Kubitschek, 'Königs-, Priester-, Eponymen-, Beamtenverzeichnisse als Grundlage chronographischer Systeme', *Paulys Real-Encyclopädie der classischen Altertumswissenschaft*, ed. G. Wissowa et al., vol. 11, part 1 (Stuttgart, 1921), cols. 996–1033.

[13] P. Anderson, *Passages from Antiquity to Feudalism* (London, 1974), p. 131.

[14] On them e.g. G. Duby and J. Le Goff (eds.), *Famille et parenté dans l'Occident médiévale: Actes du colloque de Paris (6–8 Juin 1974)* (Collection de l'Ecole Française de Rome 30, Rome, 1977); L. Genicot, *Les Généalogies* (Typologie des sources du Moyen Age occidental 15, Turnhout, 1975); K.J. Leyser, 'The German Aristocracy from the Ninth to the Early Twelfth Century: A Historical and Cultural Sketch', *Past and Present* 41 (1968), pp. 25–53 reprinted in *Medieval Germany and its Neighbours, 900–1250* (London, 1982), pp. 161–89.

Ruthard sat twenty years. The fifth Henry reigned for twenty-one years. Bishop Adalbert sat twenty-six years. Lothar reigned for fourteen years. The younger Adalbert sat three years, two months.[15]

In spite of his reasonable chronological proximity to these personages and their reigns, the compiler sacrificed accuracy for the sake of symmetry. Although the lengths attributed to the reigns of the archbishops are correct,[16] the regnal years of the emperors are all miscalculated. Archbishop Wezilo (1084–88) has been omitted, and Archbishop Adalbert II (1138–41) was not elected until the reign of Conrad III.[17] Late classical and medieval lists of bishops abound with such inaccuracies,[18] and we shall return to considering some of the consequences. In another case,

[15] 'Heinricus huius nominis III. regnavit annis 16. Sigifridus episcopus sedit annos 24. Heinricus quartus regnavit annis 51. Ruthardus episcopus sedit annos 20. Heinricus quintus regnavit annis 21. Adelbertus episcopus sedit annos 26. Lotharius regnavit annis 14. Adelbertus iunior sedit annos 3, menses 2.' O. Holder-Egger (ed.), *Series archiepiscoporum Moguntinorum*, part 5, *Series sancti Iacobi Moguntini*, MGH SS 13, p. 314.

[16] P. Gams, *Series Episcoporum Ecclesiae Catholicae* (Graz, reprinted 1957), p. 289 and F. Jürgensmeier, *Das Bistum Mainz: Von der Römerzeit bis zum II. Vatikanischen Konzil* (Beiträge zur Mainzer Kirchengeschichte 2, Frankfurt, 1988), pp. 75–87.

[17] On these bishops see H. Thomas, 'Erzbischof Siegfried I. von Mainz und die Tradition seiner Kirche. Ein Beitrag zur Wahl Rudolfs von Rheinfelden', *Deutsches Archiv für Erforschung des Mittelalters* 26 (1970), pp. 368–99; R. Schieffer, 'Die Zeit der späten Salier (1056–1125)' and O. Engels, 'Die Stauferzeit' in *Hohes Mittelalter* (Rheinische Geschichte, ed. F. Petri and G. Droege 1/3, Düsseldorf, 1983), pp. 127–46, 205–12; P. Rassow, 'Über Erzbischof Ruthard von Mainz (1089–1109)', *Die geschichtliche Einheit des Abendlandes: Reden und Aufsätze* (Kölner Historische Abhandlungen 2, Cologne, 1960), pp. 255–62; H. Büttner, 'Erzbischof Adalbert von Mainz, die Kurie und das Reich in den Jahren 1118 bis 1122', *Investiturstreit und Reichsverfassung*, ed. J. Fleckenstein (Vorträge und Forschungen 17, Sigmaringen, 1973), pp. 395–410; L. Speer, *Kaiser Lothar III. und Erzbischof Adalbert von Mainz: Eine Untersuchung zur Geschichte des deutschen Reiches im frühen zwölften Jahrhundert* (Dissertationen zur mittelalterlichen Geschichte 3, Cologne, 1983); W. Petke, *Kanzlei, Kapelle und königliche Kurie unter Lothar III (1125–1137)* (Forschungen zur Kaiser- und Papstgeschichte des Mittelalters. Beihefte zu J.F. Böhmer, Regesta Imperii 5, Cologne, 1985), pp. 13–16, 100–5, 204–5, 269–302; J. Ehlers, 'Verfassungs- und sozialgeschichtliche Studien zum Bildungsgang Erzbischof Adalberts II. von Mainz', *Rheinische Vierteljahrsblätter* 42 (1978), pp. 161–84; *Anselmi Havelbergensis Vita Adelberti II. Moguntini*, ed. P. Jaffé, *Monumenta Moguntina* (Bibliotheca rerum Germanicarum 3, Berlin, 1866), pp. 565–603.

[18] The classic work which considered this problem was L. Duchesne, *Fastes épiscopaux de l'ancienne Gaule*, 2 vols. (Paris, 2nd. edn., 1907–10).

the significant Saxon chronicle compiled at St. Michael's in Lüneburg in the thirteenth century was followed in the same hand by a list of the monastery's founding family as well as its abbots: in the first column the five dukes of the Billung line (936–1106) with four of their sons who were counts; in the second, eleven wives and daughters of the Billung house; in the third, the first nine abbots of St. Michael's, with later continuations.[19] Late in the reign of Frederick Barbarossa, a monk of Echternach attempted what the author of the Mainz list had failed to achieve; to match correctly the regnal years of abbots and rulers in parallel lists of the twenty-eight abbots since St. Willibrord (c. 698–739) and the twenty-nine rulers since Pepin of Herstal (687–714) by means of fifty-one transverse lines scored across the page between the appropriate names.[20]

If the utility of such lists for medieval biographers and annalists tended to be marred by errors, then we should remember that the principal motive for constructing sacred pedigrees was not chronographical but religious. As Leo Koep pointed out, 'the sequence of bishops' names for an episcopal see back to its foundation is of an importance beyond specific local history above all if, reaching back to the time of the early church, it validates apostolic origin for the see'.[21] Several German sees believed that they possessed just such an apostolic descent, but the oldest authentic list to claim this in the western church concerned the Roman see itself. Before the end of the second century, Bishop Irenaeus of Lyons inserted in his *Adversus omnes haereses* an annotated list of popes stretching back to St. Peter in order to prove that current Roman doctrine derived uncontaminated by heresy from the apostles

---

[19] O. Holder-Egger (ed.), *Tabula gentis Billingorum et series abbatum sancti Michaelis Luneburgensis*, MGH SS 13, p. 344. See G. Althoff, *Adels- und Königsfamilien im Spiegel ihrer Memorialüberlieferung: Studien zum Totengedenken der Billunger und Ottonen* (Münstersche Mittelalter-Schriften 47, Munich, 1984), pp. 46–51. The source also contains (p. 343) a list of forty bishops of Verden.

[20] G. Waitz (ed.), *Catalogi abbatum Epternacensium. Series regum et abbatum*, MGH SS 13, p. 742. The lists are remarkably accurate; see C. Wampach, 'Echternach', *Dictionnaire d'histoire et de géographie ecclésiastiques*, ed. R. Aubert and E. van Cauwenbergh, vol. 14 (Paris, 1960), col. 1374.

[21] 'Bischofsliste', *Lexikon für Theologie und Kirche*, ed. J. Höfer and K. Rahner (Freiburg, 1958), vol. 2, col. 507: '. . . die Namenfolge der Bischöfe eines Bischofssitzes bis hinauf zu seiner Gründung, ist von Bedeutung über die jeweilige Lokalgeschichte hinaus, vor allem wenn sie, bis auf die Zeit der Urkirche zurückgehend, apostolischer Ursprung für den Bischofssitz geltend macht'.

themselves.[22] Later and more elaborate lists such as the fourth-century Liberian Catalogue provided a credible chronological framework for the Roman *Liber pontificalis* inaugurated in the sixth century. These biographical exercises are thought to have provided the prototype for the written *gesta* of bishops and abbots north of the Alps as well.[23] Citing as illustrative examples the tenth-century *Catalogus abbatum* of Fulda Abbey and the eleventh-century *Series episcoporum* of Hamburg-Bremen,[24] Michel Sot has aptly said that 'the most elementary form of the *Gesta* is the series, list or catalogue of prelates, more or less enriched with mention of the buildings, gifts, acquisitions or reforms of the church during each reign'.[25]

Episcopal and abbatial lists thus served as ancillary material for a more developed form of ecclesiastical historiography, but it is worth noting that in one of the German sees which did use its lists to claim apostolic descent from St. Peter, catalogues also included a purpose similar to Irenaeus of Lyons' series, to warn against heresy. In the 1160s Thiodericus, *aedituus* of Deutz Abbey on the Rhine, drew up a catalogue of the bishops of Cologne,[26] recording an early incumbent as follows: 'Effrata hereticus damnatus. Sub Gratiano imperatore. (The condemned heretic Euphrates. Under Emperor Gratian).' Gratian reigned from 367 to 383, so Thiodericus has mistaken him for Constantius II (337–61) under whom Bishop Euphrates was supposed to have been removed for his

[22] A. Rousseau and L. Doutreleau (ed.), *Irénée de Lyon. Contre les hérésies, Livre III* (Sources chrétiennes 210–11, Paris, 1974), vol. 1, pp. 223–39 and vol. 2, pp. 31–39.

[23] These connexions are explored by M. Sot, *Gesta episcoporum. Gesta abbatum* (Typologie des sources du Moyen Age occidental 37, Turnhout, 1981), especially pp. 32–41. See also F.-J. Schmale with H.-W. Goetz, *Funktionen und Formen mittelalterlicher Geschichtsschreibung: Eine Einführung* (Darmstadt, 1985), pp. 105–23, 136–38, 186–89.

[24] G. Waitz (ed.), *Catalogus abbatum Fuldensium*, MGH SS 13, pp. 272–74 and J. Lappenberg (ed.), *Chronicon breve Bremense*, MGH SS 7, pp. 389–92. See M. Sandmann, 'Die Folge der Äbte', *Die Klostergemeinschaft von Fulda im früheren Mittelalter*, ed. K. Schmid (Münstersche Mittelalter-Schriften 8/1, Munich, 1978), pp. 178–204, 212–15 and W. Seegrün and T. Schieffer, *Provincia Hammaburgo-Bremensis* (Regesta Pontificum Romanorum, Germania Pontificia 6, Göttingen, 1981), pp. 1–90.

[25] Sot, *Gesta*, p. 15: '. . . la forme la plus élémentaire des *gesta* est la série, la liste ou le catalogue de prélats, plus ou moins enrichis de mentions concernant les constructions, les dons, les acquisitions ou les réformes de l'église sous chaque gouvernement'.

[26] O. Holder-Egger (ed.), *Series archiepiscoporum Coloniensium*, MGH SS 13, p. 286. The Cologne lists are discussed by F.W. Oediger, *Die Regesten der Erzbischöfe von Köln im Mittelalter, 313–1099* (Publikationen der Gesellschaft für Rheinische Geschichtskunde 21, Düsseldorf, 2nd. edn., 1978), pp. 17*–20*.

heterodox christology by a local council in 346.[27] This council is almost certainly a fiction,[28] and the legendary list of Gallic bishops who are said to have attended has itself bedevilled the chronology for the incumbency of several sees.[29] The author of the principal thirteenth-century catalogue drawn up at Cologne preserves the myth that Maternus, the first bishop of Cologne, was a disciple of St. Peter, and then continues: 'Thereafter none is found to have presided over the church of Cologne until the heretic Euphrates who is not placed in the catalogue, seeing that he polluted the church by the pestiferous doctrine of heretics in his very beginning.'[30]

Thiodericus of Deutz's list is also in the form which matches the see's incumbents with the reigning emperors, such as 'Bruno primus, annis 12, episcopus. Sub Ottone I, ipsius fratre (Bruno I, for twelve years bishop. Under Otto I, his own brother)', or 'Fridericus I, annis 32, episcopus. Sub Heinrico IIII. et Heinrico V. et Lothario. (Frederick I, thirty-two years bishop. Under Henry IV and Henry V and Lothar)'. It breaks out into a *gesta* for the heresy trial of 1163. Eleven Cathars, *Catafrigae sive Cathari*, six men, two women, and their three heresiarchs, were arrested in Cologne.[31] 'Judged and anathematised by the clergy, they were burned

ꞏ

[27] H. von Petrikovits, *Altertum* (Rheinische Geschichte, ed. F. Petri and G. Droege 1/1, Düsseldorf, 1978), pp. 257–59; C. Munier, *Concilia Galliae A. 314-A. 506* (Corpus Christianorum. Series Latina 148, Turnhout, 1963), pp. 26–29; J. Gaudemet, *Conciles gaulois du IVe siècle* (Sources chrétiennes 241, Paris, 1977), pp. 68–79.

[28] H.C. Brennecke, 'Synodum congregavit contra Euphratam nefandissimum episcopum. Zur angeblichen Kölner Synod gegen Euphrates', *Zeitschrift für Kirchengeschichte* 90 (1979), pp. 176–200.

[29] This problem is now discussed by C. Brühl, 'Studien zu den Bischofslisten der rheinischen Bistümer', *Politik, Gesellschaft, Geschichtsschreibung: Giessener Festgabe für František Graus*, ed. H. Ludat and R.C. Schwinges (Cologne, 1982), pp. 39–48 and in his *Aus Mittelalter und Diplomatik* (as n. 3), vol. 1, pp. 177–82. See also J. Dubois, 'La Composition des anciennes listes épiscopales', *Bulletin de la Société Nationale des Antiquaires de France* (1967), pp. 74–104.

[30] 'Deinde usque ad Eufraten hereticum nullus Coloniensi ecclesie prefuisse invenitur, qui ideo in katalogo non ponitur, quoniam pestifero hereticorum dogmate in ipso inicio ecclesiam fedavit.' H. Cardauns (ed.), *Catalogi archiepiscoporum Coloniensium*, MGH SS 24, p. 336. This work is analysed by F.-J. Schmale in W. Wattenbach and Schmale, *Deutschlands Geschichtsquellen im Mittelalter: Vom Tode Kaiser Heinrichs V. bis zum Ende des Interregnum* (Darmstadt, 1976), vol. 1, pp. 361–64, with criticism of Cardauns' edition.

[31] *Series archiepiscoporum Coloniensium* (as n. 26), pp. 286–87: 'Qui a clero diiudicati et anathematizati, a iudicibus et populo civitatis, cum fidem catholicam recipere et suam profanam sectam nollent abicere, in colle qui Iudaicus appellatur iuxta Iudeorum sepulturas igni cremati sunt, tanta diaboli instinctu in suo proposito usi pertinatia, ut quidam ipsorum furentibus flammis se ipsos inicerent'. For this incident see A. Borst, *Die Katharer* (MGH Schriften 12, Stuttgart, 1953), pp. 94–95. For the word *Catafrigae*,

by the magistrates and townsmen at the Jewish hill next to the cemetery of the Jews, since they did not wish to accept the Catholic faith and to renounce their profane belief. So stubbornly did they hold by instigation of the devil to his premises that certain of them flung themselves of their own accord into the raging fire'.

The occasional manipulation of episcopal lists to combat the horrid spectre of heresy aptly supported the principal purpose in compiling such series, to authenticate the orthodox descent of ecclesiastical authority and its exercise over the diocese. In the case of Cologne it was boldly claimed that such authority stemmed from the apostles,[32] and the theory may well have been advertised to the laity through the medium of such vernacular works as the *Annolied*, verses commemorating Archbishop Anno II of Cologne (1056–75) and the greatness of his bishopric.[33] No one knows who composed the *Annolied* or when it was finished,[34] and the milieu in which it may have been recited is also uncertain.

by which was intended a derogatory pun for Cathar, 'burned to ashes' or 'consumed by disease', see ibid., pp. 240–41 and note 6.

[32] See W. Levison, 'Die Anfänge rheinischer Bistümer in der Legende', *Annalen des Historischen Vereins für den Niederrhein* 116 (1930), pp. 5–28 and in his *Aus rheinischer und fränkischer Frühzeit: Ausgewählte Aufsätze* (Düsseldorf, 1948), pp. 7–27, and Oediger, *Regesten* (as n. 26), pp. 1–10. On the reality, see E. Ewig, 'Das Bistum Köln im Frühmittelalter' and 'Beobachtungen zur Frühgeschichte des Bistums Köln', *Spätantikes und fränkisches Gallien: Gesammelte Schriften (1952–1973)*, ed. H. Atsma (Beihefte der Francia 3/2, Zürich, 1979), pp. 91–125, 126–53, and E. Hegel, 'Die rheinische Kirche in römischer und frühfränkischer Zeit', *Ecclesiastica Rhenana: Aufsätze zur rheinischen Kirchengeschichte*, ed. S. Corsten and G. Knopp (Veröffentlichungen des Historischen Vereins für den Niederrhein 16, Bonn, 1986), pp. 9–29.

[33] See the editions by M. Roediger, *Das Annolied* (MGH Deutsche Chroniken und andere Geschichtsbücher des Mittelalters 1/2, Hanover, 1895), pp. 63–145; E. Nellmann, *Das Annolied: Mittelhochdeutsch und Neuhochdeutsch* (Reclams Universal-Bibliothek 1416, Stuttgart, 1975); F. Maurer, 'Annolied', *Die religiösen Dichtungen des 11. und 12. Jahrhunderts* (Tübingen, 1965), vol. 2, pp. 3–45.

[34] Opinion varies; compare W. Beinert's explicit claim in *Die Kirche – Gottes Heil in der Welt: Die Lehre von der Kirche nach den Schriften des Rupert von Deutz, Honorius Augustodunensis und Gerhoch von Reichersberg* (Beiträge zur Geschichte der Philosophie und Theologie des Mittelalters, neue Folge 13, Münster, 1973), p. 20 about Abbot Kuno of Siegburg (1105–1126) that 'Unter seinem Einfluß, wenn nicht sogar durch seine Feder, ist das *Annolied* und die *Kaiserchronik* entstanden' with the much more cautious views of A. Haverkamp, *Typik und Politik im Annolied: Zum 'Konflikt der Interpretationen' im Mittelalter* (Stuttgart, 1979), pp. 79–88 and J. Bumke, *Mäzene im Mittelalter: Die Gönner und Auftraggeber der höfischen Literatur in Deutschland 1150–1300* (Munich, 1979), pp. 82–83.

Gisela Vollmann-Profe argues persuasively that the author's intense preoccupation with the importance of Cologne[35] means that the poem 'under a particular but central aspect stands . . . as a first example of "urban" literature in Germany',[36] although it is likely that the author was a monk at Siegburg Abbey, Archbishop Anno II's principal foundation and the site of his tomb.[37] In a marvellous compression of apostolic history, the *Annolied*'s author delivers the city of Rome to the spiritual mastery of St. Peter, who promptly employs three missionaries, Eucharius, Valerius, and Maternus, to convert the Rhineland:[38]

> dannin santir drî heilige man,
> ci predigenne den Vrankan.

Having converted Trier they move on to Cologne, where Maternus is established as first bishop.[39] This tradition, making common cause with Trier's conversion, was also found in the *Gesta Treverorum* completed in 1101,[40] and is preserved in Cologne's episcopal list of the thirteenth

---

[35] Roediger, *Annolied*, lines 109–20; for the theory, H. Kugler, *Die Vorstellung der Stadt in der Literatur des deutschen Mittelalters* (Munich, 1986), pp. 88–90 and for the reality, R. Schieffer, 'Der Bischof zwischen Civitas und Königshof (4. bis 9. Jahrhundert)' and O. Engels, 'Der Reichsbischof (10. und 11. Jahrhundert)', both in *Der Bischof in seiner Zeit: Bischofstypus und Bischofsideal im Spiegel der Kölner Kirche. Festgabe für Joseph Kardinal Höffner, Erzbischof von Köln,* ed. P. Berglar and O. Engels (Cologne, 1986), pp. 17–39, 41–94.

[36] G. Vollmann-Profe, 'Wiederbeginn volkssprachiger Schriftlichkeit im hohen Mittelalter (1050/60–1160/70)', *Von den Anfängen zum hohen Mittelalter*, ed. J. Heinzle (Geschichte der deutschen Literatur von den Anfängen bis zum Beginn der Neuzeit 1/2, Königstein, 1986), p. 38: 'Unter einem bestimmten, aber zentralen Aspekt stellt somit das 'Annolied' ein erstes Beispiel 'städtischer' Literatur in Deutschland dar'.

[37] E. Wisplinghoff, *Die Benediktinerabtei Siegburg* (Germania Sacra, neue Folge 9/2: Das Erzbistum Köln 2, Berlin, 1975), pp. 21–28; *Urkunden und Quellen zur Geschichte von Stadt und Abtei Siegburg 1, (948) 1065–1399* (Siegburg, 2nd. edn., 1985), nos. 2–12, pp. 3–26.

[38] 'From there (Rome) he sent three holy men to preach to the Franks': Roediger, *Annolied*, lines 539–40.

[39] Ibid., lines 557–60.

[40] G. Waitz (ed.), *Gesta Treverorum*, MGH SS 8, pp. 143–48. For the reality, see H. Thomas, *Studien zur Trierer Geschichtsschreibung des 11. Jahrhunderts insbesondere zu den Gesta Treverorum* (Rheinisches Archiv 68, Bonn, 1968); E. Ewig, *Trier im Merowingerreich: Civitas, Stadt, Bistum* (Trier, 1954), esp. pp. 28–60, 88–143 and his 'Kaiserliche und apostolische Tradition im mittelalterlichen Trier', *Gallien* (as n. 32), pp. 51–90; H. Heinen, *Trier und das Treverland in römischer Zeit: 2000 Jahre Trier* (Trier, 1985), vol. 1, pp. 282–85, 327–47, 381–84, 417–20.

century.[41] As it stands the story is a myth, but Maternus is genuinely attested in 313 and 314 as the first bishop of Cologne,[42] and both Trier and Cologne cathedrals were in reality dedicated to St. Peter, encouraging belief in special links with the Roman see.

The author of the *Annolied* was himself familiar with the enumeration of episcopal reigns which brought Archbishop Anno II out as thirty-third incumbent at Cologne, an incorrect calculation also accepted in lists drawn up subsequently. When the archbishop was laid to rest at Siegburg in December 1075, lead tablets were buried with him, their inscriptions including the words:[43] 'Hic requiescit domnus Anno secundus, Coloniensis ecclesiae tricesimus tercius archiepiscopus. (Here lies the lord Anno II, thirty-third archbishop of the church of Cologne)'. In the *Annolied* the number thirty-three was then exploited to make an explicit hagiographical comparison between the archbishop's sufferings and those of Christ, who was known to have undergone crucifixion when thirty-three years of age. In the thirty-third stanza Anno II is characterised as thirty-third bishop,[44] one of whose tribulations, his expulsion from Cologne by a rising of the townsmen in 1074,[45] is described as follows:[46]

> ci jungis niwart daz niht virmidin,
> her niwurde mit gewêfinin ûze dir burg virtribin,
> als Absalôn wîlin
> virtreib vater sînin,
> den vili guotin Dâvîd.
> disiu zuei dinc, harti si wârin gelîch.
> leidis unte arbeide genuog

---

[41] *Catalogus primus* (as n. 30), p. 336.

[42] See Schieffer, 'Bischof' (as n. 35), pp. 17–18; von Petrikovits, *Altertum* (as n. 27), p. 257; Brühl, 'Studien' (as n. 29), pp. 180–81.

[43] They were found and recorded in 1183; R. Koepke (ed.), *Translatio sancti Annonis archiepiscopi*, MGH SS 11, p. 517.

[44] On the symbolic importance of numerals in the *Annolied*, see W. Haug, *Literaturtheorie im deutschen Mittelalter: Von den Anfängen bis zum Ende des 13. Jahrhunderts* (Germanistische Einführungen, Darmstadt, 1985), pp. 62–63.

[45] The best source is Lampert of Hersfeld's *Annales*, ed. O. Holder-Egger, *Lamperti monachi Hersfeldensis opera* (MGH SRG Hanover, 1894), pp. 185–93, and see U. Ewald, 'Köln im Investiturstreit', *Investiturstreit* (as n. 17), pp. 382–84.

[46] 'At length it was unavoidable that he was driven out of the town by armed force as Absalom once drove out his father, the excellent David. These two things were equally hard to bear. The good lord (Anno) bore enough suffering and punishment after Christ's holy pattern. God atoned for this from heaven': Roediger, *Annolied*, lines 665–74.

genîhte sich der hêirro guot
al nâh dis heiligin Cristis bilide.
duo suont iz got van himile.[47]

For Anno II the lists of Cologne's pastors compiled at Mönchengladbach and Brauweiler held to the same computation as the grave tablet and the *Annolied*. The Werden list, however, counted him as the thirty-fourth bishop because it still included the heretic Euphrates, absurdly inserting him into the late ninth century.[48] The important thirteenth-century *Catalogus primus*, which also preserved biographical material about the archbishops, reflects the hagiographical tradition as follows:[49] 'Tricesimus tercius sanctus Anno, flos et nova lux totius Germaniae, qui cunctos antecessores suos in augmentacione Coloniensis ecclesie precessit. (Thirty-third was St. Anno, flower and new light of all Germany, who outdid all his predecessors in fostering the church of Cologne)'. It goes on to praise his wisdom, his ecclesiastical foundations, and the miracles attested at his tomb.[50] Certainly Anno II was successful in his acquisitions, especially at the expense of the counts-palatine of Lotharingia and of the crown.[51] Whatever the hagiographical significance of counting Anno II as thirty-third bishop may have been, modern scholarship reckons him to have been the thirty-sixth, not counting Euphrates.[52]

The cathedral church of Cologne may have considered itself to have been a genuine apostolic foundation, but by far the most ambitious

---

[47] On these comparisons see Haverkamp, *Typik und Politik*, pp. 59–71, 104–6 and W. Fechter, 'Absalom als Vergleichs- und Beispielfigur im mittelhochdeutschen Schrifttum', *Beiträge zur Geschichte der deutschen Sprache und Literatur* 83 (1961), pp. 302–16. The archbishop was also compared to Moses (Roediger, *Annolied*, lines 853–78), who explicitly prefigured Christ in medieval exegesis: see J. Châtillon, 'Moïse figure du Christ et modèle de la vie parfaite: Brèves remarques sur quelques thèmes médiévaux', *D'Isidore de Séville à saint Thomas d'Aquin: Etudes d'histoire et de théologie* (London, 1985), part III.

[48] *Series* (as n. 26), pp. 284–85

[49] *Catalogus primus* (as n. 30), p. 340.

[50] *Nova lux* is drawn from the epitaph in the *Vita* of Anno (MGH SS 11, pp. 509, 1104–1105) composed at Siegburg Abbey.

[51] G. Jenal, *Erzbischof Anno II. von Köln (1056–75) und sein politisches Wirken: Ein Beitrag zur Geschichte der Reichs- und Territorialpolitik im 11. Jahrhundert* (Monographien zur Geschichte des Mittelalters 8/1, Munich, 1974), pp. 56–154; U. Lewald, 'Die Ezzonen: Das Schicksal eines rheinischen Fürstengeschlechtes', *Rheinisches Vierteljahrsblätter* 43 (1979), pp. 120–68; D H IV 104 (1063).

[52] S. Weinfurter and O. Engels (eds.), *Archiepiscopatus Coloniensis* (Series episcoporum ecclesiae catholicae occidentalis ab initio usque ad annum MCXCVIII, 5/1, Stuttgart, 1982), pp. 7–27.

attempt to gain apostolic status for a German see by means of fabricating an episcopal catalogue of fictions occurred at Passau in the mid thirteenth century. Simple episcopal series drawn up in monasteries of the diocese, Heiligenkreuz, Niederalteich and Göttweig, had correctly identified Vivilo as first bishop of Passau, reigning from 723 to 745.[53] Then some time before 1254 the most distinguished of the cathedral canons, Albert Behaim of Böhaming, who had been dean of the chapter since 1246 and papal legate in Germany since 1239,[54] confected an elaborate new catalogue adorned with historical *pièces justificatives* which attempted to prove that Passau was really a Roman archiepiscopal see at Lauriacum, now Lorch on the River Enns in Austria, founded by missionaries sent out by St. Peter, lavishly endowed by the emperor Philip the Arab (244–49), and later forced by Avar and other barbarian incursions to retreat to Passau.[55] The immediate motive for enshrining these extraordinary claims in an episcopal catalogue was inspired by Passau's fear of a new bishopric which it was proposed to set up in Vienna at the expense of the diocese of Passau. The idea was mooted by Dukes Leopold VI (1198–1230) and Frederick II (1230–46) of Austria, and in 1207 Pope Innocent III had warned Bishop Manegold of Passau of the Austrian claim that Lorch itself had merely been the daughter church of Vienna, which was the true see overrun by the barbarians and ought now to be restored.[56]

[53] O. Holder-Egger (ed.), *Series episcoporum Pataviensium*, MGH SS 13, pp. 361–64 and K. Reindel, 'Christentum und Kirche: Die Errichtung einer neuen Bistumsorganisation', *Handbuch der bayerischen Geschichte, 1: Das alte Bayern; Das Stammesherzogtum bis zum Ausgang des 12. Jahrhunderts*, ed. M. Spindler (Munich, 2nd edn., 1981), pp. 226–33.

[54] P. Herde, 'Albert Behaim', *Lexikon des Mittelalters*, vol. 1, col. 288 and G. Schwertl, *Die Beziehungen der Herzöge von Bayern und Pfalzgrafen bei Rhein zur Kirche (1180–1294)* (Miscellanea Bavarica Monacensia 9, Munich, 1968), pp. 17–42.

[55] The catalogue was edited by G. Waitz as *Historia episcoporum Pataviensium et ducum Bavariae*, MGH SS 25, pp. 617–27; for the relation of this to the other fragments by Albert Behaim, see G. Leidinger, *Untersuchungen zur Passauer Geschichtschreibung des Mittelalters* (Sitzungsberichte der Königlich Bayerischen Akademie der Wissenschaften, phil.-hist. Klasse, Abhandlungen 9, Munich, 1915); P. Uiblein, 'Studien zur Passauer Geschichtschreibung des Mittelalters', *Archiv für österreichische Geschichte* 121 (1956), pp. 93–180; Wattenbach and Schmale, *Deutschlands Geschichtsquellen*, pp. 172–78; K. Schnith, 'Bayerische Geschichtsschreibung im Spätmittelalter: Eine Studie zu den Quellen von Passau-Kremsmünster', *Historisches Jahrbuch* 97–98 (1978), pp. 194–212.

[56] A. Potthast, *Regesta pontificium Romanorum inde . . . MCXCVIII ad . . . MCCCIV* (Berlin, 1874), vol. 1, no. 3085, p. 262; see K. Lechner, *Die Babenberger: Markgrafen und Herzoge von Osterreich 976–1246* (Veröffentlichungen des Instituts für österreichische Geschichtsforschung 23, Vienna, 1976), pp. 200–3, 293, 372, 408–9.

To outface the ambitions of Vienna, Albert Behaim, who had himself been archdeacon of Lorch since 1226, undertook the responsibility for demonstrating Passau's apostolic and archiepiscopal status once and for all. This myth had a respectable history at Passau. With the recovery of the eastern marches of Bavaria after the victory over the Magyars at the Lech in 955,[57] Bishop Pilgrim of Passau (971–91) sought to re-establish ecclesiastical rule in rivalry with Salzburg by means of forged papal bulls ascribed to popes as far back as Symmachus in the fifth century.[58] On the basis of sources such as the late fifth-century *Vita sancti Severini* which was known at Passau,[59] Bishop Pilgrim appears genuinely to have believed that Lorch was the original ecclesiastical metropolis of Pannonia and Noricum,[60] and that Passau was its refugee descendant, rather in the manner of Bremen's retreat from Hamburg in the ninth century. In 977 Otto II gave property at Ennsburg and Lorch to Bishop Pilgrim, the charter accepting that the church at Lorch was 'ubi antiquis etiam temporibus prima sedes episcopalis habebatur (where in ancient times the first episcopal see was sited)'. He did not accept the bishop's more extravagant claim, outlined in the first version of the charter, that before the desolation of Bavaria by barbarian invasions, Lorch rather than Salzburg was the mother church and episcopal cathedral for the whole duchy, and would now be restored by imperial and canonical authority to its pristine honour.[61] With Salzburg as a much more powerful episcopal rival, and with the establishment of Esztergom as Hungary's metropolitan see in 1001, Passau's pretensions had little future. Nevertheless, the papal bulls of Bishop Pilgrim's invention were taken as genuine in the twelfth century; Magnus of Reichersberg, for example, used them in good faith in his annals.[62]

---

[57] See K.J. Leyser, 'The Battle at the Lech, 955: A Study in Tenth-Century Warfare', *History* 50 (1965), pp. 1–25, reprinted in *Medieval Germany*, pp. 43–67.

[58] E. Zöllner, 'Die Lorcher Tradition im Wandel der Jahrhunderte', *Mitteilungen des Instituts für österreichische Geschichtsforschung* 71 (1963), p. 228.

[59] T. Mommsen, *Eugippii Vita Severini* (MGH SRG, Berlin, 1898); see Zöllner, 'Lorcher Tradition', pp. 227–28.

[60] In modern historiography I. Zibermayr in *Noricum, Bayern und Osterreich: Lorch als Hauptstadt und die Einführung des Christentums* (Horn, 2nd. edn., 1956) made much of the evidence for Lorch in such a role, but this is rejected by E. Zöllner in *Mitteilungen des Instituts für österreichische Geschichtsforschung* 66 (1958), pp. 129–33.

[61] D O II 167 A and B.

[62] W. Wattenbach (ed.), *Magni presbyteri Annales Reicherspergenses*, MGH SS 17, p. 481; for the reality in Passau diocese, L. Veit, *Passau: Das Hochstift* (Historischer Atlas von Bayern, Teil Altbayern, 35, Munich, 1978), pp. 6–85.

In the catalogue designed by Albert Behaim, the distinction between his 'modernisation' of Passau's Lorch tradition and outright forgery is difficult to discern. Apart from distancing Passau from the authority of its metropolitan at Salzburg, another motive was to authenticate apostolic descent for the see. But a difficulty arose in that the legend preserved no name before the supposed reign of Archbishop Eutherius in the third century. Nothing daunted, the dean improved upon the hints in the forged papal bulls of the tenth century to claim explicitly that St. Peter had sent missionaries to convert Lorch in the year 47, and to establish a see.[63] This explanation is given a different twist in the actual introduction to his catalogue, where Lorch is listed with nineteen other archiepiscopal sees, including Trier, Cologne, and Mainz, which he claims were founded at St. Peter's behest.[64] This apostolic pedigree, the forged bulls ascribed to earlier popes, and his own archiepiscopal series from the third to the thirteenth centuries still did not seem enough. Lorch, and a fortiori Passau, must be endowed with a vast archdiocese, immense property and no less than twenty-two suffragan bishoprics including Grado, Würzburg, and Prague.

All this was justified by a fictional donation ascribed to the Emperor Philip, who was widely considered in late antiquity and in medieval times to have been a Christian.[65] We learn that the huge patrimony bequeathed by this emperor stretched north from the Adriatic to include what had been the Roman provinces of Pannonia and Noricum as well as half of Rhaetia, the name Moesia being imaginatively applied by our author to the Bavarian Nordgau, Bohemia and Moravia into the bargain.[66] Here it is difficult to believe that Albert Behaim was not improving upon the legend by direct fabrication. He claimed that he had himself seen Emperor Philip's tomb in Rome, actually quoting its 'inscription' testifying that these provinces had indeed been donated to Lorch.[67] The point, of course,

[63] This occurs in another of Albert's fragments, Uiblein, 'Studien', p. 101 f.: 'Qui beatus Petrus quarto anno sui adventus (hoc est ab incarnatione Domini XLVII anno) suis predicatoribus Laureacensem urbem per fidem katholicam visitavit. Et quia metropolis prothoflaminum prius fuerat ethnicorum, ad katholicam fidem conversa ydola et simulacra deorum igni tradens, metropolim katholicorum fundavit ibidem'.

[64] *Historia episcoporum Pataviensium* (as n. 55), p. 617.

[65] For the reality, see X. Loriot, 'Chronologie du règne de Philippe l'Arabe (244–249 après J. C.)', *Principat,* Aufstieg und Niedergang der römischen Welt, ed. H. Temporini, (Berlin, 1975), part 2, vol. 2, pp. 788–97.

[66] *Historia episcoporum Pataviensium* (as n. 55), pp. 618–19.

[67] Leidinger, 'Untersuchungen', p. 9; Zöllner, 'Lorcher Tradition', p. 230.

was to destroy Salzburg's rights as the actual metropolitan of Bavaria, Carinthia, Styria and Austria. By modern standards Albert Behaim was a forger;[68] by thirteenth-century standards he was a good one. Instead of attempting to match the high prestige and instant authority of a series of forged papal and imperial privileges, he grasped that a workmanlike genre without pretensions, the episcopal catalogue, could more credibly be presented as a solid piece of contemporary historiography for which the original sources had, as Albert explains, unfortunately disappeared at the time of Odoacer and Theoderic.

Having brought his readers thus far, the dean gives a list of archbishops and bishops of Lorch and Passau from the third century to his own day, explaining that it was after the unexpected death of 'Archbishop' Urolf in 806 that Bishop Arn of Salzburg (785–821) misled the pope and purloined the pallium from Passau by *trufas et bufas*, 'deceits and trickeries'.[69] In appended notes, Albert goes on to praise or castigate the bishops of Passau according to whether they had fought for or neglected the rights of their see, including the coveted pallium. Urolf's successor Hatto (806–17) for example, did nothing but eat, caring little for the dignity of the pallium. Naturally enough, 'Archbishop' Pilgrim received a good notice as a saint who had governed his church with vigour, recovered its property, with imperial assistance, from the depredations suffered under the Magyars, and likewise made good the damage sustained by the chapter.[70]

Collecting unadorned lists of bishops' names and dates was a less exciting enterprise than Albert Behaim's fantasy, but such catalogues did provide a valuable basis for more advanced historiographical, literary and cultural exercises. As Franz-Josef Schmale and Irene Schmale-Ott have pointed out,[71] lists of bishops' rights served as material and framework for

[68] From the large literature on medieval forgery, see especially H. Fuhrmann, 'Die Fälschungen im Mittelalter – Überlegungen zum mittelalterlichen Wahrheitsbegriff', *Historische Zeitschrift* 197 (1963), pp. 529–601; W. Speyer, *Die literarische Fälschung im heidnischen und christlichen Altertum: Ein Versuch ihrer Deutung* (Handbuch der Altertumswissenschaft 1/2, Munich, 1971), especially pp. 13–106, 171–303; G. Constable, 'Forgery and Plagiarism in the Middle Ages', *Archiv für Diplomatik* 29 (1983), pp. 1–41; A. Gawlik, 'Fälschungen', *Lexikon des Mittelalters*, vol. 4, cols. 246–51; the five-volume collection *Fälschungen im Mittelalter: Internationaler Kongress der Monumenta Germaniae Historica, München, 16–19. September 1986* (MGH Schriften 33/1–5, Hanover, 1988).

[69] *Historia episcoporum Pataviensium* (as n. 55), p. 620.

[70] Ibid., pp. 623–24.

[71] Wattenbach and Schmale, *Deutschlands Geschichtsquellen* (as n. 30), pp. 171, 269–71, 340–44.

episcopal histories at Gurk, Augsburg, and Strasbourg,[72] amongst other sees. An ambitious attempt to integrate chronology based upon series of episcopal names with biographical and political history was undertaken at Cologne in the thirteenth century.[73] In Cologne's tradition of historiography, this work stands between the more striking universality of the *Chronica regia Coloniensis*,[74] whose first recension carried the account of imperial history down to the end of the twelfth century, and the onset of an urban historiography with Gottfried Hagen's *Boich van der stede Colne*.[75]

At first sight, the episcopal catalogues appear to grudge much assistance towards an understanding of the religious and cultural history of Germany in the middle ages. However, they do betray new insights especially when their compilers descended to subterfuge or repeated errors, often in good faith, which were in origin designed to promote the prominence of the see in question. When the catalogues preserve traditions of apostolic foundation by the authority of St. Peter, they are unconsciously matching another myth, the theory of *translatio imperii*, that is, the direct descent of Roman imperial authority from the Caesars to the Franks and the Germans as the final guardians of the fourth Danielic empire before the collapse of human history and society at the millenium. This historiographical oddity, which received serious attention from the best minds of medieval times,[76] underpinned one of the justifications for imperial authority in Europe in the middle ages. Many a chronicler therefore numbered the German emperors in direct series of succession to Augustus, without arousing incredulity or ridicule. So it is not surprising that ecclesiastical compilers opportunistically attempted to link their founders with supposed disciples of St. Peter as well.

[72] W. Wattenbach (ed.), *Chronicon Gurcense*, MGH SS 23, pp. 8–10; G. Waitz (ed.), *Catalogus episcoporum Augustensium et abbatum Sanctae Afrae*, MGH SS 13, pp. 278–80, and *Chronicon breve episcoporum Augustensium*, MGH SS 14, pp. 556–59; P. Jaffé (ed.), *Ellenhardi Argentinensis Annales et Chronica*, MGH SS 17, pp. 91–141.

[73] See n. 30 above; *Catalogi*, pp. 332–67.

[74] G. Waitz (ed.), *Chronica regia Coloniensis (Annales maximi Colonienses)* (MGH SRG, Hanover, 1880); the *Catalogus primus*, p. 313, refers to the tradition in its account of Archbishop Rainald (1159–1167): . . . 'multa et cronice regie dignissime inserenda per omnem Ytaliam operatus est'.

[75] H. Cardauns, *Die Chroniken der niederrheinischen Städte: Cöln* (Die Chroniken der deutschen Städte 12, Leipzig, 2nd. edn., 1875), vol. 1, pp. 3–236.

[76] See W. Goez, *Translatio Imperii: Ein Beitrag zur Geschichte des Geschichtsdenkens und politischen Theorien im Mittelalter und in der frühen Neuzeit* (Tübingen, 1958), pp. 37–198.

5

Episcopi cum sua militia: The Prelate as Warrior in the Early Staufer Era

Timothy Reuter

Caesarius of Heisterbach, writing in the 1220s, told of a Paris student who claimed to be able to believe anything except that a German bishop could achieve salvation. Caesarius glossed this by saying that almost all the German bishops wield both the spiritual and material sword, and hence, since they exercise blood-justice and wage war, must give more thought to the wages of their troops than to the souls of their flocks.[1] The theme of the militant German ecclesiastic was a favourite one with twelfth-century moralists. Gerhoch of Reichersberg, writing in the 1130s, complained of bishops who busied themselves with the defence of their terrestrial possessions by secular methods and snatched the alms from the poor in order to maintain their contingents of troops for the defence of their secular possessions.[2] Two decades later Abbot Ruthard of Eberbach wrote to Archbishop Arnold of Mainz to remind him that he would have to answer for his soul and for the souls of those committed to his care, and that it would not go well for him if it could be said that the poor hungered at

---

[1] *Dialogus Miraculorum* II 27, ed J. Strange (Cologne, 1851), vol. 1, p. 99; essentially the same story with the same moral in a sermon of Caesarius', *Die Wundergeschichten des Caesarius von Heisterbach*, ed. A. Hilka (Bonn, 1933), vol. 1, p. 127–28.

[2] *Liber de aedificio Dei* c. 7, Migne PL 194, cols. 1217–20. See P. Classen, *Gerhoch von Reichersberg: Eine Biographie* (Wiesbaden, 1960), pp. 40–44; E.-D. Hehl, *Klerus und Krieg im 12. Jahrhundert* (Stuttgart, 1971), pp. 54–56.

his gate while inside the *pueri tyrannorum* lived in unrestricted luxury.[3] The archbishops of Mainz seem to have been particularly vulnerable to such criticism: two letters survive in the collection of Guido of Gembloux attacking Archbishop Christian (1165–83) for being more devoted to Mars than to Martin (the patron of Mainz cathedral) and for being much more punctilious in giving to Caesar what was Caesar's than in giving to God what was God's.[4] The letter-collection of Wibald, abbot of Stavelot and Corvey, contains much on the theme. Monks, in Wibald's view, should have nothing to do with military matters. This is the implicit charge raised against many of his opponents and those who supported them: his deposed predecessor as abbot of Corvey, Henry of Northeim; Henry's sister Judith, abbess of Kemnade; and Abbot Hillin of Pegau, who had given Henry aid and comfort.[5] A generation later Caesarius was to offer similar criticisms of an abbot of Corvey.[6] Caesarius, traditionally enough, saw worldly wealth and power, and the worldly involvement needed to gain and keep them, as fatal to piety: he adduced them as the reason for the decline of religion in royal monasteries,[7] and he saw Archbishop Engelbert of Cologne, murdered in 1225, as 'bonus dux sed non bonus episcopus'.[8]

Modern ethics might see no essential difference between organising and directing contingents of troops in war and personal participation in

---

[3] *Mainzer Urkundenbuch II: Die Urkunden seit dem Tode Erzbischof Adalberts I. (1137) bis zum Tode Erzbischof Konrads (1200)*, ed. P. Acht (Darmstadt, 1968), vol. 1, pp. 428–30, no. 237 (1153 × 1158).

[4] Ibid., vol. 2, p. 645, no. 392 (an anonymous Cistercian abbot to the clergy of Mainz); p. 1109, no. 676 (Guido of Gembloux to Conrad of Mainz); both were probably written by Guido himself.

[5] Here and henceforth I shall cite Wibald's correspondence by the text and number of the edition I am preparing for the MGH, with a reference to the edition by P. Jaffé, *Monumenta Corbeiensia* (Bibliotheca rerum Germanicarum 1, Berlin, 1864), pp. 76–607. The convent of Corvey to the papal chancellor Guido, ep. 7 (= Jaffé, no. 37, p. 118): Henry was 'plus militaribus insignibus deditus quam monastice institutioni intentus'; letters from Bernard of Hildesheim and Abbot Werner of Amelungsborn to Pope Eugenius III, epp. 46 and 52 (= Jaffé, no. 69 and 75, pp. 145, 150): Judith gave away the lands of Kemnade to 'militibus atque amatoribus suis'. Hillin of Pegau was drowned while on the crusade led by Bernard of Plötzke, which was in Wibald's view a judgement both on his having deserted his monastery and on his support for Henry, ep. 124 (= Jaffé, no. 150, p. 244).

[6] *Dialogus* XII 40 (as n. 1), vol. 2, p. 349.

[7] *Wundergeschichten*, p. 156. These views were shared by Wibald, who ought to have known: ep. 104 (= Jaffé, no. 126, p. 202).

[8] *Wundergeschichten*, p. 154. Later he was commissioned to write a Life of Engelbert, in which he took a rather different line.

battle, but this distinction was undoubtedly felt in the twelfth century. Probably not many prelates swung a sword or a battle-axe in anger, but certainly Rainald of Dassel did so on his tour through eastern Italy with Otto of Wittelsbach in 1158 and again at Tusculum in 1167, when he was already consecrated archbishop of Cologne.[9] Even worse was Christian of Mainz: 'Christian only in name', 'not Christian but Antichrist', 'not like a cleric but like a tyrant' – of course, people called Christian do better to be virtuous. He led imperial troops in Italy for twenty years and on occasion fought in person, and that from choice, not from necessity;[10] even those who benefitted from his activities were troubled. At the end of his life Christian helped to restore Alexander III and Lucius III to the *patrimonium Petri*, yet the letter in which Pope Lucius III announced his death to the prelates of Germany in 1183 did not say that Christian had achieved salvation by practising warfare in a just cause. This had perhaps helped to redeem his earlier career, but he still needed the prayers of all 'in order that the divine clemency may forgive him the blemishes which still adhere to him from the contamination of this world'.[11] In the face of such examples it is perhaps not surprising that the *topos* of the militant German ecclesiastic has been frequently drawn on by modern historians, including the present writer.[12] There is a good deal of truth in the notion, but it will bear closer examination. We may begin by looking

[9] R. Knipping (ed.), *Die Regesten der Erzbischöfe von Köln im Mittelalter, 2: 1100–1205* (Bonn, 1901), pp. 112, no. 675 and 156, no. 893; for the bishops of Liège see J.-L. Kupper, *Liège et l'église impériale, XIe-XIIe siècles* (Brussels, 1981), p. 452.

[10] The quotations are taken from Boncompagno, *Liber de Obsidione Ancone*, ed. G.C. Zimolo (Rerum Italicarum Scriptores, nuova edizione 6/3, Bologna, 1937), p. 11; *The Letters of John of Salisbury: The Later Letters (1163–1180)*, ed. W.J. Millor and C.N.L. Brooke (Oxford, 1979), p. 54 no. 152; Robert de Monte, *Cronica*, MGH SS 6, p. 533–34 (*s.a.* 1182). For an epitaph in the same vein from the *regnum Teutonicum* see Arnold of Lübeck, *Cronica Slavorum* II 2, ed. J.M. Lappenberg (MGH SRG, Hanover, 1868), p. 38: 'neglectis ovibus sibi commissis magis tributa cesaris quam lucra Christi colligebat'. On Christian's career see C. Varrentrapp, *Erzbischof Christian I. von Mainz* (Berlin, 1867), who is rightly sceptical about some of the more bloody anecdotes, for example the stories recounted two generations later by Albert of Stade, *Annales Stadenses*, MGH SS 16, p. 347 (*s.a.* 1172, 1173) on the authority of Henry, *scholasticus* of Bremen, Christian's notary at the time.

[11] *Mainzer Urkundenbuch* (as n. 3), vol. 2, pp. 740–41, no. 457 (2 September, 1183).

[12] T. Reuter, 'The Imperial Church System of the Ottonian and Salian rulers: a Reconsideration', *Journal of Ecclesiastical History* 33 (1982), p. 368. See most recently the survey by B. Arnold, 'German Bishops and their Military Retinues in the Medieval Empire', *German History* 7 (1989), pp. 161–83, with much material from the thirteenth to fifteenth centuries.

at the contribution made by prelates and their followers to Staufer armies, before turning to the militant ecclesiastic on his home ground.

In his continuation of Otto of Freising's *Gesta Friderici* Rahewin described how in the autumn of 1157, when Frederick Barbarossa was in Burgundy, Louis VII moved towards Dijon with the intention of meeting him. No such meeting took place; Rahewin stressed that the two rulers exchanged courtesies through intermediaries, but he wrote also that he had heard from Bishop Henry of Troyes that Louis had not wanted to meet Frederick. Instead he had prepared for war, to such an extent that Henry could recall nine bishops with their military followings passing through Troyes.[13] Though Rahewin had good sources and a meeting may have been planned, it does not seem very plausible that Louis put an army together largely from episcopal contingents.[14] But it presumably reflects the realities of Rahewin's own world, with prelates providing their ruler with substantial military forces. Some idea of the size of followings which could be expected from German prelates may be found in a list included in the early thirteenth-century *Historia Ducum Veneticorum* of those attending the peace-conference at Venice in 1177.[15] Leaving aside the archbishops for a moment, we find two bishops, those of Augsburg and Bamberg, with 100 men; three, those of Basle, Gurk and Passau, with fifty; four, those of Brandenburg, Merseburg, Osnabrück and Worms, with thirty; and four, those of Halberstadt, Lübeck (with an unidentified colleague) and Minden, with twenty or fewer. Of the abbots who can be identified in the face of the Venetian writer's mis-spelling of German names, we find Naumburg with ten, Nienburg and Memleben with twenty-five, Salzburg and St. Veit with five; there were also a number of provosts and lesser dignitaries (including some members of the royal chapel and chancery) with followings ranging in size from seven to forty. The archbishops, most of whom are listed as having a group of lay and

[13] *Ottonis et Rahewini Gesta Friderici I. imperatoris* III 12, ed. G. Waitz and B. von Simson (MGH SRG, Hanover, 3rd. edn., 1912), p. 180–81: 'novem episcopos cum sua militia'. For Frederick's itinerary at this time and a letter of his to Louis VII which may date from the autumn of 1157 see *Die Regesten des Königreichs unter Friedrich I. 1152 (1122)–1158*, ed. F. Opll (J.F. Böhmer, Regesta Imperii 4/2, Vienna, 1980), nos. 508, 509. Henry of Troyes was a Cistercian like Rahewin's patron Bishop Otto of Freising, to whom he was distantly related: G. Wunder, 'Die Verwandtschaft Erzbischof Friedrichs I. von Köln', *Annalen des historischen Vereins für den Niederrhein* 166 (1964), pp. 34–35, 42.

[14] See below, p. 84 at n. 21.

[15] MGH SS 14, pp. 85–89.

ecclesiastical followers, had contingents on a quite different scale: Ulrich of Aquileia brought 300, Phillip of Cologne 400, Christian of Mainz 300, and Wichmann of Magdeburg 300. The archbishop of Trier brought fifty, and the archbishop of Salzburg sixty, besides which there was a Wittelsbach contingent of 125 under Otto, count palatine of Bavaria and his brother Conrad, archbishop of Mainz and cardinal bishop of Sabina, who was to be made archbishop of Salzburg at the conference.

These archiepiscopal contingents were far larger than the largest of those led by lay magnates (Leopold of Austria with 160, Hermann of Carinthia and Otto of Wittelsbach with 125). It is admittedly doubtful whether the figures indicate fighting strength, though they have often been so read;[16] the formula used is *cum hominibus*, which is more likely to mean 'vassals' than simply 'bodies', but on the other hand it is unlikely that the mediators sent by the kings of France and England, the bishop of Clermont and the abbot of Bonnevaux, who had contingents of thirty and thirteen *homines* respectively, turned up with armed followings. On the other hand the numbers do not necessarily define the upper limit on what a prelate could call up for service.[17] They are of interest above all as a guide to relative strengths: it seems intuitively plausible that the archbishop of Mainz had a following ten times the size of that of the bishops of Worms or of Osnabrück. Gislebert of Mons' account of the great assembly at Mainz in 1184 offers a cross-check. He speaks of a total of 70,000 knights attending, including contingents of 2000 under the duke of Bohemia, 500 under the duke of Austria, 1000 under the count palatine of the Rhine. Of the ecclesiastics, the archbishops of Mainz and Cologne had 1000 and 1700 knights respectively, while the archbishop of Magdeburg had 600 and the abbot of Fulda 500.[18] The contingents of magnates for which an explicit figure is given total some 10,000 knights, leaving 60,000 to be accounted for by a further thirty-odd princes, an average of 200. The absolute figures are grotesquely high compared with those given for Venice, but they confirm the proportions reasonably

---

[16] Notably by K.F. Werner, 'Heeresorganisation und Kriegführung im deutschen Königreich des 10. und 11. Jahrhunderts', *Ordinamenti Militari in Occidente nell'alto medioevo* (Settimane di studio del centro italiano di studi sull'alto medioevo 15, Spoleto, 1968), p. 835, and by C. Brühl, *Fodrum, Gistum, Servitium Regis* (Cologne, 1968), p. 529–30 (though see also p. 525 and n. 417).

[17] Kupper, *Liège* (as n. 9), pp. 450–51, estimates that on his home ground the bishop of Liège could draw on up to 700 warriors for campaigns.

[18] *La chronique de Gislebert de Mons*, c. 109, ed. L. Vanderkindere (Brussels, 1904), pp. 157–58.

well: the archbishop of Cologne had rather more than the archbishop of Mainz, who in turn had about twice the numbers of the duke of Austria, while both had five to ten times the followings of most other prelates.

The overall proportions are also of interest. The ratio of lay to ecclesiastical troops is about 1:2.5 in Gislebert's account, and 1:4.5 in the Venetian list. Something like the latter ratio is also found in a list of the late tenth century,[19] which suggests a certain continuity. Although lay magnates probably did more than that indicates,[20] there is still a striking contrast with the figures from England, where it was lay, not ecclesiastical, contingents which amounted to between two-thirds and four-fifths of the whole. This is somewhat surprising in view of the fact that the Domesday Book figures for landed wealth give the greater churches some 40 per cent of the total held by tenants-in-chief, but it probably reflects broadly accurate proportions of obligation and of service: where leaders of contingents are mentioned in narrative sources they are lay magnates, though muster-rolls of the thirteenth century refer to personal service by prelates.[21] Here of course we are dealing more with fiscal obligations than with military performance: the number of knight's fees on which scutage might be levied is not automatically to be equated with the number of armed bodies a lord could call on, and we are not at all well informed about the actual sizes of contingents provided by tenants-in-chief on those occasions when they sent troops rather than paying scutage. In France the Capetians did comparatively little campaigning in the last three-quarters of the twelfth century, though more than would appear from the accounts of some of their modern historians. Though bishops were said in Philip Augustus's time to owe service in the host, *exercitum*, this was for defensive warfare. There is no sign of ecclesiastical contingents on the Toulouse expedition of 1159, the one occasion when Louis VII really left his home base to fight, and even in the campaigns

[19] 'Indiculus Loricatorum', *Constitutiones et Acta Publica 1, 911–1197*, ed. L. Weiland (MGH Legum 4/1, Hannover, 1893), p. 633–34, no. 436.

[20] G. Gattermann, *Die deutschen Fürsten auf der Reichsheerfahrt* (Diss., Frankfurt, 1956), vol. 1, pp. 100–3, 208–15; see also below at n. 55.

[21] The most recent study, with useful tables, is T.K. Keefe, *Feudal Assessments and the Political Community under Henry II and his Sons* (Berkeley, 1983); see also H.M. Chew, *The English Ecclesiastical Tenants-in-Chief and Knight Service* (Oxford, 1932), pp. 1–74, and I.J. Sanders, *Feudal Military Service in England* (Oxford, 1956), pp. 3, 16–19, 108–14. The figures for Domesday wealth I have taken from W.F. Corbett, 'The Development of the Duchy of Normandy and the Norman Conquest of England', *Contest of Empire and Papacy*, ed. C.W. Previté-Orton (The Cambridge Mediaeval History 5, Cambridge, 1926), pp. 507–10.

against the German invasions of 1124 and of 1214 such troops apparently played little part.[22]

The idea that German ecclesiastics could do more for their rulers militarily than their French or English counterparts is supported by their behaviour on their home ground. Here the building and purchase of castles appears as one of their primary concerns. The three Rhenish archbishops invested very large sums in this. Conrad of Mainz, for example, spent over 5000 marks in five years on recovering pledged castles and buying others, while Philip of Cologne's burial inscription records the sum of 50,000 marks for the purchase of the duchy of Westfalia and other rights;[23] the Third Crusade in particular offered a good opportunity to acquire castles and other rights from crusaders who needed ready cash. The bishops of Liège and Utrecht also pursued an active *Burgenpolitik*.[24] These prelates were interested as much in control as in ownership; like the Capetian rulers of France and unlike the Angevins, they sought agreements with the possessors of fortifications which allowed them to use the fortifications in times of war or feud.[25] Bishops took part in the

---

[22] M. Pacaut, *Louis VII et son royaume* (Paris, 1964), pp. 67–117 (Louis and the church), 185–86 (Toulouse) is conspicuous by its silence. For 1124 see Suger, *Vie de Louis VI le Gros*, c. 28, ed. H. Waquet (Paris, 2nd. edn., 1964), pp. 222–24, whose account lists no ecclesiastical contingents as such except that of Saint-Denis; even on the campaign against the excommunicated Thomas of Marle the clergy are mentioned separately from the army, ibid., c. 24, pp. 174–76. For 1214 see J.W. Baldwin, *The Government of Philip Augustus* (Berkeley, 1986), pp. 450–53, and pp. 281–89 for the military service owed the Capetians and the Norman dukes in the twelfth century.

[23] *Mainzer Urkundenbuch* (as n. 3), vol. 2, pp. 877–85, no. 531 (1189 × 1190). On Trier see I. Bodsch, *Burg und Herrschaft: Zur Territorial- und Burgenpolitik der Erzbischöfe von Trier im Hochmittelalter bis zum Tod Dieters von Nassau (†1307)* (Boppard, 1989), pp. 61–111; on Cologne see most recently H. Stehkämper, 'Der Reichsbischof und Territorialfürst (12. und 13. Jahrhundert)', *Der Bischof in seiner Zeit*, ed. P. Berglar and O. Engels (Cologne, 1986), pp. 95–184, here 135–37, and also Knipping, *Regesten*, p. 277–82, no. 1386, for Philip's extensive acquisitions.

[24] Kupper, *Liège* (as n. 9), pp. 428–33, 523–27; S. Muller and A.C Bouman (ed.), *Oorkondenboek van het Sticht Utrecht tot 1301* (Utrecht, 1920), vol. 1, pp. 384–86. no. 428 (1159), 402–5, no. 449 (1165).

[25] For early examples of such 'open house' (*Offenhaus*) agreements see F. Hillebrand, *Das Öffnungsrecht bei Burgen* (Diss., Tübingen, 1967), pp. 11–45, with twelfth-century examples from Hildesheim, Trier, Cologne and Utrecht. The notion seems to correspond pretty exactly to 'rendability', on which see C.H. Coulson, 'Fortress-Policy in Capetian Tradition and Angevin Practice: Aspects of the Conquest of Normandy by Philip II', *Anglo-Norman Studies* 6 (1984), pp. 13–38. Characteristically, the discussions of the Anglo-French phenomenon and of the German phenomenon seem to have been carried on without reference to each other.

major conflicts of the 1160s, the coalition against Henry the Lion in the north (the archbishops of Magdeburg, Cologne and Bremen) and against the count palatine of Tübingen in the south (the bishops of Worms, Speyer and Augsburg), and in the campaigns against Henry the Lion after his condemnation in 1180 (again, the archbishops of Magdeburg and Cologne, as well as the bishops of Halberstadt and Bamberg and a number of royal abbots).[26] They also pursued feuds of their own, without respect of persons: Archbishop Albero of Trier explicitly provided for hostilities against the abbot of Prüm in one of his agreements.[27] For these purposes they could draw on their unfree military vassals, the *ministeriales*, and here too it looks as if they differed from their counterparts further west, who were reducing their armed retinues and commuting their military obligation for cash payments.[28] Besides warfare on this larger scale, prelates whose churches possessed immunities or comital rights also wielded the *gladius materialis* in another way, by exercising blood justice, as Caesarius pointed out. They did not normally do this directly, but some at least in the late twelfth century were buying out the rights of the men who had previously done this for them, the advocates, and committing judicial powers to men more directly responsible to them.

Yet all this is by no means the whole story. Most prelates did not take part, at least in person, in most royal campaigns of the twelfth century, either to the east or to the south. The archbishop of Salzburg did not serve between 1125 and 1198, and his suffragans hardly at all; nor did the suffragans of Trier or of Magdeburg. Few churches were represented by their prelates on more than one or two of the dozen or so royal campaigns against rebels or beyond the frontiers of the *regnum Teutonicum* in this period. A preliminary list would include the archbishops of Mainz, Cologne, Trier, Bremen and Magdeburg and the

---

[26] K. Schmid, *Graf Rudolf von Pfullendorf und Kaiser Friedrich I.* (Freiburg im Breisgau, 1954), pp. 158–68; K. Jordan, *Henry the Lion* (Oxford, 1979), pp. 99–106, 166–78.

[27] H. Beyer (ed.), *Mittelrheinisches Urkundenbuch* (Coblenz, 1860), vol. 1, p. 612, no. 551 (*c.* 1148). For a characteristic example see the feud between Baldwin of Utrecht and Count Otto I of Guelders, recorded in a letter from Conrad of Mainz to Dietrich of Münster, *Mainzer Urkundenbuch* (as n. 3), pp. 828–30, no. 508 (1187 × 1188), and in the agreement between count and bishop, *Oorkondenboek Utrecht* (as n. 24), pp. 467–68, no. 528 (1187 × 1188).

[28] See Arnold, 'Bishops' (as n. 12), pp. 169–75 (though the statement at p. 172 that 'by the twelfth century the armed retinues serving the German bishops consisted almost entirely of *ministeriales* sustained by hereditary fiefs' goes too far), and his *German Knighthood, 1050–1300* (Oxford, 1985).

bishops of Bamberg, Hildesheim, Speyer, Strasbourg, Verden, Worms, Würzburg, Liège, Merseburg and Zeitz;[29] but the participation of many, especially on Italian expeditions, is known only from their presence as witnesses in royal diplomata, and it is by no means a certain inference that they were at the head of troop contingents. These should not readily be assumed if they are not explicitly recorded, for their cost was not trivial: at the going rate of a mark a month a contingent of forty *ministeriales* south of the Alps would have cost 500 marks a year, quite apart from the costs of the prelate's own upkeep.[30] No doubt for this reason Staufer armies in the course of the twelfth century were manned increasingly by imperial *ministeriales* and by mercenaries, with not too much time-lag behind Angevin and Capetian practice.[31] German churchmen helped to finance these, but that hardly made them different from their English and French counterparts.

There has been much debate about the nature and basis of the obligation to military service, of necessity inconclusive, though it is clear that there was nothing like a forty-day limit as there was further west.[32] There is evidence for quotas for some bishoprics, but it is hardly compelling, especially as it seems to have been so common not to serve.[33] In the absence of records we can only surmise about the extent to which prelates paid scutage if they did not come themselves. There are a few references to such payments, either in money or in kind.[34] There were one or two diplomata which release either a prelate or his church from the obligation to serve. There were also occasions where Barbarossa

[29] See the tables in Gattermann, *Reichsheerfahrt*, vol. 2.

[30] That was the going rate in Cologne in the 1160s. A century earlier the *ministeriales* of Bamberg got a horse and three pounds each. See Arnold, *Knighthood* (as n. 28), pp. 41, 83, 86, for references. Gattermann, *Reichsheerfahrt*, vol. 1, p. 200, estimates Rainald of Dassel's expenses in 1161–62 at 7–8000 marks.

[31] Gattermann, *Reichsheerfahrt*, vol. 1, pp. 111–21; on mercenaries see H. Grundmann, 'Rotten und Brabanzonen', *Deutsches Archiv für die Erforschung des Mittelalters* 5 (1942), pp. 419–92.

[32] Gattermann, *Reichsheerfahrt*, vol. 1, pp. 196–97, sums up the older controversy about obligation and length of service.

[33] The works by Werner and Brühl cited in n. 16 discuss this.

[34] K. Jänicke, *Urkundenbuch des Hochstifts Hildesheim I: Bis 1221*, (Leipzig, 1896), p. 322–23, no. 337 (1166): the bishop of Hildesheim pays Barbarossa 400 marks. In 1157 the bishop of Speyer recorded that he had granted Conrad III's son Frederick of Rothenburg an estate in return for exemption from the expedition sworn in 1151: R. Scholz, *Beiträge zur Geschichte der Hoheitsrechte des deutschen Königs zur Zeit der ersten Staufer (1138–1197)* (Leipzig, 1896), p. 42.

put pressure on a prelate to serve in person.[35] All this is not enough to force us to suppose that all prelates served by payment or in person on each expedition. Those who did serve will often have done so because of particular obligations – they needed either the ruler's protection or his favour. To seek 'closeness to the king' (*Königsnähe*) was a strategy almost compulsory for the prelates of the tenth and eleventh centuries, but less attractive in the twelfth, when it offered little to many prelates.[36] The strategy was still pursued by some: several of the bishoprics get into the list above through the military activities of a single prelate. Verden, for example, was only active in imperial military service under Hermann I, a man close to Frederick Barbarossa, while the careers of Henry of Liège, a Barbarossa supporter, and his successor Rudolf, who was rarely seen at court or in imperial armies, nicely illustrate the alternative strategies of *Königsnähe* and *Königsferne* now open to a bishop.[37]

Pledges left by prelates as security for loans for campaigns have left traces in a number of charters, but this evidence is not as straightforward as it looks. Sometimes the charters have survived in the archives of those from whom they raised the money, showing that the pledge was never redeemed: thus Werner of Minden borrowed from the collegiate church of St. Martin's, Minden, and Arnold of Mainz borrowed from the church of Würzburg.[38] Even in cases like these we may suspect that grants or the disposal of distant estates lay behind seeming pledges, and there are other explanations. Letters from Barbarossa ordering the canons of Würzburg to lend money against the security of episcopal revenues so that their bishops could serve in Italy, and those in favour of Wichmann of Magdeburg for the same purpose, were issued for a simple reason.[39] Chapters wanted guarantees, should their bishop die on the campaign, that Barbarossa would not take the lands pledged to them into his own

---

[35] For exemptions see Scholz, *Beiträge*, p. 42. For pressure on Arnold of Mainz see *Mainzer Urkundenbuch* (as n. 3), vol. 1, pp. 421–32, nos. 234, 236, 238 (1158); for that on Eberhard of Salzburg see D F I 327; 341: 'tua dignitas non solum qualicumque pecunia, sed et personis et armatura laboribus nostris adesse debeat'; 346 (all 1161); and see also D F I 439 (1164). Both Arnold and Eberhard offered money for exemption, which was refused.

[36] Reuter, 'Imperial Church System' (as n. 12), p. 360.

[37] O. Wurst, *Bischof Hermann von Verden, 1148–67* (Hildesheim, 1972); for Liège see the works by Kupper cited in n. 40 below.

[38] H.A. Erhard (ed.), *Westfälisches Urkundenbuch, accedit Codex Diplomaticus* (Münster, 1851), vol. 2, codex diplomaticus p. 91, no. 318 (1161); for Mainz see n. 35.

[39] D F I 345 (1161), 645 (1175), 822 (1182).

hands as *spolia*. Rudolf of Liège raised 1000 marks before the Legnano campaign and pledged episcopal estates to do so; but in effect he used the monies to buy from Barbarossa the imperial lands beyond the Meuse.[40] The loans raised by Philip of Cologne on several large estates show that even Philip was not capable of meeting the large sums required from his petty cash, but one must take into account also the chronic shortage of specie in the Reich at this time.[41] Loans needed sureties, but were not inherently a sign that prelates were being drawn on so heavily that they were becoming impoverished. Philip's revenues were in the medium term not only up to redeeming the loans but also to further purchases and recuperations. So were those of the archbishop of Mainz: within five years of taking office in 1183 Conrad had been able to redeem most of the alienations and pledges which had been made by Christian – presumably to finance his career as Barbarossa's general.[42] It is worth noting that Christian had borrowed some of the money from Barbarossa himself and his son Henry VI.

German medieval historians often take refuge behind regional differences to avoid having to generalise, but here the bishops of the north-west of the Reich really were rather different from the rest. It was here above all that the Staufer still sought to exercise control over episcopal elections, whereas elsewhere they were usually content to confirm the candidate chosen locally.[43] Mainz and Cologne especially were rich enough for their incumbents to be able to hire soldiers: Philip of Heinsberg led an army of 3000 mercenaries against Henry the Lion in 1179, for example, and it was largely mercenaries whom Christian of Mainz commanded in Italy.[44] The bishops of Liège also made extensive use of their financial resources in building up their territories.[45] These, incidentally, were also the sees with which western observers, who supply not a little of the anecdotal evidence for militant prelates, were most familiar. Robert of Torigny, John of Salisbury and Richard of Cornwall all wrote about

[40] D F I 663 (1176); cf. Kupper, *Liège* (as n. 9), pp. 478–85, and idem, *Raoul de Zähringen, évêque de Liège, 1167–1191* (Brussels, 1974), pp. 69–79.

[41] J. Barrow, 'German Cathedrals and the Monetary Economy in the Twelfth Century', *Journal of Medieval History* 16 (1990), pp. 13–38. For Philip's loans see D F I 649 (1176), 1006 (1189).

[42] See the references in n. 22.

[43] See B. Töpfer, 'Friedrich Barbarossa und der deutsche Episkopat', *Friedrich Barbarossa*, ed. A. Haverkamp (Vorträge und Forschungen 40, Sigmaringen, forthcoming).

[44] Grundmann, 'Rotten' (as n. 31), pp. 420–24, 456–57.

[45] Kupper, *Liège* (as n. 9), pp. 453–56.

the archbishops of Cologne and Mainz, as did Gislebert of Mons and Caesarius of Heisterbach.[46]

More sweeping generalisations seem plausible because German prelates were undoubtedly more locked into their aristocratic environment than English or French ones. This was not simply a question of the notorious aristocratic exclusiveness of the German high churches. Prelates' relationships of vassalage with lay magnates were not merely instrumental, however difficult they might be at times. The major and minor vassals of German bishops and abbots normally witnessed their charters, whereas in England only the lay household officials of the bishops did so with any regularity, and the same appears to be true of France.[47] German episcopal charters often say that a prelate had acted with the advice and consent of his vassals and *ministeriales*.[48] There were dividing lines here which were difficult to draw, and probably not at all easy for outsiders to grasp.[49] When Wibald wished to annoy Bishop Henry of Minden, with whom he was in conflict over the transfer of the nunnery of Kemnade to Corvey, he wrote that he was prepared to appeal to the pope, in spite of the (otherwise unknown) fate of an abbot of the diocese: 'your laymen are accustomed to judge of appeals to the lord pope with drawn swords'.[50] This stung, as it was meant to. Henry denied the charge indignantly, and added the *tu quoque* that Wibald, should he wish to appeal, was surrounded by enough armed retainers to do so without fear.[51] But he also pointed out that a prelate's vassals and *ministeriales* were owed respect and consultation,

[46] See n. 10 above; for Richard of Cornwall, who was impressed by the Rhenish bishops, see Arnold, 'Bishops', p. 167.

[47] For England see K. Major, 'The *Familia* of Stephen Langton', *EHR* 48 (1933), pp. 529–53; D.M. Smith (ed.), *English Episcopal Acta 1: Lincoln 1067–1185* (London, 1980), pp. xxxix–xxliii; F. Barlow, *Thomas Becket* (London, 1986), pp. 77–83; and the essay by P. Brand in the present volume. More work is needed on France; the generalisation in the text is based on some casual observations and on the evidence for those few bishops whose charters have been systematically collected, for example A. de Florival, *Barthélemy de Vir, évêque de Laon* (Paris, 1877).

[48] Typical is the phrase *faventibus cleris et laicis ministerialibus* in a charter of Otto of Eichstätt of 1191: F. Heidingsfelder, *Die Regesten der Bischöfe von Eichstätt* (Erlangen, 1915–38), p. 157, no. 494; cf. also ibid., no. 492: *ex sententia chori cleri et ministerialium*.

[49] On the difficulties French and English observers of the twelfth century experienced in analysing German society see T. Reuter, 'John of Salisbury and the Germans', *The World of John of Salisbury*, ed. D.E. Luscombe, C.N.L. Brooke, M.J. Wilks (Oxford, 1984), pp. 415–25.

[50] Ep. 236 (= Jaffé, pp. 385–87, no. 260).

[51] Ep. 238 (= Jaffé, pp. 389–90, no. 262).

something that Wibald himself acknowledged in other, less polemical contexts.[52]

Such a social atmosphere had a different feel from that with which western observers were familiar. It would be wrong to deduce from this that prelates presided over an officers' mess; most of them managed at best the status of honorary colonel of the regiment. German bishops died violent deaths more frequently in the eleventh and twelfth centuries than their French and English counterparts,[53] but this was not because they lived by the sword but because they were vulnerable: Arnold of Mainz (1160), Albert of Liège (1192), Conrad of Würzburg (1202), and Engelbert of Cologne (1225) were all killed by vassals and/or *ministeriales* of the bishopric.[54] The fact that so much church property was held in vassalage enabled prelates to dispose, seemingly, over large forces: the abbot of Fulda had a large part of the German high aristocracy, from Frederick Barbarossa downwards, as his vassals.[55] A prelate's vassals might, where honour and group solidarity was concerned, lend him their support.[56] They might also serve under him on royal campaigns, one reason why

[52] Ep. 124 (= Jaffé, no. 150, pp. 235, 246); ep. 128 (= Jaffé, no. 152, p. 257); ep. 295 (= Jaffé, no. 314, p. 443). Caesarius noted this too, but deplored it: *Wundergeschichten* (as n. 1), p. 127.

[53] For the Salian era see my 'Unruhestiftung, Fehde, Rebellion, Widerstand: Gewalt und Frieden in der Politik der Salierzeit', *Die Salier und das Reich*, ed. S. Weinfurter (Sigmaringen, 1991), vol. 3, pp. 297–325.

[54] For Arnold see W. Schöntag, *Untersuchungen zur Geschichte des Erzbistums Mainz unter den Erzbischöfen Arnold und Christian I (1153–1183)* (Diss., Marburg, Darmstadt, 1973), pp. 29–35; for Albert see R.H. Schmandt, 'The Election and Assassination of Albert of Louvain, Bishop of Liège', *Speculum* 42 (1967), pp. 649–53; for Conrad see A. Wendehorst, *Die Bischofsreihe bis 1254* (Germania Sacra, neue Folge 1, Das Bistum Würzburg, Teil 1, Berlin, 1962), pp. 193–94, 196–99; for Engelbert see Stehkämper, 'Reichsbischof' (as n. 23), pp. 137–38. In the case of Albert and Conrad the ruler was also said to be implicated; but the killing was done by locals.

[55] *Gesta Marcuardi Abbatis Fuldensis*, ed. J.F. Böhmer, *Fontes rerum Germanicarum* (Stuttgart, 1853), vol. 3, pp. 172–73. William of Malmesbury was also impressed by the power of the abbot of Fulda, who owed the emperor sixty knights' service: *Gesta Regum* II 192, ed. W. Stubbs (Rolls Series, London, 1887–89), vol. 1, pp. 233–34.

[56] See the story in Arnold of Lübeck, *Chronica* III 9, pp. 87–90, about the vassals who backed Philip of Cologne in a dispute with the abbot of Fulda at the great assembly at Mainz in 1184 about who should sit at Barbarossa's left hand; for a similar dispute between the followers of the abbot of Fulda and of the bishop of Hildesheim in 1063, which ended in bloodshed, see Lampert of Hersfeld, *Annales*, ed. O. Holder-Egger (MGH SRG, Hanover, 1894), pp. 81–82. See also the anecdote of William of Malmesbury referred to in the previous note.

ecclesiastical contingents seem so large by comparison with England and France, where men of equivalent social standing would normally be recorded separately.[57] But they were not his men in the sense of being his private army, any more than, say, John the Marshal was Becket's man.[58]

Contemporary criticisms of militant prelates might be described, in Max Weber's famous distinction, as *Gesinnungsethik* ('the morality of feeling'). Those in higher positions could show what Weber called *Verantwortungsethik* ('the morality of responsibility'), as did Innocent III, who explicitly condemned the notion put forward by Caesarius's Paris student.[59] *Verantwortungsethik* was both practised and explicitly defended in the twelfth century. The morality of responsibility was of course often equated with the morals of the responsible, much as it is today; but even Caesarius contrasted the earlier archbishops of Cologne, who had pulled down castles and built monasteries, with their contemporary successors who did the reverse.[60] In Wibald's view the king's service included service *in expeditione*, and this and other kinds of service were necessary to secure the king's favour and support for the churches of which he was in charge.[61] Activities which might seem to have been devoted to the maintenance of worldly power like those of any other magnate are depicted in Baldwin's biography of Albero of Trier, or in the *Triumphus Sancti Lamberti* recording the victory of the Liège episcopal forces in 1141 under the archdeacon and future bishop, Henry, or in Archbishop Arnold II of Cologne's defence of his siege and capture of Sayn, as being carried out in the service of peace and thus as proper work for a prelate.[62] Perhaps they were indeed that. Abbot Marcward of Fulda,

[57] See the letter of Wibald cited in n. 60, and the Venetian list cited at n. 14.

[58] Barlow, *Becket* (as n. 47), pp. 98, 108–10.

[59] Migne PL 215, col. 806, cited by Stehkämper, 'Reichsbischof' (as n. 23), p. 160.

[60] *Wundergeschichten* (as n. 1), p. 128.

[61] Ep. 124 (= Jaffé, no. 150, p. 239), and cf. also Wibald to Frederick Barbarossa, ep. 416 (= Jaffé, no. 446, p. 578): 'de occisione Thiderici comitis de Huxara, qui in expeditione vestra Italica nobis strennue ac fideliter servivit'. On Wibald's attitude to royal service see ep. 261 (= Jaffé, no. 286, p. 414) and the commentary by F.-J. Jakobi, *Wibald von Stablo* (Münster, 1979), pp. 234, 255.

[62] On Balderic's *Vita Adalberonis* (MGH SS 8, 243–60) see Hehl, *Klerus und Krieg* (as n. 2), pp. 51–52 and Bodsch, *Burg und Herrschaft* (as n. 23), pp. 61–75. For Henry of Liège see *Triumphus Sancti Lamberti de castro Bullonio*, MGH SS 20, pp. 497–518. For Arnold of Cologne see his letter to Wibald, ep. 360 (= Jaffé, no. 385, p. 517), with a long defence of his siege of the castle of Sayn, and Wibald's letter to him, ep. 356 (= Jaffé, no. 381, p. 512): 'castrum, quod nuper gloriose expugnastis'.

recording his castle-building, said: 'Not that it is proper that monks should inhabit anything but monasteries or fight battles other than spiritual ones; but the evil in the world cannot be defeated except by resistance'.[63] Nor did the money spent in purchasing castles and *Offenhaus* agreements necessarily guarantee successful territorial control. They were investments in prestige as much as in power, and the typical technique in the dioceses of Mainz, Trier and Cologne of purchasing a castle which was then held by the previous owner as a fief could just as well be interpreted as an attempt to buy peace from lay magnates. For the twelfth century at least, *Territorialpolitik* is often a much too grand and principled term for what were often very ad hoc and defensive measures.

Caesarius's Paris student has often been cited as a contemporary aphorism on the worldliness of German prelates, but both the student and Caesarius were primarily concerned with the moral problem for the prelates themselves: 'a great fear sits on them', as Caesarius wrote.[64] This fear does indeed seem to have been felt, and those who seemed not to feel it were reminded of it, as we have seen. That alone shows that there was not a radically different ethos of prelacy in Germany from that current in England or France.[65] German bishops and abbots differed as least as much from each other as they did from their western colleagues. They might possess the *gladius materialis*, but in owning and delegating rights of blood justice they were hardly more reprehensible from the point of view of canon law or current moral theology than for example those English prelates who acted, usually without qualms, as sheriffs and judges for the king.[66] They might serve in royal armies or conduct their own campaigns, but few were particularly prominent or successful as warriors and troop-leaders and it would be wrong to populate the twelfth-century Reich with Christians of Mainz and Rainalds of Dassel,

---

[63] *Gesta Marcuardi* (as n. 54), p. 167.

[64] *Wundergeschichten* (as n. 1), p. 127. Note Caesarius's story about Christian of Mainz's conversation with an Italian bishop who knew the names of all his flock, whereas Christian did not, ibid., p. 129 (echoing the epitaph of Arnold of Lübeck cited in n. 10).

[65] O. Engels, 'Der Reichsbischof (10. und 11. Jahrhundert)', *Der Bischof in seiner Zeit* (as n. 23), pp. 41–94, and 'Der Reichsbischof in ottonischer und frühsalischer Zeit', *Beiträge zu Geschichte und Struktur der mittelalterlichen Germania Sacra*, ed. I. Crusius (Göttingen, 1989), pp. 135–75, argues for a change in the episcopal ideal from the eleventh century from a primarily monastic one towards that of a territorial lord. His conclusions need examining in the light of twelfth-century *vitae*.

[66] Cf. R.V. Turner, 'Clerical Judges in English Secular Courts: The Ideal Versus the Reality', *Medievalia et Humanistica*, new series 3 (1972), pp. 75–98.

any more than England and France were filled with Odos of Bayeux and Williams of Savoy. On the whole they bore the sword in vain, and they found it difficult to find others who would bear it for them reliably; almost invariably they came off worse in clashes with their advocates and other local notables.[67] In the course of the territorialisation which set in in the *regnum Teutonicum* in the twelfth century and was largely completed by the fourteenth, not many were to achieve control of much more than their episcopal or monastic city together with a small patch of the immediately surrounding countryside. If any of them lost their souls in the process, they did so without gaining the whole world in return.

[67] I intend to deal with this topic at greater length elsewhere.

6

Lanfranc's Supposed Purge of the Anglo-Saxon Calendar

Richard W. Pfaff

Among the cardinal questions in the relationship between lay and ecclesiastical power in the high middle ages is that of designating which departed members of the body of Christ were to be venerated as saints.[1] The consequences of such veneration are so many and obvious that it is not necessary even to adumbrate them here. The purpose of this essay is to consider one widely-held view about the way this power was exercised at the time of the Norman Conquest of England.

It is a commonplace that among the ecclesiastical effects wrought by the Norman Conquest was a marked diminution in the number of saints venerated in the English church: a diminution which, furthermore, is said to have been the result of a deliberate policy on the part of Lanfranc, from 1070 on William the Conqueror's new (and first Norman) archbishop of Canterbury. Exactly how this notion came to have currency in the modern world is not clear; but the *locus classicus* from which

---

[1] The general subject of saints and sainthood is one which has been intensively worked on in recent decades. The main thrust of much of this work, summed up in such phrases as 'the role of the holy man in society', is not at all my concern here, which is rather to clear some ground between older liturgical scholarship of e.g. Edmund Bishop and Francis Wormald on one hand and current investigations like those of Susan Ridyard (see nn. 33 and 50) and David Rollason (see n. 48) on the other. Much of the work for this essay was completed before the books of the two last-named scholars were published, though I am glad to see that we are in general agreement.

the idea ultimately arose is without question the passage in Eadmer's *Life of Anselm* which relates the well-known conversation in, it seems, 1079 between the saint (while still abbot of Bec) and the archbishop. The focus of the discussion was one saint only, albeit an important one: Alphege (Ælfheah), the archbishop slaughtered by drunken Danes in 1012.[2] Anselm's defence convinced Lanfranc, who thereupon promised to 'worship and venerate the saint with all my heart', and indeed commissioned Osbern of Canterbury to write a life 'not only in plain prose for reading but also put . . . to music for singing; and Lanfranc himself for the love of the martyr gave it the seal of his eminent approval . . .'[3]

The implication is, of course, that Lanfranc could have withheld his 'eminent approval'; and, had he done so, that Alphege would thenceforth have been out of the calendar of the English church. And the impression given by this implication is intensified by a sentence at the beginning of this chapter of Eadmer's work (c. 30) where the biographer speaks of *quaedam institutiones* which Lanfranc found in England and some of which he changed 'simply by the imposition of his own authority (sola auctoritatis suae deliberatione)'. That this statement is followed immediately by an account of the conversation with Anselm – 'itaque dum illarum mutatione intenderet' – and that the general topic of the conversation *appears* to be that of English saints about whose sanctity he has doubts, seems to have led to a natural conclusion that though Alphege escaped, others were purged. In fact, Eadmer says nothing of the sort; so though it is his account out of which the idea seems to have developed, the notion of a 'Lanfrancian purge' cannot be substantiated from his words. The first question we need to ask is whether it can be substantiated at all.

Modern scholars of generally impeccable reliability have gone on retailing this idea.[4] Among the earliest, and probably the most influential, has been Edmund Bishop, who, in his investigation of the calendar of

---

[2] Saints' names are generally given in the forms of the main entries in D.H. Farmer (ed.), *The Oxford Dictionary of Saints* (Oxford, 1978).

[3] *Eadmer's Vita Sancti Anselmi*, ed. and trans. R.W. Southern (Edinburgh, 1952), pp. 50–54 especially 54.

[4] For example, F.M. Stenton, *Anglo-Saxon England* (Oxford, 1943), p. 664: 'The revised calendar which he [Lanfranc] imposed on them omitted the names of many saints whose cult had been traditional in that church'.

the Bosworth Psalter (London, British Library, MS Additional 37517) in a book of that name published in 1908, included a section entitled 'The Changes at Canterbury under Lanfranc.'[5] Here he argued, from a comparison between, on the one hand, four Christ Church calendars of the thirteenth to fifteenth centuries (all in the British Library: MSS Cotton Tiberius B. III; Egerton 2867; Additional 6160; and Sloane 3887) and on the other the calendar of the Bosworth book (*c.* 1000), that there had been 'a singular and extensive series of changes'. He found the key document in explaining these changes to be the calendar of the Arundel Psalter (London, British Library, MS Arundel 155).

After characterising Arundel's calendar as 'the post-Conquest calendar of Winchester', he went on to account for its particular nature in this way: 'that during the archiepiscopate of Lanfranc, that great and strenuous prelate abolished the existing and traditional calendar of his church at Canterbury and substituted for it by his authority that of the church of the capital of his master's newly acquired kingdom, Winchester' (p. 31). Bishop then repeated the story of the conversation about Alphege, and cited two other pieces of evidence, a supposed suppression of the feast of the Conception of Mary and a favouring of the Gallican feast day for (the Translation of) Benedict on 11 July over the old English date of 21 March (we shall notice both of these later). His conclusion – for our purposes – was that 'the calendar of Arundel 155 as originally drawn up is a record of the primitive and "rude" phase of Lanfranc's liturgical reformation in the ancient Church of which he was now archbishop' (p. 32).

What Edmund Bishop, superlative scholar though he was in most respects, did not realise is that the Arundel Psalter was written not in the later eleventh century but between 1012 and 1023 by Eadui Basan, the prize monk-scribe of Christ Church in the first quarter or third of the eleventh century.[6] Its calendar was extensively altered in the middle of the twelfth century (and later, in both the thirteenth and the fifteenth centuries), but in the form in which Eadui wrote it – which can be

---

5 [F.A. Gasquet and] E. Bishop, *The Bosworth Psalter* (London, 1908), pp. 27–34.

6 Alphege's martyrdom on 19 April, 1012 is included, his Translation on 8 June, 1023 is not. On this manuscript see E. Temple, *Anglo-Saxon Manuscripts, 900–1066* (London, 1976), no. 66, and J. Backhouse and others, *The Golden Age of Anglo-Saxon Art* (London, 1984), no. 57. The identification of Eadui Basan as the scribe of this and other manuscripts (his hand has been found in at least eleven) was made by T.A.M. Bishop, *English Caroline Minuscule* (Oxford, 1971), p. 22. See now R.W. Pfaff, 'Eadui Basan: *Scriptorum Princeps*?', in *England in the Eleventh Century*. Proceedings of the Harlaxton Conference 1990, ed. C. Hicks (Woodbridge, forthcoming).

ascertained without too much difficulty – it is a document which antedates Lanfranc's time by a good half century.

There seems to be no other relevant anecdotal evidence for any Lanfrancian purge of Anglo-Saxon saints as such.[7] The principal source for what might be termed his liturgical attitudes is his *Monastic Constitutions*,[8] directed ostensibly at the monks of Christ Church but extendible as far as persuasion and influence might stretch: for example, to the newly-established monks at Durham Cathedral *c.* 1083.[9] These Constitutions do not specify any sort of calendar, but some information can be inferred about the feasts deemed most important. Besides the five greatest occasions (Christmas, Easter, Pentecost, Assumption, and the *festivitas loci*), which were celebrated with immense elaboration, there is a list of fifteen others (plus the octaves of Easter and Pentecost) to be kept 'magnifice . . . quamuis non aequaliter'. Of these fifteen, five are feasts of Christ or Mary (Epiphany, Purification, Annunciation, Ascension, Nativity of the Virgin); five are the ancient major solemnities of John the Baptist, Peter and Paul, Michael, All Saints, and Andrew; and five speak directly to Christ Church tradition: Gregory, Augustine of Canterbury, Benedict, Alphege (as a consequence, we assume, of Anselm's eloquent defence), and the Dedication of the church. That Lanfranc is aware of 'Englishness' as a factor here seems to be indicated by his specifying that the feast of Gregory is included among the greatest 'quia nostrae, id est, Anglorum gentis apostolus est' – which Knowles calls 'one of the few recognisable touches of Lanfranc's own hand'.[10]

The fifteen feasts (plus Octave of the Assumption) of the third rank, celebrated a good deal less solemnly, were concerned largely with New Testament figures (Conversion of Paul, Philip and James [the Less], James, Peter's Chains, Bartholomew, Beheading of John the Baptist, Matthew, Simon and Jude, Thomas) or the Cross (Invention, Exaltation). Three of the remaining five are of greater antiquity than most of the

[7] The mid twelfth-century *Vita Lanfranci* attributed to Milo Crispin (see M. Gibson, *Lanfranc of Bec* [Oxford, 1978], pp. 196–97) tells the same story as Eadmer's *Life of Anselm* had but at somewhat greater length, including a comparison between Alphege's sanctity and that of John the Baptist. The text, edited by L. D'Achery in 1648, is available in Migne, PL 150, cols. 56–57.

[8] *Decreta Lanfranci monachis Cantuariensibus transmissa*, ed. and transl. D. Knowles (Edinburgh, 1951); a revised edition by Knowles is in the *Corpus Consuetudinum Monasticarum*, vol. 3 (Siegburg, 1967).

[9] D. Knowles, *The Monastic Order in England* (Cambridge, 2nd edn., 1963), p. 123.

[10] *Decreta* (as n. 8), p. 61.

feasts of the apostles – Vincent, Laurence, Martin. There is also, slightly surprisingly, Augustine of Hippo; and the list closes with a vague 'aliae festiuitates ita celebrari instituantur', which leaves open the possibility that others may be added.

Taken as a whole, these three groups of major feasts have only one striking element about them: the presence of Alphege and of Augustine of Canterbury (and perhaps of Augustine of Hippo). Certainly we would not expect to find any other Anglo-Saxon saints among this select group of two to three dozen (Dunstan is the only possible exception).[11] Equally certainly there is no indication of a systematic exclusion of anyone who might have reminded the Christ Church monks of their English past.

If there is little direct evidence for a Lanfrancian policy of purging Anglo-Saxon saints from the calendar, is there indirect or inferential evidence from the calendars themselves? In trying to answer this question one runs up against a pair of historiographical difficulties. The first is that very few English calendars survive from the last quarter of the eleventh and first quarter of the twelfth centuries: the period during which such a policy, had it existed, would have been reflected most clearly. The other, and related, problem is that though Francis Wormald published a corpus of all the English calendars known to him which dated from before 1100 (for the most part, from before the Conquest),[12] for the period after 1100 he limited his field of collection to localisable Benedictine calendars only – and of them was able to publish only two of three projected volumes.[13] This means that the pre-1100 evidence appears to have a kind of discreteness lacking for that of the later period.

---

[11] See Gibson, *Lanfranc*, pp. 171–72. Her suggestion that the *festivitas loci* was the feast of Dunstan 'rather than (as we might expect) the feast of the Trinity' deserves consideration, especially in the light of the fact that it is extremely unlikely to have been Trinity Sunday, an observance scarcely known anywhere in Christendom at that time.

[12] *English Kalendars before A.D. 1100* (Henry Bradshaw Society 72, London, 1934). To the twenty there listed may be added Paris, Bibliothèque Nationale, MS latin 7299, but it is not clear whether this distinctly sparse calendar was written in England or merely descends from an English exemplar: see B. Barker-Benfield in *Medieval Learning and Literature: Essays Presented to R.W. Hunt*, ed. J.J.G. Alexander and M.T. Gibson (Oxford, 1976), p. 152. Its entries (for information about which I am indebted to Professor Michael Lapidge and Dr. Patricia Stirnemann) add little to the present argument.

[13] *English Benedictine Kalendars after A.D. 1100* (Henry Bradshaw Society 77 and 81, London, 1939 and 1946). Publication of the third volume has been taken in hand by Dr. N.J. Morgan.

Because the amount of calendarial evidence directly relevant to our enquiry is very limited, it is difficult to compare calendars used in the same places, or at least areas, immediately before and soon after Lanfranc's time. This would be a desirable procedure above all for Christ Church itself: yet to set alongside the Arundel Psalter, clearly designed for that house and almost without question reflecting its traditions between 1012 and 1023,[14] there is no Christ Church document earlier than the mid twelfth century. From this time there survive three witnesses, one of them being the extensively added-to calendar of the Arundel Psalter itself.[15] The resulting gap of roughly sixty years is too wide to permit conclusive argument to be advanced as to calendarial developments in Lanfranc's own house.

Similar problems exist in trying to ascertain the situation in other establishments of primary importance: monastic houses like St. Augustine's, St. Albans, Bury St. Edmunds, Ely, Glastonbury, Westminster, Worcester and the Old and New Minsters at Winchester among monastic churches, and London, Exeter, Salisbury and perhaps Hereford among secular cathedrals. To lay out the whole of even the limited evidence that exists for pre- and post-Conquest calendarial usages at each of these places, with necessary analysis of the manuscripts involved, would far exceed the scope of this essay. All that can be done here it to try to give as accurate a sampling as possible from a cross-section of the available documents.

Before we do that, however, it will be convenient to establish a rough list of the Anglo-Saxon saints who appear in the great majority of surviving Anglo-Saxon calendars. Such a list can itself be divided into three groups. First come seven 'ancient' saints (one, indeed, pre-English): Cuthbert 20 March (with translation, 4 September), Guthlac 11 April, Augustine 26 May, Boniface 5 June, Alban 22 June, Etheldreda 23 June (with a widely-observed translation on 17 October), Oswald 5 August. Then there are three recent martyrs: Edmund 20 November (869), Edward 18 March (978) and Alphege 19 April (1012), who appear almost universally

---

[14] Cf. N. Brooks, *The Early History of the Church of Canterbury* (Leicester, 1984), p. 265: 'The Arundel calendar . . . marks the beginning of a medieval Benedictine community's jealous reliance upon its own traditions'. But it is not enough to see this calendar, as Brooks does, primarily as a calendar of Winchester origin.

[15] These three – the added-to Arundel Psalter, the Eadwine Psalter (Cambridge, Trinity College, MS R. 17.1), and a now-detached calendar in Oxford, Bodleian Library, MS Additional C.260 – are analyzed in detail in R.W. Pfaff, 'The Calendar', in *The Eadwine Psalter*, ed. M. Gibson, T.A. Heslop, R.W. Pfaff (London, forthcoming).

from the time of their deaths. Finally, among the many saints who had a strong local cult are three or four who stand out because their connections are with places of the greatest importance. One, Dunstan 19 May (d. 988), is from Christ Church (and also Glastonbury); the others represent Winchester Old Minster: Swithun 2 July (d. 862, translated 15 July 971); Birinus, in some sense the first bishop of Winchester, 3 December (d. 650, translated 4 September, 980); and Ethelwold 1 August (d. 984).

Several other figures were widely observed, notably those connected with the New Minster at Winchester (Judoc, whose deposition feast was 13 December and translation 9 January, and Grimbald 8 July); and with Ely (especially Ermengild 13 February, as well as Etheldreda), Lichfield (Chad 2 March), London (Erkenwald 30 April), and York-plus-Rochester (Paulinus 10 October). But let us in caution use as the basis for our comparisons primarily the fourteen persons identified above as almost always present in pre-Conquest calendars, so as to avoid possible skewing by the inclusion of markedly obscure or predominantly local figures.

It would be unnecessarily tedious to lay this comparison out in chart form. By stretching as far as the third quarter of the twelfth century (and in one case to *c.* 1200 and in another to *c.* 1300), we can establish five localisable pairs, which among them represent (the first one listed is pre-, the second is post-Conquest) these places:

Canterbury Christ Church: London, British Library, MS Arundel 155 (1012–23)[16] and Cambridge, Trinity College, MS R.17.1 (987; Eadwine Psalter).[17]

Ely: Rouen, Bibliothèque municipale, MS Y.6 (probably pre-1012)[18] and Milan, Biblioteca Nazionale Braidense, MS AF.XI.9 (pre-1170).[19]

---

[16] Wormald, *Kalendars before 1100*, no. 13.

[17] Facsimile in *The Canterbury Psalter*, ed. M.R. James (Canterbury, 1935); this is the only one of the three witnesses mentioned above which has not been extensively added to: see the discussion in Pfaff (as n. 15).

[18] *The Missal of Robert of Jumièges*, ed. H.A. Wilson (Henry Bradshaw Society 11, London, 1896); this is not printed in Wormald, *Kalendars before 1100*, though it is listed there.

[19] MS D in Wormald's collation of Ely calendars in *Kalendars after 1100*, vol. 2, pp. 8–19.

Winchester Old Minster (= St. Swithun's): London, British Library, MS Cotton Vitellius E. XVIII (probably 1060s)[20] and Madrid, Biblioteca Nacional, MS Vit. 23–8 (mid twelfth century).[21]

Winchester New Minster (from 1110, Hyde Abbey): London, British Library, MS Cotton Titus D. XXVII (1023–32)[22] and Oxford, Bodleian Library, MS Gough liturg. 8 (*c.* 1300).[23]

Worcester: Cambridge, Corpus Christi College, MS 9 (*c.* 1025–50)[24] and Oxford, Magdalen College, MS 100 (*c.* 1225).[25]

For all of the comparisons the results are similar. From the fourteen figures on our list, those missing from the later calendar of each pair number between one and four, along with an occasional translation feast. The saints lacking from the later calendars are for Ely, Edward the Martyr and Ethelwold; for Winchester Old Minster, Guthlac, Dunstan and Boniface; for Hyde, only Guthlac; for Worcester, Boniface (and Ethelwold, not in the earlier calendar either) and the translations of Swithun, Birinus and Etheldreda. Canterbury alone has lost as many as four: of saints present in the Arundel Psalter calendar, that in the Eadwine Psalter lacks Guthlac, Boniface, Swithun and Birinus, along with the translations of Swithun and of Cuthbert and Birinus (Ethelwold and the Translation of Etheldreda are not present in either calendar).[26]

It must be stressed that these comparisons are not, and from the limitations of the evidence cannot be, either exhaustive or wholly scientific. Nonetheless, it is reasonably clear that there was neither a massive nor a systematic loss of the principal Anglo-Saxon saints – of, that is, those most universally venerated in the pre-Conquest English church. Between

---

[20] Wormald, *Kalendars before 1100*, no. 12. There is some possibility that the calendar may have originated at the New Minster instead.

[21] The English entries are listed in F. Wormald, 'Liturgical Note', in H. Buchthal, *Miniature Painting in the Latin Kingdom of Jerusalem* (Oxford, 1957), pp. 122–23. Though again it has been suggested that this is a Hyde Abbey calendar, Wormald concludes that 'it was unquestionably written for the Cathedral Priory'.

[22] Wormald, *Kalendars before 1100*, no. 9.

[23] *The Monastic Breviary of Hyde Abbey*, vol. 5, ed. J.B.L. Tolhurst (Henry Bradshaw Society 71, London, 1934).

[24] Wormald, *Kalendars before 1100*, no. 18.

[25] The calendar is printed as column 4 in the table in *The Leofric Collectar*, ed. E.S. Dewick and W.H. Frere (Henry Bradshaw Society 56, London, 1921), pp. 589–600.

[26] The situation at Canterbury was probably unusually complex, and indeed there seem to be three calendarial traditions apparent at Christ Church in the middle of the eleventh century: see Pfaff, 'Calendar' (as n. 15).

ten and thirteen of the fourteen saints who have formed the basis of our comparison were still present in the later documents. Furthermore, had any systematic 'purge' of the kind often alluded to taken place, surely the same saints would have been removed everywhere: say, Guthlac (lost at the two Winchester houses and at Christ Church but kept at both Ely and Worcester) or Edward the Martyr (lost only at Ely).

Almost certainly, however, two things did happen which among them resulted in the loss of quite a number of entries present in many pre-Conquest calendars; it seems likely that between them these two are responsible for much of the widespread if erroneous impression we have been considering. One is the removal of numerous saints, whether Anglo-Saxon or not, who in the age of Early Scholasticism (Lanfranc's period and after) must have seemed hopelessly obscure or confused. A good example is the saints who appear in most pre-Conquest calendars on January 19 (or sometimes 20) either as Mary and Martha or as a family of Persian martyrs called Marius, Martha, Audifax and Abbacuc.[27] Whereas of the twenty pre-1100 calendars printed by Wormald only six lacked an entry of this sort, of a dozen twelfth-century calendars he printed or collated in his later collection, any such commemoration is evident in manuscripts from only two houses, Durham[28] and Ely.[29] Whatever the reason for the dwindling away of this confused commemoration, it cannot have been because the figures involved were Anglo-Saxon. (It is somewhat ironical that the saint who came to be almost universally present on 19 January in English calendars from the early thirteenth century on was the last Anglo-Saxon bishop, Wulfstan of Worcester, canonised in 1203.)

To be sure, among those lost in this process were numerous Anglo-Saxon 'saints'. Some are so obscure as to defy identification: figures like the *Athelmodus confessor* on 9 January in an unlocalised Wessex calendar;[30] or the Othulph whose translation is recorded on 10 October along with Ecgwin's in one mid eleventh-century Worcester calendar[31] but in no others, pre- or post-Conquest. To be sure also, some regional royal or semi-royal personages disappeared as a consequence of both the passage of time and the existence of a national (and Anglo-Norman)

---

[27] A study of this curious phenomenon by the present author is near completion.

[28] Durham, Cathedral Library, MS Hunter 100 (soon after 1100): *Marii et Marthae* on the 19th; Cambridge, Jesus College, MS Q.B.6 (mid twelfth century), has the same entry on the 20th.

[29] The calendar now in Milan (see n. 19), on the 20th.

[30] London, British Library, MS Cotton Nero A. II.

[31] Oxford, Bodleian Library, MS Hatton 113.

monarchy;[32] though there is evidence that at some places, perhaps most notably at Ely, their memory survived tenaciously.

The other category of observance which seems to have been to a large extent lost after the Norman Conquest – although again there seems no reason to speak of a systematic purge – is that of three or four distinctively if somewhat inexplicably Anglo-Saxon feasts none of which has a logical connection with England. These are the Ordination of Gregory, the Conception of John the Baptist, one of two Translations of Benedict and the Oblation of the Virgin Mary (possibly the feast of the Conception should be included here also).[33] How these come to be distinctive features of Anglo-Saxon calendars is not part of the present investigation. We need to note here only the following facts.

The Ordination of Gregory appears in about three-fifths of pre-Conquest calendars on March 29 (eight of Wormald's twenty) or March 30 (four more). This date, liturgically inconvenient (it will always fall within Lent or Eastertide, and very often within Holy Week or the Paschal octave), apparently derives from the translation of some relics of Gregory's to Soissons in 826.[34] In any case, after the Conquest the feast was widely found in English calendars not in late March but on 3 September, a date both more historically accurate (Gregory seems to have been ordained Bishop of Rome on that day in 590) and more liturgically feasible.[35] That this change can plausibly be ascribed to Lanfranc seems most unlikely. The new date is not to be found in the mid thirteenth-century calendar of Bec,[36] nor in the early thirteenth-century calendar of St. Neots, which was a cell of Bec.[37] It was, however, added

[32] Some of these, particularly those connected with Ely and with Winchester, are studied in detail by S.J. Ridyard in her important book, *The Royal Saints of Anglo-Saxon England* (Cambridge, 1988); but her emphasis is primarily on their character as royal rather than as some among many possibilities for liturgical commemoration.

[33] The two Marian feasts will not be treated here because it is by no means clear that they were feasts of anything like widespread observance in Anglo-Saxon England. The evidence that exists seems to point only to Winchester and Canterbury; see E. Bishop, 'On the Origins of the Feast of the Conception', in his *Liturgica Historica* (Oxford, 1916), pp. 238–59, at 258–59, and R.W. Pfaff, *New Liturgical Feasts in Later Medieval England* (Oxford, 1970), pp. 103–15.

[34] See the account by Odilo of St. Medard's, printed in Migne, PL 132, cols. 579–622.

[35] It seems to remain at 29 March only in a Chester calendar of the late twelfth century, Oxford, Bodleian Library, MS Tanner 169*.

[36] *Missale Beccense*, ed. A. Hughes (Henry Bradshaw Society 94, London 1963).

[37] London, Lambeth Palace, MS 563; collated in Wormald, *Kalendars after 1100*, vol. 2, p. 115.

in an eleventh-century hand to the Glastonbury calendar which forms part of the so-called Leofric Missal,[38] and it was noticed in the very late eleventh-century St. Augustine's mass-book through the insertion, by a hand which has made many contemporary annotations, of the words 'De ordinatione sancti gregorii require in ordinatione sancti martini'.[39]

The situation is similar with the Conception of John the Baptist, except that here it is not a matter of an alternative date. That feast, appearing in all twenty of Wormald's pre-1100 calendars on 24 September, is almost as uniformly absent from those of the early post-Conquest period. Perhaps its earliest (re-)appearance is in three calendars of second half of the twelfth century, from Chester, Ely and Gloucester.[40] At other places where it is known to have been included before the Conquest – notably Christ Church and Worcester – there look to be no traces of it afterwards.[41]

This leaves us with the observance which Edmund Bishop took as the most symptomatic of Lanfrancian purge, that of 'his own patriarch St. Benedict, and his own compatriot too in a sense;' here 'Lanfranc simply trampled under foot the old English tradition of honouring with high observance the feast of 21 March . . . and puts instead of it in the place of honour, among the most "magnificent" feasts of the year, the Gallican feast of St. Benedict, the translation in July' (July 11th).[42] Bishop's 'instead of it' implies that the March feast was done away with: but of course it is not usually the case that a translation feast supplants that of the deposition. Nor was this so with Benedict, though once again the date of the latter, 21 March, put it in danger of being often overshadowed by seasonal observances.

In fact, there was no supplanting whatever. Both feasts are present in all twenty of the pre-1100 witnesses used by Wormald.[43] What changed

---

38 Oxford, Bodleian Library, MS 579; ed. F.E. Warren (Oxford, 1883).

39 *The Missal of St. Augustine's Abbey Canterbury*, ed. M. Rule (Cambridge, 1896), p. 108.

40 Respectively, Oxford, Bodleian Library, MS Tanner 169*, Milan, Biblioteca Nazionale Braidense, MS AF.XI.19 (but not the other twelfth-century Ely calendars), and Oxford, Jesus College, MS 10.

41 One later Christ Church calendar does – inexplicably – contain the feast, Paris, Bibliothèque Nationale, Nouvelles acquisitions latins 1670, a psalter of *c*. 1200: Bishop, *Bosworth Psalter*, p. 107.

42 *Bosworth Psalter*, p. 32.

43 The Translation is not included in the calendar of the Robert of Jumièges sacramentary (probably from Ely, Rouen, Bibliothèque Municipale, Y.6) but its mass is in the *sanctorale*; the same thing is true of Dunstan.

was rather that a second translation, on 4 December,[44] which is present in thirteen of these documents, seems to disappear almost wholly after the Conquest.[45] The 21 March feast continued with complete regularity. Bishop was right that Lanfranc did not include it in his list of greater feasts, undoubtedly for the commonsense reason noted above; but to speak of 'trampling under foot' an old English tradition of high observance is fanciful to say the least.[46]

It may seem odd to devote attention largely to arguing that something did not happen; a verdict of Not Proven is, even if correct, never very exciting. Though absence of proof can never be as conclusive as proof positive, in this case it seems amply clear that there was no 'Lanfrancian purge' of the Anglo-Saxon calendar. That statement in itself, however, contains the seeds of several large questions which, though they cannot be pursued here, deserve to be laid out.

The first is, was there any meaningful sense in which there was such a thing as 'the Anglo-Saxon calendar' in the years just before the Norman Conquest. Literally, of course, the answer is no; there is no mid eleventh-century equivalent of the position the Use of Sarum came to have in England in the years just before the Reformation. Yet there may be some signs that a kind of Canterbury–Winchester mix (with perhaps a dash of Worcester) was coming to predominate in terms not only of the basically monastic character of the calendar – witness the two translations of Benedict – but also of the presence of an increasingly discrete body of English saints and other observances like the Conception of John the Baptist. It is certainly a question worth pursuing.[47]

---

[44] The controverted and knotty question of which translations took place on which days, to say nothing of which (if any) were of Benedict's genuine relics, cannot be discussed here. A judicious, if somewhat dated, treatment of the matter is J. McCann, *Saint Benedict* (London, 1937; revised paperback edition 1958), especially pp. 168–69.

[45] It appears, again with no conceivable explanation, in a late fourteenth-century calendar for Dunster Priory, London, British Library, MS Additional 10628: Wormald, *Kalendars after 1100*, vol. 1, p. 160.

[46] Very few of the pre-1100 calendars are graded in anything like the sense we come to encounter with later documents. In those that are there is no preponderance of dignity one way or the other. In perhaps the most noteworthy case (because the one so badly misunderstood by Bishop), Arundel 155 has the March feast graded 'II' but the July one as 'III', among the six highest.

[47] I have not seen the unpublished Ph. D. thesis of V.N. Ortenberg, 'Aspects of Monastic Devotions to the Saints in England, *c*. 950 to *c*. 1100: The Liturgical and Iconographic Evidence' (Cambridge, 1987).

The next such question is, what then happened to account for the fact that English calendars do look somewhat different in, say, the mid twelfth century from the way they looked in the mid eleventh? Some attempt has been made here to indicate partial answers, but it must be admitted that this is a particularly difficult area to treat because of a curious counter-phenomenon to any slimming (though not purging) of late Anglo-Saxon calendars. This is the resurgence, or perhaps better revitalisation, of the tradition of hagiographical writing about English saints which took place in the generation after the Norman Conquest. A mere mention of the names of Goscelin, Osbern and Eadmer – each sometimes called 'of Canterbury' – is sufficient reminder that in a sense the culmination of Anglo-Saxon hagiography (albeit expressed in Latin) lay in the two decades or so on either side of the year 1100.[48] Full appreciation of this phenomenon is to be welcomed, but it may be useful to recall another contemporary development alluded to earlier: that the age of Lanfranc (d. 1089) and Eadmer (d. *c.* 1128) was also that often associated with the phrase Early Scholasticism. The critical mentality involved was inevitably confronted by questions of saints' cults and relics; the kind of attitude expressed by Abelard towards the relics of St. Denis is likely to have crossed the Channel and to have had consequences for the persistence of some of the less well-attested English saints in Anglo-Norman calendars.

'Less well-attested' does not only mean not supported by a Life, preferably one in Latin. It may also mean not supported by a place in the sanctorale of a mass-book. This observation leads to the next open-ended question: what the relationship was between the presence of a saint in a liturgical calendar (especially given the fact that many early liturgical calendars exist in the context not of service books but of *computistica*) and in a liturgical book, most often a mass-book. Too few pre-Conquest mass-books survive for this question to be investigated systematically,[49] but it is a consideration which must be kept in mind in the light of the general (modern) presumption that a saint will be 'culted' in part by having a place in the sanctoral cycle.

[48] On this see above all D. Rollason, *Saints and Relics in Anglo-Saxon England* (Oxford, 1989), especially chap. 9, 'Englishness and the Wider World'.

[49] There are only eight (and two fragmentary ones) in the listing by H. Gneuss, 'Liturgical Books in Anglo-Saxon England and their Old English Terminology', *Learning and Literature in Anglo-Saxon England: Studies Presented to Peter Clemoes*, ed. M. Lapidge and H. Gneuss (Cambridge, 1985), pp. 91–141, at 101–2. Only four of the eight have calendars.

A fourth question, again only to be adumbrated here, is how to account for the undoubted revival of Anglo-Saxon saints, sometimes of considerable obscurity, in the thirteenth century and thereafter. Part of the reason why it is necessary to be so cautious in the comparison of pre- and post-Conquest calendars is that the further one gets from the late eleventh century the likelier one is to encounter Anglo-Saxon saints of less than the greatest visibility: figures like Wenefred, Frideswide and John of Beverley are more prominent in the fifteenth century than at any earlier time.

This is in turn a separable question from our final one, the very large matter of how 'useful' – culturally and politically as well as ecclesiastically – Anglo-Saxon saints were in Anglo-Norman England. The logic of the matter is simple enough: that the more important the saint, the more potentially useful to those running the new ecclesiastical regime; and that, conversely, the saints likeliest to drop by the wayside were those not of the greatest potential import (e.g., an Alphege) but those of the greatest obscurity.[50] As Karl Leyser has put it with typical pithiness: 'It is characteristic of rising dynasties in this period that they sought to acquire and make the *virtus* of especially exalted and martial saints their own'.[51] An Alphege, an Oswald, an Etheldreda or any of the others of the most prominent (though not necessarily martial, save that a martyr is always *miles Christi*) Anglo-Saxon saints fall, of course, into this category.

A full consideration of all the uses the Anglo-Normans may have had for these saints would make for a large and fascinating study in the spiritual as well as political history of England in the late eleventh and twelfth centuries. Such a study should not be hampered by a presupposition that the starting point of Norman action was anything like a deliberate and systematic purging of the Anglo-Saxon calendar.

[50] This point is well supported by the investigations of S.J. Ridyard, especially in her article '*Condigna Veneratio*: Post-Conquest Attitudes to the Saints of the Anglo-Saxons', *Anglo-Norman Studies* 9 (1987), pp. 179–206. She considers each of four literary instances involving apparent Norman scepticism about or disrespect towards English saints, and shows that when an important figure was involved, like Alban, there was no sign of disrespect.

[51] K.J. Leyser, *Rule and Conflict in an Early Medieval Society* (London, 1979), p. 88.

7

Peter Bartholomew and the Role of 'The Poor' in the First Crusade

Randall Rogers

The significance of the Holy Lance of Antioch and its discoverer, Peter Bartholomew, for the First Crusade has perplexed historians of that expedition since the time of William of Tyre.[1] This relic, revealed to a lowly southern Frenchman by St. Andrew, played a central role in the religious and psychological preparations before the decisive battle of Antioch in June 1098. The discovery of the Lance and the crusaders' victory over Kherbogha of Mosul confirmed the promise of supernatural support which crusaders considered central to their endeavour, and this is widely reflected in contemporary sources. The Lance became a potent symbol in the faction fighting and wrangling over policy and objectives which overshadowed the crusade from the capture of Antioch until the abandonment of the siege of Arqua in May 1099. Throughout this period the discoverer of the Lance reported St. Andrew's continued admonitions, which he learned though a series of visions, to the expedition's leaders. The death of the relic's finder in the wake of a public ordeal intended to demonstrate his veracity doubtless diminished the Lance's appeal, particularly among contingents hostile to the leadership of Raymond of St. Gilles.[2]

[1] William of Tyre, *Historia rerum in partibus transmarinis gestarum* VII 18 (Receuil des Historiens des Croisades, Historiens Occidentaux, Paris 1844), vol. 1, pp. 304–5.

[2] S. Runciman, 'The Holy Lance found at Antioch', *Analecta Bollandiana* 68 (1950), pp. 197–209; B. Ward, *Miracles and the Medieval Mind* (Philadelphia, 1982), pp. 203–4;

Yet the outcome of the ordeal was not unambiguous, and the relic remained important at least for the count and his followers. The Lance was utilised in the large-scale preparations for the major assault on Jerusalem in July 1099 and figured in the propitiation before the battle of Ascalon on August 12.[3] Moreover the Lance was cited in the so-called 'official' letter of the crusade's leaders to the pope which outlined the expedition's paramount achievements.[4] The Lance's subsequent history is clouded: it was probably lost in Anatolia in 1101 although portions may have been saved before the ill-fated crusade of 1101.[5] Yet it is clear that the Lance's significance for the First Crusade was overshadowed by the discovery of the True Cross between 15 July and 12 August 1099 in Jerusalem. This became the nascent kingdom's chief relic until its capture by Saladin in 1187. Despite its prominence in the expedition and in accounts of it, the Lance never became important in the shrines or politics which stemmed from the First Crusade.

That crusaders had doubts about the Lance is evident from its unearthing in the newly consecrated church of St. Peter at Antioch.[6] Foremost among the relic's early doubters, though he apparently came to change his opinion, was the papal legate Adémar of Le Puy. While other versions – or perhaps portions – of this relic may have been known to crusade leaders, generating misgivings about this particular relic, the principal factor which undermined the Lance's credibility was its finder, Peter Bartholomew. An unlettered servant of a southern French pilgrim, who had left the main expedition at least twice before June 1098, Peter inspired little confidence in Adémar of Le Puy. Peter's death following an ordeal by fire in April 1099 confirmed the opinion of those who believed him to have been fraudulent since the outset of the affair. However, Peter

J. Riley-Smith, *The First Crusade and the Idea of Crusading* (London, 1986), chapters 3 and 4.

[3] Raymond of Aguilers, *Le Liber de Raymond d'Aguilers*, ed. J.H. and L.L. Hill (Paris, 1969), pp. 156; Peter Tudebode, *Historia de Hierosolymitano itinere*, ed. J.H. and L.L. Hill (Paris, 1977), pp. 145–46.

[4] H. Hagenmeyer, *Die Kreuzzugsbriefe aus den Jahren 1088–1108* (Innsbruck, 1901), pp. 167–74.

[5] Riley-Smith, *First Crusade*, p. 97.

[6] Ralph of Caen, *Gesta Tancredi* (Receuil des Historiens des Croisades, Historiens Occidentaux, Paris, 1856), vol. 3, pp. 676–678; Fulcher of Chartres, *Historia Hierosolymitana* I 18, ed. H. Hagenmeyer (Heidelberg, 1913), pp. 236–39; Albert of Aachen, *Historia Hierosolymitana* V 32 (Receuil des Historiens des Croisades, Historiens Occidentaux, Paris, 1879), vol. 4, p. 452.

died some two weeks after his ordeal, and Raymond of Aguilers illustrates how this event could be interpreted to support Peter as a true man of God. The count of St. Gilles observed Peter's somewhat bizarre admonitions concerning ritual baptism in the river Jordan, indicating that the count as well as his chaplain continued to believe in Peter's legitimacy.[7] Bewilderment about the genuineness of Peter's claims was doubtless widespread in the spring of 1099, as William of Tyre surmised. Whatever doubts Peter's fate may have engendered were rendered unimportant by the capture of Jerusalem, victory at Ascalon and discovery of the True Cross. Raymond of Aguilers, however, clearly believed that the importance of the Lance and Peter needed to be made manifest, and wrote his history of the First Crusade accordingly. Raymond did not attempt to distance the relic from its finder, and viewed both as manifestations of supernatural influence in the crusade.

As Ward and Riley-Smith note, the story of the Lance became rapidly and deeply embedded in the historical writing surrounding the First Crusade.[8] Thus the Lance became part of the tradition of the first great armed pilgrimage which so profoundly affected the medieval west. This episode of the First Crusade has been viewed by some as representative of the religious climate of the age. That a relic should become central in maintaining morale and commitment in such a disparate group of Latin Christians as the first crusaders is in no way surprising, particularly since one of the many secondary aims of the expedition was the retrieval of the west's religious heritage. That a symbol of spiritual power and authority was harnessed to military operations is also much in keeping with the religiosity of the age. Yet in explaining this phenomena historians have concentrated more upon the Lance and the psychological and religious needs of the crusade than on Peter Bartholomew. Peter has been perceived as an unwitting tool of either the count of St. Gilles or of clerics attempting to influence him; as one of the few straightforward visionary frauds of the age; as possessed of metal divining abilities; or as a manifestation of the challenges bishops of the period faced.[9] While Morris's recent study has noted the seriousness with which Raymond of

---

[7] Raymond of Aguilers, *Liber*, pp. 119–24, 156.

[8] Ward, *Miracles*, p. 204; Riley-Smith, *First Crusade*, pp. 95–96.

[9] Ward, *Miracles*, pp. 203–5; J.H. and L.L. Hill, *Raymond IV of St. Gilles, Count of Toulouse* (New York, 1962), pp. 77–78; Runciman, 'Holy Lance' (as n. 2); Riley-Smith, *First Crusade*, p. 96. P. Dinzelbacher, *Vision und Visionsliteratur im Mittelalter* (Stuttgart, 1981), pp. 57–60, depends entirely upon Runciman.

Aguilers regarded the Lance, he pays little attention to the relic's finder and his relation to events.[10] Thus in understanding the 'affair of the Lance', it seems appropriate to focus on Peter Bartholomew and reactions to his prominent role in the expedition.

There is little doubt that Adémar of Le Puy's well-known early scepticism about St. Andrew's messages to the crusaders via Peter Bartholomew, which referred to the Lance as a token of the renewal of divine aid, stemmed from the legate's impression of the visionary's character. Although he was to become a charismatic leader, Peter Bartholomew was a servant of an undistinguished southern Frenchman who had no known connection with the 'popular crusade' of Peter the Hermit. It is likely that Peter's story confronted Adémar with the usual difficulties which eleventh-century popular religion presented to ecclesiastical authorities. Not affiliated to any established religious community or prominent cleric, Peter clearly came from the fringes of the First Crusade. In this regard he resembled similar figures of eleventh- and twelfth-century Europe who on occasion vexed ecclesiastical authorities as a result of popular religious energies. It is of course possible that, as some of his contemporaries suggested, Peter Bartholomew was an outright fraud. Neither the course of events nor what Raymond of Aguilers shows us of the Provencal's psychology make this seem likely. As Morris has pointed out, no one should be surprised that excavators found a metal object in a venerable church in Antioch.[11] Even if Peter knowingly fabricated the relic, it remains true that many in the expedition including important and powerful leaders came to have credence in the Lance and its finder. Peter has also been depicted as an unwitting or at least confused tool of religious and political leaders among the southern French. The Hills have argued that the Lance was promoted primarily by a group of clerics around Raymond of St. Gilles who wanted to influence policy. It is not possible to identify these men, with the exception of the historian Raymond of Aguilers, and any control over Peter that they may have exercised soon evaporated.

Because the relic was linked to the count of St. Gilles even before its discovery, since the time of the First Crusade some have seen 'the cult of the Lance' as part of Raymond of St. Gilles attempt to assert his leadership

[10] C. Morris, 'Policy and Visions. The Case of the Holy Lance at Antioch', *War and Government in the Middle Ages: Essays in Honour of J.O. Prestwich*, ed. J. Gillingham and J.C. Holt (Cambridge, 1984), pp. 33–45.

[11] Morris, 'Policy and Visions', p. 36 n. 9.

over the expedition. There seems little doubt that the count tried to utilise the relic and its discoverer towards these ends during the course of the crusade. This does not necessarily mean that the Lance was unearthed for these purposes. It seems likely that Raymond employed the Lance once it had established a following, since otherwise he appears as an especially far-sighted as well as cynical politician. Peter's rebukes to the count on several occasions, including after his ordeal, and the content of his later visions make it difficult to view him as a pliable tool of crusade policy making.[12]

It is certain that the Lance's legitimacy and Peter's prominence in the expedition were due to the extraordinary circumstances of that phase of the First Crusade. The plight of the crusaders caught between Antioch's citadel and a powerful relieving force camped outside the city walls shook the crusading movement and its developing ideology to its core, and doubtless contributed to a climate in which messages of renewed divine support for the endeavour were seized upon. Moreover Peter's visions and the discovery of the Lance were linked to the visions of a priest, Stephen of Valence, during the time of the crusaders' entrapment. Stephen's vision, which had as its core a restoration of divine aid and a soon to be visible token of such support, was widely disseminated within the expedition as the existence of several accounts of it testifies. Raymond of Aguilers' account suggests that Stephen certainly believed in the Lance, as his later vision outside Arqua shows.[13] Stephen's vision at Antioch, Raymond of St. Gilles' support for the relic and the needs of the moment overcame, or at least quietened, Adémar's objections and the Lance became a symbol of the renewal of divine favour for the *expeditio Dei*.[14] The Lance became central in the large-scale religious exercises organised by the clergy intended to propitiate the Almighty. These ceremonies and processions also maintained morale and prepared the crusaders psychologically for the coming battle. The culmination of the Lance's role in these activities was when it was carried on to the field of battle on 28 July 1098. The decisive victory which followed confirmed crusaders' belief that theirs was an expedition especially favoured by

---

[12] Raymond of Aguilers, *Liber*, pp. 123–24.

[13] Ibid., pp. 125–26.

[14] While Riley-Smith argues that Adémar maintained ambivalence until his death, Morris's interpretation, that the bishop's doubts were confined to a period immediately after its discovery, is better supported by the evidence. Riley-Smith, *First Crusade*, pp. 96–97; Morris, 'Policy and Visions', pp. 44–45.

God and his saints. Even the sober-minded *Gesta Francorum* reported that SS. Mercury, Demetrios, and George led the central charge of the battle.[15] Whatever the direct participation of supernatural combatants in this conflict, the triumph confirmed the Lance as a genuine token of divine aid. It also catapulted its discoverer, Peter Bartholomew, into the highest echelons of the crusade. The confirmation of the Lance in the wake of the ceremonies in which it had played a part, Peter's rise, and the vacuum of leadership which developed during the summer of 1098 also brought another group into the wrangling over policy characteristic of this stage of the crusade: the *vulgus*.

In understanding how the Lance and its finder became identified with the amorphous group of non-knightly crusaders emerging at this stage of the crusade, it is important to examine some of the particular elements of Peter's visions. It may be noted that the Hills have attributed most of the content of Peter's revelations to the creativity of Raymond of Aguilers. In particular they stress the historian's consistent employment of contemporary forms and representations in his descriptions.[16] These elements of celestial visitation stemmed much more from the accounts of the visionary than from the historian seeking to establish as venerable a tradition as possible for these phenomena. While the historian doubtless arranged what was related, and added appropriate scriptural material, we should not understand the accounts of Peter's visions as primarily the work of Raymond of Aguilers. If nothing else the extraordinary nature of the material related and Peter's eventual fate argue against the Hills.

Ceremonies and rituals organised during periods of crisis sought to ameliorate some of the acute symptoms as well as restore the expedition to divine favour. The first such major response to a developing famine occurred at the end of December 1097 in the camps outside Antioch. Alms were encouraged and sinners, especially money-changers and prostitutes, scourged.[17] Whatever the effects of such actions on the practices of the expedition, they at least confirmed clerical leadership, and Adémar of Le Puy played a prominent role in organising them. Such responses to major difficulties maintained the crusaders' ultimate belief that their

[15] *Gesta Francorum et Aliorum Hierosolimitanorum* IX, ed. R. Hill (Oxford, 1962), p. 69.

[16] Most of their points are made in footnotes to their English translation of Raymond of Aguilers' work. J.H. and L.L. Hill, *Historia Francorum qui ceperunt Iherusalem* (Philadelphia, 1968).

[17] W. Porges, 'The Clergy, the Poor, and the Non-combatants on the First Crusade', *Speculum* 21 (1946), pp. 1–20.

expedition was a manifestation of God's will. If the sins of participants were the root causes of difficulties, stopping the causes of sin would improve matters. Although the crusaders' logistical problems were not eased until mid February 1098, and departures by the indigent, including Peter the Hermit and Peter Bartholomew, were attempted, most of the expedition maintained its cohesion outside Antioch's walls. The most dramatic episode of mass penance was the great procession around Jerusalem on 8 July 1099 which travelled from Mount Zion to the Mount of Olives where the expedition was addressed by forceful preachers.[18] While closely focused on penance and propitiation as well as the imminent assault, this procession was in keeping with established models. There are a number of obvious religious and psychological impulses behind this remarkable event. However, we should not overlook the effects of the fate of Peter Bartholomew on the expedition's confidence and solidarity in convincing leaders that a large-scale communal action was necessary.

Kherbogha's siege of June 1098 threatened the expedition as well as the beliefs underpinning it far more than earlier crises of supply. The information related in Peter's visions and the actions they called for were broadly in keeping with earlier patterns. Sins were to be discontinued, the date of the Lance's discovery was to be kept as a holy day, propitiation organised, alms given. From the outset St. Andrew had a special regard for the poor. All were to participate in alms giving, and those without funds were to say Pater Nosters.[19] All members of the expedition were thus to be involved in these activities, emphasising the crusade's structure not as a hierarchically organised expedition but as a common venture of pilgrims. Moreover, Peter's central vision ended with a call to military action. While not containing specific tactical advice, it did connect the Lance and the ceremonies around it closely with the forthcoming battle, and consequently the victory which ensued.

In understanding the rapid rise of the Lance it may be appropriate to consider possible parallels from other cultures. There appear some very broad similarities between the affair of the Lance and the 'military millennial movements' studied by social anthropologists. In such phenomena charismatic figures arise preaching a new prophecy which, while anchored in traditional beliefs and practices, promises a new dispensation

---

[18] While widely reported, Tudebode gives the most detailed account. Peter Tudebode, *Historia*, pp. 135–38; Raymond of Aguilers, *Liber*, pp. 144–46; *Gesta Francorum* X, p. 90; Hagenmeyer, *Kreuzzugsbriefe*, pp. 170–74.

[19] Raymond of Aguilers, *Liber*, pp. 82–84.

through direct supernatural aid in military affairs. In the movements which have been analysed, groups with a shared tradition but which have been divided amongst themselves unite in a common purpose involving military action. What are perceived as miraculous successes bind followers into a powerfully motivated force, in which the originality of the new prophecy and seeming triumph promote considerable unity at all levels. While the professors of such messages seem usually not to direct operations, as prophets they provide a focus for common beliefs, enthusiasm, and actions. Such leaders and their movements usually collapse when promised supernatural aid is not manifested on a crucial battlefield.[20] While the religious traditions of the eleventh-century Latin west had its own military prophets, some of the forces behind the rise of the Lance may be better understood with this comparison in mind. The Lance was a newly discovered relic, and one closely associated with a great military victory. It appears that elements within the crusade hitherto unorganised collected together in part around the Lance and its discoverer. Adémar of Le Puy's initial reaction to Peter Bartholomew was also consonant with established patterns. He may have been virtually compelled by circumstances to recognise the Lance, but the enthusiasm of the *vulgus* was the primary mover.

Non-knightly personnel constituted a significant number of the first crusaders.[21] While the 'popular' contingents of Walter the Penniless and Peter the Hermit were wiped out as independent units in May 1097, there were survivors, including Peter the Hermit. Some of the princely contingents which concentrated at Constantinople in 1097 included appreciable numbers of pilgrims. This was particularly true of Raymond of St. Gilles' followers, as the earlier popular crusades had been drawn from northern France and the Rhineland and not the south.

These crusaders usually termed the poor or pilgrims included men, women and children and clerics without bellicose tendencies as well as the aged and infirm. They also included some participants who cannot be strictly classified as non-combatants, though they were clearly not knights. Peter Bartholomew – who claimed to have been involved in the fighting outside Antioch during Kherbogha's siege – and his lord, William Peter are two such examples.[22] Impoverished knights doubtless travelled

[20] For a survey of these movements, see B.R. Wilson, *Magic and the Millennium* (St. Albans, 1975), pp. 221–71, 292–308.
[21] Porges, 'Clergy, Poor and Noncombatants'; Riley-Smith, *First Crusade*, pp. 74–80.
[22] Raymond of Aguilers, *Liber*, p. 68.

and lived in these groups during times of shortage. Such personnel were probably soon taken into the service of more prominent crusaders once resources and especially horses became available. While the pilgrims played little bellicose role before the later stages of the siege of Antioch, their presence in military affairs subsequently is notable.

That such crusaders were a burden to the expedition on the march and in field battles is manifest in the sources and a not infrequent observation of historians of less successful later crusades. Their provisioning was a continual logistical challenge, especially during protracted siege operations. Famine is mentioned in connection with the siege of Nicea early in the crusade, and presented a major challenge during several periods of the siege of Antioch. There was a food shortage at Marra in 1098; cannibalism was reported in the aftermath of that siege. Arqua's besiegers seem to have been relatively better supplied perhaps because of the season and also due to the payments made to Raymond of St. Gilles by nearby Muslim rulers. It is clear that food was not always unavailable during these sieges; rather, it was too highly priced. Jerusalem's besiegers seem to have had sufficient food although water was scarce. This gave the poor a means of earning funds which they probably used to buy food. At Jerusalem, as was probably the case at Arqua, fiscal resources meant the difference between adequate supplies and famine.

Events at Jerusalem illustrate one of the military dimensions of these personnel usually overlooked: their role in siege warfare. The poor played little role in operations at Nicea and at Antioch, and it may be noted that there were relatively few large-scale machinery assaults at the latter siege. However, they were involved in storming Marra and in carrying the city despite attempts to arrange a negotiated surrender. At Jerusalem they were invaluable, not only in bringing water but in providing the manual labour crusader operations at Jerusalem required. In particular the moving of partially assembled siege engines by the northern division would not have been possible without this labour. As at Marra, the poor entered Jerusalem in the wake of the main assault and contributed significantly to the terrible sack of the city. It should be noted that the particular thoroughness with which the poor and pilgrims conducted their sackings were in part a consequence of the structure of the expedition and the economic impulses of crusading. Looting captured cities was a primary source of the income so essential for continued crusading. While valid for all crusaders, this was particularly so for the poor and pilgrims unattached to a prominent leader. Alexius I recognised this with his payment to crusade leaders as a compensation for the surrender of Nicea to imperial forces before a general sack occurred. It may be noted that the economics of crusader siege warfare in part explains the determination of the poor and pilgrims to complete the conquest of cities.[23]

The coalescence of elements of the poor and pilgrims into an interest group within the crusade and the rise of Peter Bartholomew are clearly linked. The death of Adémar of Le Puy on 1 August 1098 was a factor in the formation of this group as he had taken an interest in the welfare of the poor since the food crisis of December 1097. The expedition was already racked with internal conflicts and faction fighting regarding the establishments of lordships in Syria and the next military goals of the crusade.[24] While Bohemond sought the full lordship of Antioch and its establishment as a base for further operations, Raymond of St. Gilles retained possession of a section of the city, focusing his quarrels with the Italian-Norman leader. Godfrey of Bouillon joined his brother Baldwin in Edessa, and the expedition to Jerusalem appeared to be in danger of falling apart. This wrangling was exacerbated by supply difficulties, particularly in providing the poor with the wherewithal to purchase food. For them movement to areas not yet picked clean by foragers was a minimum requirement: they had little to gain and much to lose by remaining in northern Syria. In this context the non-knightly crusaders became another faction attempting to influence policy.

The crusader attacks on Albara and Marra in the winter of 1098 stemmed from the interplay of these interests and struggles as well as from a need to pursue some common action. Although Albara was quickly overrun, Marra offered firmer resistance and a full-scale siege developed in December 1098 while Raymond of St. Gilles had assault machinery constructed. Food shortages and high prices are reported and the spectre of famine once again overshadowed the crusade.

Peter Bartholomew was once more visited by St. Andrew who admonished the crusaders concerning marriage and the need for alms and charity. The saint also assured Peter that the imminent assault on the city would be successful. The southern French participant Peter Tudebode reports that St. Andrew also told the expedition, or at least Raymond of St. Gilles' contingent, how the spoils of Marra should be divided: one quarter each to the bishop of Albara, priests, the church, and the poor.[25]

---

[23] R. Rogers, 'Latin Siege Warfare in the Twelfth Century' (Oxford D. Phil. thesis, 1984), chapter 1.

[24] J. France, 'The Crisis of the First Crusade', *Byzantion* 40 (1970), pp. 276–308.

[25] Raymond of Aguilers, *Liber*, pp. 95–97; Peter Tudebode, *Historia*, p. 122.

The crusaders established control of a section of the city's defences on 11 December with the aid of a wall-dominating siege tower. Nightfall and attempts to negotiate a surrender resulted in a cessation of hostilities by some of the attackers. Elements of the poor, however, continued their attacks during the night, forcing their way into residences. Despite their determination, the poor did not acquire sufficient plunder from the city. Perhaps Bohemond's cunning and deceit in luring inhabitants to the central mosque siphoned off much movable wealth; perhaps Marra never possessed the wealth necessary to sustain the crusade. In any event food shortages continued although large-scale famine did not result.[26]

Dissatisfaction with the spoils of Marra and with the continued bickering between Bohemond and Raymond of St. Gilles resulted in one of the most bizarre episodes of the First Crusade: cannibalism. While this was to become almost a leitmotif of later twelfth-century accounts, particularly of the poor at Antioch, it is clear from the participant historians that cannibalism was restricted to the siege of Marra. Sources agree that this occurred after the siege and in the context of continued high food prices. Some of the recently slaughtered inhabitants of Marra were taken from the swamp in which they had been cast and eaten. The corpses exhumed and devoured were searched for hidden wealth and doubtless subjected to degradation.[27] While compelled by necessity, there also seems an element of protest in these actions, that is to say they may have been intended as much to shock crusade leaders and compel some kind of relief as to meet the food shortage. The sources are in agreement that it was the poor only who indulged in these activities.

It should also be noted that this episode may mark the origin of the group known in later accounts as the Tafurs.[28] Lowly crusaders led by a debased Norman knight known for their bravery and savagery in fighting, the Tafurs were also defined by their cannibalism, which they practised enthusiastically even when other provisions were available. Whether their 'customary' cannibalism reflected events or the legends which grew up around them, it is likely that they had their origins in the food crisis and faction fighting of the siege of Marra.

---

[26] Rogers, *Siege Warfare*, pp. 106–16.

[27] Raymond of Aguilers, *Liber*, pp. 94–96: *Gesta Francorum*, p. 80; Peter Tudebode, *Historia*, pp. 121, 124–5.

[28] L.A. M. Sumberg, 'The "Tafurs" and the First Crusade', *Medieval Studies*, 21 (1959), pp. 224–46

Whatever the extent of crusader cannibalism, the poor took matters into their own hands in January 1098, when they began destroying Marra's fortifications to compel Raymond of St. Gilles to abandon attempts to found a lordship in Syria and resume the march to Jerusalem.[29] The count rushed back from the council of war he had organised but found little left upon which to build or that could be used to bargain with Bohemond. Having accepted the leadership of the poor and the Holy Lance, a barefoot Raymond of St. Gilles led substantial elements on the road to Jerusalem on 13 January 1099.

This period of the crusade was the high watermark of the count's general leadership as other leaders made their way south to join him. The fearsome reputation earned by the crusaders made it possible for Raymond of St. Gilles to extort payments from local rulers in the hope that the expedition would leave them unmolested. Peter Bartholomew experienced another vision in which he was told how these funds should be appropriated among the expedition, with a substantial quantity going to the poor. Intriguingly, Peter the Hermit was named custodian of these funds, perhaps as a balance against Peter Bartholomew or perhaps reflecting his status in the expedition.[30] It is noteworthy that this was his first prominent role in the crusade involving some kind of authority since the debacle of Nicomedia. He appears to have attempted to leave the expedition in January 1098 – doubtless like many of the destitute – but was brought back by Bohemond's followers.[31]

Raymond of St. Gilles' march south stopped at Arqua which was besieged in part to extort further payments from the emir of Tripoli. Although some efforts were made to overcome the well-protected defences, nothing on the scale of operations at Marra was attempted.[32] This may reflect the stronger natural position of Arqua and better provisioning of the town as well as lack of consensus about the importance of taking Arqua.

As the siege dragged on Peter Bartholomew experienced another vision of St. Andrew in which the saint called for an end to sinning, propitiation, alms, and military action. There were elements which differed significantly from earlier admonitions. Peter Bartholomew's last great vision did not reinforce common bonds within the expedition. Rather it

[29] Raymond of Aguilers, *Liber*, pp. 94–94, 99–102.
[30] Ibid., p. 111.
[31] *Gesta Francorum* VI, p. 33.
[32] Rogers, 'Siege Warfare', pp. 118–21.

called for a means of identifying true, fainthearted, and false crusaders, and for the severest punishment for the third group. The dissemination of the contents of this vision triggered the public dissent which culminated in Peter's decision to undergo an ordeal.[33]

As we have seen, the outcome of the ordeal was not decisive in determining the opinion of the majority of the expedition. Rather it confirmed what individuals and groups already believed. Thus the authenticity of Peter Bartholomew and the Lance he discovered remained valid for a significant number of the first crusaders. Peter's death clearly undermined the wider authority of those who had linked themselves to the man and relic: it effectively ended Raymond of St. Gilles' bid for overall leadership, but as well as the role of the poor in determining policy. While non-knightly crusaders played an important role in operations at Jerusalem, they served largely within the two main divisions organised against the city's defences. The poor exercised no independent political role subsequent to the fall of Peter Bartholomew. The fortunes of that group were too closely linked to Peter to survive him.

It has been suggested here that the affair of the Lance and Peter Bartholomew has some similarities with 'military millennial movements', particularly in the rapid rise of the Lance and the way in which elements of the poor coalesced around it. It is also clear that the affair of the Lance had a number of parallels in eleventh- and twelfth-century Latin Europe. Popular religious enthusiasms which developed around a pious individual or charismatic religious figure were well known during the period, as Guibert of Nogent among others went to some length to point out.[34] While some religious establishments on occasion supported these movements, others, perhaps threatened by the birth of a new local centre of spirituality and pilgrimage, opposed them, questioning their legitimacy. The episode of the Lance may be seen in this context; were patterns on crusade not to have resembled those prevalent in contemporary Latin Europe we would indeed be surprised. But there were also differences.

Relics were enmeshed in the political relations of the period, as the possession of physical remains of a common Christian heritage reflected status and on occasion were indicators of position and authority.[35] They

---

[33] Raymond of Aguilers, *Liber*, p. 98.

[34] C. Morris, 'A Critique of Popular Religion: Guibert of Nogent on the Relics of the Saints', *Studies in Church History* 8 (1972), pp. 55–60.

[35] K.J. Leyser, 'Frederick Barbarossa, Henry II and the Hand of St. James', *Medieval Germany and its Neighbours, 900–1250* (London, 1982), pp. 215–40.

thus played a role in the relations of secular rulers as well as in ecclesiastical politics. Yet the role of the Lance among the secular leaders of the First Crusade resembled more the relations between rival religious houses than those between political rulers. Possession of a widely venerated relic defined status and authority. While the wealth and wonder-working manifestation of supernatural power was not at stake in the First Crusade, questions of primacy within a remarkably fluid leadership were.

The Lance involved a religious figure who was not alien to the period but associated more often with other forms of popular religiosity. Charismatic figures from the fringes of society who inspired a popular following through a reputation for miracle working and an occasional anti-clericalism were as much a part of the late eleventh-century religious landscape as the cult of relics. The First Crusade was in part the result of such men, and that one should rise from obscurity to prominence among participants is not unexpected.

The importance of the Lance in the expedition and in accounts of it and the prominence afforded Peter Bartholomew also reflect another dimension of the First Crusade, the role of often poor pilgrims in the expedition. Although they were a hindrance on the march and unable to fight as knights, they did perform military functions, particularly in siege operations during the second half of the expedition. They also constituted one of the various groups which made up the crusade and tried to influence its course. Although providing for them vexed the expedition, it was clearly a responsibility which many took seriously. Given the structure of the First Crusade and its separate contingents, these pilgrims ultimately provided for themselves during protracted operations. Militarily they played an important role in the rapid, labour intensive assaults on Marra and Jerusalem. While their psychological effects upon their opponents cannot be measured, one is tempted to believe that they inspired fears in crusade leaders similar to those Wellington's troops are said to have done in their commander. Whether or not those attacked by the crusaders knew about their reputation for man-eating, elements of the poor clearly terrified opponents as much as did their better armoured colleagues. Ultimately in the First Crusade, *laboratores*, inspired by religious leaders not always in the clerical hierarchy, as well as the economic forces of the expedition, were important in the successes of the *bellatores*.

8

The Survival of a Notion of *Reconquista* in Late Tenth- and Eleventh-Century León

Felipe Fernández-Armesto

In the final scene of Francesco Conti's *Don Quixote in Sierra Morena*, the hero is wheeled onstage in a cage, from which, in the intervals of self-doubt, he reproaches the world outside with insanity. The scene could be taken as an image of how traditional historiography, Spanish and foreign alike, has treated Spain. After a long period of chivalric self-absorption in the middle ages, and an ultimately unsuccessful foray into world-wide knight-errantry in the early modern period, Spaniards are thought to have declined into an isolated and introspective world of their own, alternately reviling and envying their materially successful but spiritually impoverished neighbours. The supposed uniqueness of Spain's historical experience, compared with that of the rest of western Europe – the conviction that 'Spain is Different'[1] – dominated the historical tradition until the 1970s. Dissident voices, of which the loudest in the mid sixties was Otis Green's,[2] cried in an unresponsive wilderness (and today seem to echo with the sound of prophecies scorned).

Most attempted histories of Spain that have not been purely narrative or descriptive have indeed been conceived as attempts to 'explain'

[1] Anti-Francoists made this innocuous tourist-board slogan into a reproach of Spanish traditionalism and 'the advertising slogan of Francoism'. R. Carr and J.P. Fusi, *Spain from Dictatorship to Democracy* (London, 1979), p. vii.

[2] O.H. Green, *Spain and the Western Tradition*, 4 vols. (New York, 1964).

Spain's differentness. Sometimes the search for origins has led back to an autochthonous, or at least very early, Spanish race, endowed with distinctively Spanish qualities.[3] More generally, since most of Roman Spain was heavily Romanised and Visigothic Spain evidently part of the barbarian west, it has been to the period from the eighth century onwards that the beginnings of Spain's supposedly characteristic peculiarity have been ascribed. The country has been seen as differentiated, in one way or another, by the presence of the Moors, either as the product of symbiosis between western and oriental cultures or as forged in the white heat of a long credal conflict.

Today's historians look back from a Spain which no longer seems different. The oddities of, say, thirty years ago have been obliterated by industrialisation, consumerism and democracy,[4] so that Spain now seems a typical western European country – by which I mean that it seems no more different from its fellow-members of the European Community than each of them does from the others. The syncopations that formerly made Spanish history look out of step with that of neighbouring countries are, apparently, over and done with. In as much as one can talk about a 'typical' western European past, Spain has had it and is now at last seen to have had it: a pre-Roman, Celtic culture; a Roman conquest; an impressively thorough Romanisation; barbarian invasions which led to the creation of sub-Roman states by relatively small migrant elites, which included those of the Moors; medieval *Staatsbildung* by means of the expansion of initially small political centres; the 'unification' of what was to become 'national' territory within frontiers which were determined by a combination of geography and dynastic accident with the limitations imposed by the formation of other strong states nearby; the creation of what was in effect a single and 'unitary' state in tension with separatist or devolutionist tendencies at the periphery; colonial expansion overseas, followed by the traumatic severance of empire; the conflict of 'constitutionalist' and 'absolutist' politics, ending at last in the triumph of the former; industrialisation; and the rise of parliamentary democracy under an effectively sovereign representative legislature.

[3] See the critiques of A. Castro, *La realidad histórica de España* (Mexico City, 1966), pp. 1–7, 21–25 and C. Sánchez-Albornoz, *España: un enigma histórico*, 2 vols. (Buenos Aires 1956), vol. 1, pp. 104–13. Certainty that 'the Spanish character' is not immutable or 'racial' does not, however, prevent Sánchez-Albornoz from classifying Seneca, for example, as Spanish or tracing what he calls *homo hispanus* to pre-Roman origins.

[4] Carr and Fusi, *Spain* (as n. 1), pp. 49–78, 127–33, 207–58; J. Hooper, *The Spaniards* (London, 1986), pp. 26, 29, 38–46.

Realisation of this and anticipation of some aspects of it have inspired, in the last twenty years, a thorough-going revision by medievalists of the supposed quirks of Spanish history in their period. Some of the results have been salutary, especially on agrarian history and in the study of notions and institutions of lordship and dependence.[5] The trouble with revisionism, however, is that it pulls the plug pretty violently, and ideas which still have bright futures before them can be swirled away like the baby with the bath water. The most surprising casualty of recent debate in Spanish medieval history has been the traditional doctrine that warfare between Christian and Moorish states was inspired or animated by an ideology of *Reconquista* – that is, that it was waged with credal self-consciousness on the Christian side and that it was part of a long-term strategy for recovering all the soil of Spain from unbelieving usurpers. Enshrined in text-books and school history-courses, this doctrine had become, by the 1960s, one of the most widely held and dearly loved assumptions about the middle ages in Spain. Since then, it has been so thoroughly undermined by professional historians that the traditional understanding of the term *Reconquista* is now in imminent danger of being irretrievably lost or unrecognisably transmuted.

My purpose in this essay is to suggest that the old doctrine may have heen prematurely condemned. The formulation of a programme of *Reconquista* in texts of the eighth and ninth centuries is not in doubt; it is generally acknowledged to have been reformulated or revived in the twelfth century, partly or wholly as a result of the influence of the crusades. Advocacy of a continuous *Reconquista* tradition, however, has been inhibited by an embarrassingly long gap in the tenth and early and mid eleventh centuries, when the idea of *Reconquista* was apparently

[5] This is best represented by the work of late medievalists, especially those working on Andalusia, associated with such periodicals as *Historia, instituciones, documentos; Norba*; and *En la España medieval*. For recent summaries on Andalusia see M. Ladero Quesada, *Los muéjdares de Castilla y otros estudios de la historia medieval andaluza* (Granada, 1989), pp. 235–36, 242–45, 257–82, and E. Cabrera, 'The Medieval Origins of the Great Landed Estates of the Guadalquivir Valley', *Economic History Review*, second series 42 (1989), pp. 465–83. Work on the high middle ages has tended to be distracted by a search for a 'scientific' typology. See for example, R. Pastor, *Resistencias y luchas campesinas en la época del crecimiento y consolidación de la formación feudal* (Madrid, 1980), and J. Valdeón Baruque, 'El feudalismo ibérico: interpretaciones y métodos', *Estudios de historia de España en homenaje a M. Tuñón de Lara* (Madrid, 1981), pp. 7–62. J.A. García de Cortázar y Ruiz de Aguirre and C. Díez Herrera, *La formación de la sociedad hispano-cristiana del Cantábrico al Ebro en los siglos VIII a XI* (Santander, 1982), while not entirely free of this tendency, represents a notable advance.

dormant or extinct.[6] I hope to suggest that there were times during this critical period when its survival as a notion can be detected in authentic texts. It may appear outrageous cheek for a very late medievalist to try to adjust his sights in this specialists' shooting-gallery, but the opportunity of honouring Karl Leyser has emboldened me to return to a period for which he inspired me with great love, and in which I have always retained a keen amateur interest.[7] I have two points to make: first, that some pieces of evidence in favour of the *Reconquista* tradition, mainly in the chronicle of Sampiro, have been overlooked, and others unfairly minimised; secondly, that the debate on the *Reconquista* has been in part politically motivated – which does not of course mean that its conclusions are wrong, but does call them into question.

To understand the context of the debate it is necessary to go back to the attack on the traditional understanding of the importance of the *Reconquista* in Spanish history mounted by Américo Castro in 1948.[8] Castro's vision of Spain as 'the land of three religions', with a culture produced by cross-pollenation between western and oriental influences, transformed the Moor from 'other' to 'brother' and presented the making of Spain as a collaborative enterprise instead of a productive conflict. The thesis was curiously limited in some ways: it included the Jews as oriental contributors to Spanish civilisation but left out the gypsies. Nor did it amount to the historiographical revolution for which it has generally been mistaken. It was proposed as an answer to the traditional question about the differentness of Spain and appropriated a foreigners' perception of very long standing, in which Spain is represented as a sort of honorary oriental land which has somehow got washed up on the wrong shore of the Mediterranean.[9] In this tradition, best represented

[6] D.W. Lomax, *La reconquista* (Barcelona, 1984) p. 225; R.A. Fletcher, 'Reconquest and Crusade in Spain, *c*. 1050–1150', *Transactions of the Royal Historical Society*, fifth series 37 (1987), p. 34.

[7] I should explain that my attention was drawn to the question partly by a commision from Oxford University Press to write a history of Spain with very wide terms of reference and partly by a debate over whether fifteenth- and sixteenth-century Spanish colonial institutions could be called 'feudal'. This made me look at the similar contorversy about the appositeness of the term in the context of early and high medieval Spain. See F. Fernández-Armesto, *Before Columbus* (London, 1987), pp. 6, 215–17.

[8] A. Castro, *España en su historia: cristianos, moros y judíos* (Buenos Aires, 1948).

[9] A. Castro, 'The Meaning of Spanish Civilization', in *Américo Castro and the Meaning of Spanish Civilization*, edited by J. Rubia Barcico (Berkeley, 1976), pp. 23–40; *La realidad histórica de España* (Mexico City, 1966), p. 3.

by the picturesque visions of nineteenth-century engravers, who depict an exotic and archaic Spain peopled by swart gypsies inhabiting Moorish ruins,[10] Spain's beauties and vices alike are traced to Moorish influence. The origins of Spanish Romanesque sculpture, for instance, have been attributed to the effect of Moorish ivories,[11] the lateness of the trains to an exotic strain in the Spanish character.[12]

Against this background Américo Castro's version of the Spanish past almost totally convinced a large and cohesive band of foreign, especially American, scholars and attained by the mid seventies a status very close to orthodoxy in Spain.[13] The challenge to the *Reconquista* tradition was not pressed with any ruthless consistency by Américo Castro himself. While insisting, for instance, that the 'semi-Muslim history of Spain from 711 to 1492' should not be seen as 'a warlike enterprise, long drawn-out and laborious', he admitted that a programme to recover 'the land formerly ruled by the Visigothic kings of Toledo' was begun 'in Asturias in the eighth century'.[14] There are still scholars who uphold simultaneously a *castrista* idea of Moorish-Christian symbiosis and a more traditional view of Moorish-Christian conflict as a formative influence.[15] Castro, however, retained the *Reconquista* only as a very small part of his picture and, by insisting that its ideology was of Islamic origin, made it yet another example of alleged cross-pollenation.[16] The spread of *castrismo* prepared the ground for a drastic revision of *Reconquista* historiography, such as was proposed by A. Ubieto Arteta, who was not in general one of Castro's disciples, in an epoch-making but now little cited lecture in 1970. Ubieto reclassified episodes of tenth- and eleventh-century history,

10 See for example J.F.L. Lewis, *Sketches of Spain and Spanish Character* (London, 1836) and D. Roberts, *Picturesque Sketches in Spain* (London, 1837).

11 F. Jiménez-Placer, *Historia del arte español* (Madrid, 1955), vol. 1, p. 161; P. Palol and M. Hirmer, *Early Medieval Art in Spain* (London, 1967), p. 76; J. Pérez de Urbel, *El claustro de Silos* (Burgos, n.d.), p. 22; G. Gaillard, *La Sculpture romane espagnole* (Paris, 1946), pp. 9, 11.

12 T. Okey in R. Ford, *Gatherings from Spain* (London, 1987), p. xi; Disraeli derived Spanish 'dignity' from the same source. J. Pemble, *The Mediterranean Passion: Victorians and Edwardians in the South* (Oxford, 1987), p. 146.

13 See P. Laín Entralgo (ed.), *Estudios sobre la obra de Américo Castro* (Madrid, 1971); J.L. Gómez Martínez, *Américo Castro y el origen de los españoles* (Madrid, 1975), especially pp. 58, 74; A. Pérez, *Américo Castro y su visión de España y de Cervantes* (Madrid, 1975); J. Rubia Barcico (as n. 9).

14 *Realidad* (as n. 9), pp. 113, 163, 194.

15 B. Bennassar, *The Spanish Character* (Berkeley, 1979), pp. 81, 123–29.

16 *Realidad* (as n. 9), pp. 30, 204–206.

previously regarded as belonging to the *Reconquista*, as regional power struggles without any ideological character or long-term aims.[17] Thus, for instance, the supposed contribution to the *Reconquista* of Sancho García I of Navarre in *c.* 920 was just a characteristic lurch in the squabbles of the mixed Muslim and Christian elite of the Cuenca del Ebro. The 'reconquest' of Calahorra in 1045 was part of a war between two mixed Muslim-Christian alliances. Those of Viseu and Coimbra in 1057 and 1064 were motivated by the local power-politics of the western seaboard of the peninsula. The fatal adventure of Ramiro I of Aragon in 1063 occurred over a question of dynastic advantage and was settled by the superiority of Muslim and Christian forces in alliance. Even Alfonso VI's occupation of Toledo was not part of an anti-Islamic strategy but an extemporised response to a succession crisis. One of the few eleventh-century conflicts which Ubieto admitted to be inspired by differences of faith – the so-called Barbastro crusade of 1064 – has since been shown to have been fought without the inducement of the spiritual benefits traditionally associated with it.[18] In general, Ubieto was unwilling to admit the reemergence of a *Reconquista* ideology until after the Almoravid irredentism of the early twelfth century. Thus by implication the *Reconquista* became, as Castro had claimed, yet another of the ideas the Christians got from the Moors.

The early 1970s were the twilight years of Francoism and, in a sense, Spain's first fully post-industrial epoch. It then became possible to criticise the *Reconquista* 'myth' from an overtly 'Europeanist' perspective. Spain's similarities to other European countries could be plainly detected and clearly voiced. In a work of 1973, which has received insufficient recognition for the boldness of its originality in the Spanish context (despite a character which appears conservative when judged by the standards of European historical writing generally), J.A. García de Cortázar y Ruiz de Aguirre outlined the Spanish middle ages in terms which stressed elements of experience allegedly common to Spain and other western European countries – including some which were perhaps infelicitously chosen, like 'feudalism' and 'class struggle'.[19] In his next major work, two years later, the same author did not eliminate the concept of *Reconquista*, but presented a secularised version of it, in which it became merely a

[17] A. Ubieto Arteta, 'Valoración de la reconquista peninsular', *Príncipe de Viana* 120–22 (1970), pp. 213–20.

[18] A. Ferreiro, 'The Siege of Barbastro, 1064–5: A Reassessment', *Journal of Medieval History* 9 (1983), pp. 127–44.

[19] J.A. García de Cortázar y Ruiz de Aguirre, *La época medieval* (Madrid, 1973), especially pp. 20–21, 88, 437–41.

process of expansion without any credal or teleological character; neither the religion of its victims, nor the usurped status of the lands they occupied made any difference.[20] It was a *Reconquista* by name but not by nature. Most other studies made at about the same time and since have confirmed this picture, and amplified it, by providing determinist explanations of the expansion southwards of northern peninsular peoples as the result of demographic pressure and social and economic change.[21] Peter Linehan's brilliant critique of 1982 further weakened fellow-scholars' faith in the *Reconquista* by pointing out its association with objectionable forms of political partisanship.[22]

Of the major contributions which have followed, only that of D.W. Lomax – written, of course, outside Spain and therefore outside the contextual pressures that impelled the revisionists – remained robustly faithful to the traditional understanding of the *Reconquista*. The revised Spanish edition of his book, aggressively entitled *La Reconquista*, maintained, in 1984, an austerely lofty attitude to revisionism, leaving a specific reply still to be uttered. Lomax's narrative did not attempt to rehabilitate the *Reconquista* as an idea, except by asserting the obvious force and fidelity to some very early texts of this way of interpreting the term.[23] The danger therefore remains that the usefulness and distinct meaning of the term may be lost or displaced by a new usage, for which 'conquest' or 'expansion' might be equally serviceable. If it is to survive at all as a distinct concept, *Reconquista* has to be distinguished from other phenomena of territorial expansion. Sufficient defining characteristics (I assume in these pages) are a consciousness on the Christian side of an ultimate strategy of liberation of all the territory of the peninsula, and an awareness of a credally perceived and identified enemy.

It may be useful to make a further important distinction clear before going any further. *Reconquista* and crusade are not the same thing. To demonstrate, as shrewd critics have done,[24] that there was no concept

---

[20] *Nueva historia de España en sus documentos: edad media* (Santiago de Compostela, 1975); cf. the author's tentative language in *La época medieval* (as n. 19), pp. 154–55.

[21] See for example A. Barbero and M. Vigil, *Sobre los orígenes sociales de la reconquista* (Barcelona, 1974); J.L. Marín, *Evolución económica de la península ibérica: siglos VI-VIII* (Barcelona, 1976); Cortázar and Díez Herrera, *La formacíon* (as n. 5).

[22] P.A. Linehan, 'Religion, Nationalism and National Identity in Medieval Spain and Portugal', *Studies in Church History* 18 (1982), pp. 161–199.

[23] D.W. Lomax, *The Reconquest of Spain* (London, 1978); *La Reconquista* (Barcelona, 1984), especially pp. 10–12, 44–46, 56–59.

[24] Ferreiro, 'Siege' (as n. 18); Fletcher, 'Reconquest' (as n. 6), pp. 31–47.

of crusading in Spain until it was imported from outside in the twelfth century is not to prove that there was no *Reconquista* tradition in Spain before that. The term *Reconquista* does not mean a war sanctified by spiritual benefits or by the redemptive virtues of pilgrimage, but a war justified by the commonest of medieval doctrines in the context – that of the legitimacy of war waged for the recovery of usurped possessions.[25] It can be distinguished from other such wars by the existence of a credally defined foe. As it spread southwards to Spain's own holy ground, where the bones of martyrs cried for release from impious hands and where relics seemed to pullulate, the reconquest could, with increasing ease, be represented as a hallowed enterprise as well as a just one. It might be seen as salutary simply because divinely ordained. Yet if *Reconquista* is to retain its usefulness as a term, it has to be distinguished from crusading, not assimilated to it.

It seems to have been overlooked, in the course of what has been a very one-sided debate, that the traditional understanding of the *Reconquista* can subsist alongside the materialistic and secularised versions. Ideologies, after all, are commonly invoked to serve material ends and often generate rhetoric which comes to form and shape the activities of those who formulate or hear it. Christian rulers engaged in warfare against Muslims in tenth- and eleventh-century Spain, when the pressures and resources for expansion were weak, continued to have access to hostile images of their adversaries, created in awareness of religious differences, and to justifications of war which, by representing the rulers of al-Andalus as usurpers, pointed towards a teleological strategy for the recovery of the whole of Spain from the Moors. Propaganda in this sense from the reign of Alfonso III (866–910) was still being copied and quoted in León and Rioja in the late tenth and very early eleventh centuries.[26] His wars against Muslim adversaries spawned chronicles deeply tinged with credal odium and teleological prophecy, expressed in predictions of the expulsion of the Muslims, the 'salvation of Spain' and the 'restoration of the kingdom of the Goths'.[27]

[25] F.H. Russell, *The Just War in the Middle Ages* (Cambridge, 1975), pp. 18–19.

[26] M. Gómez-Moreno, 'Las primeras crónicas de la Reconquista', *Boletín de la Real Academia de la Historia* 100 (1932), pp. 592–93, 596; M.C. Díaz y Díaz, *Index Scriptorum Latinorum Medii Aevi Hispanorum*, 2 vols. (Salamanca, 1958), vol. 1 pp. 130–31; *Libros y libreros en la Rioja altomedieval* (Logroño, 1979), pp. 34–36, 171–72; J. Pérez de Urbel, *Sampiro, su crónica y la monarquía leonesa en el siglo X* (Madrid, 1952), p. 44.

[27] Gómez-Moreno, 'Las primeras crónicas' (as n. 26), pp. 601, 614, 623.

Not only was this material available and increasingly diffused in the late tenth and early eleventh centuries, its active influence can also be detected in sustaining a notion of *Reconquista*. The evidence lies in sources of two types: the despised Christian chroniclers; and the debated charters, which sometimes echo the chroniclers' language or which record the obscure 'imperial' aspirations of Spanish kings.

Although chronicle evidence is sparse, the surviving chronicles commonly dated to the late tenth and early or mid eleventh centuries, the chronicle of Sampiro and the so-called pseudo-Isidorean *Chronica Gothorum*,[28] disclose, in their treatment of conflicts against Muslims, strongly committed *Reconquista* attitudes. However derived, the reflection of such attitudes does suggest that a *Reconquista* tradition was kept alive and transmitted between the time of Alfonso III and the Christian resurgence of the late eleventh century, across a period when there were no enduring conquests of Moorish territory by Christian leaders and when the mood detectable in the chroniclers' language was almost unmatched by deeds.

The author of the *Chronica Gothorum* was in all probability an otherwise unknown monk of Toledo. Sampiro was a great personage in the kingdom of Léon, where he served at the courts of Vermudo II and Alfonso V, becoming bishop of Astorga in 1035, when his masters' dynasty was displaced by Navarrese invaders. Despite their different background the two writers had closely comparable views of the natural enmity of Christians and Muslims and seem to have shared a common understanding of the history of Spain in the periods they covered as dominated by credal conflict. The author of the *Chronica Gothorum* also had a strong notion of the potential unity of Spain, which it was the legitimate object of Christian warriors to restore.[29] The usefulness of his text for my present purpose is vitiated by two flaws. It cannot be shown to

---

[28] The best edition of Sampiro is in Pérez de Urbel, *Sampiro* (as n. 26), pp. 279–356, and that of the *Chronica Gothorum* is A. Benito Vidal (ed.), *Crónica pseudo-Isidoriana* (Valencia, 1961).

[29] R. Barkai, *Cristianos y musulmanes en la España medieval* (Madrid, 1984), p. 47; the author's reading both of this chronicle and Sampiro leads him (pp. 49–51) to a conclusion almost diametrically opposite to my own, that Sampiro 'does not express consciousness of the *Reconquista*' and that the *Chronica Gothorum* 'expresses a diminishing of tension'. But Dr. Barkai's approach, which is concerned with the depiction of Muslims, is made on a different front from that attempted here and is not based on a detailed examination of Sampiro's language; the examples he gives from Sampiro, on pp. 45–48, are highly selective.

131

have been used in the Christian kingdoms (although, in a general way, continuity of culture between Christian communities in both moieties of the peninsula can be assumed in this period), and its dating rests on a presumption.[30] Arguments based on it must for that reason be tentative, but it is useful to give the text at least a brief examination before turning to more solid evidence.

The writer betrays a special concern with Toledo, a tendency to exaggerate the importance of Murcia and a profound devotion and intellectual debt to St. Isidore. He was impressively well read, with a command of Muslim and Christian sources. His sense of the natural enmity of Christendom and Islam therefore proceeded from privileged and informed observation. The very fact that he should have chosen to write a history of the Visigothic kingdom implies that he possessed a sense of the unity of Spain, which was made explicit in a strongly Isidorean passage at the start of the work in which Spain was described and the term *Hispaniae* explained as relating to 'upper' and 'lower' provinces – *Hispania inferior* and *Superior Hispania* – which between them covered the whole peninsula.[31] The history closed with an account of the occupation of Spain by the Moors through a combination of force and internecine divisions smong the Visigoths. The catalogue of conquered territories – which specified Seville, Cordova, Murcia and Toledo before turning despairingly to *reliqua loca* – with its account of the slaughter of King Roderic as the outcome of the treachery of ousted princes, could have been intended as a systematic exposition of a usurpation, designed to justify a programme of reconquest. The account of the treason of Count Julian shows the writer's appreciation of the juridical differences between Christians and Muslims which governed the making of contracts between members of the two communities. 'Vis ingredi Ispaniam?', Julian is made to ask. 'Ego te ducam, quia claves maris et terre habeo et bene te dirigere possum.' 'Que fiducia', retorts Tariq, 'erit mihi in te, cum tu sis Christianus et ego Maurus?' Julian proposes his wife and children as

---

[30] C. Sánchez-Albornoz, 'San Isidoro, Rasis y la pseudo-Isidoriana', *Cuadernos de historia de España* 4 (1946), p. 73; G. Lévi Della Vida, 'The "Bronze Era" in Moslem Spain', *Journal of the American Oriental Society* 63 (1943), p. 186 n. 27, argued that the phrase *Marrochinas partes* betrayed composition after the foundation of Marrakesh, which he dated to the 'late eleventh century'. The true date seems to have been *c.* 1057 and the unknown etymology of the name leaves open the possibility that similar forms were current earlier. See *Encyclopaedia of Islam: New Edition* (Leiden, 1989), vol. 6, p. 591–92, s.v. Marrākush.

[31] *Crónica* (as n. 28), pp. 12–13.

hostages and a large pecuniary guarantee.[32] Thus, while the transaction is regulated by entirely commonplace constraints, it reflects the gulf of mutual suspicion that divided adherents of the two systems of law.

Because he dealt only with remote events, and only briefly with a period in which Muslim and Christians came into conflict, the author of the *Chronica Gothorum* could not reflect *Reconquista* notions as fully as Sampiro, whose work spanned the period from the reign of Alfonso III (866–910) to that of Vermudo II (981/5–999). In the most primitive of the surviving versions, the brief addition on Alfonso V (999–1028) and Fernando I (1038–65) is evidently of later authorship, distinct in style, tone and language. Sampiro approached his subject with profound personal reasons to feel enmity for the 'Agarenes'. In an autobiographical retrospect to a charter issued near the end of his life, in 1042, he revealed that before coming to the court of Vermudo II he was a fugitive from a Moorish raid in which he lost all his personal wealth, both his inheritance and the fruit of his efforts.[33] As he first appeared in the king's entourage in a witness-list in 992, and continued to appear as both scribe and witness regularly thereafter,[34] it is likely that he was a victim of one of the devastating series of raids launched by Almanzor into León between 987 and 990. The experience of those years left him with a conviction that Almanzor's Christian clients and collaborators were traitors to their creed as well as to their king; treachery, he maintained, was aggravated when its beneficiaries were credal foes. In 992 in a charter made in his favour – and therefore probably drafted by Sampiro himself – the 'sons of perdition' who helped Almanzor were denounced for their disloyalty, rebellion and conspiracy to deprive Vermudo of his throne 'et quod peius et malum amplius et deterius est seipsos ad regem muzlemitarum transtulerunt ut regnum christianorum diruerent'.[35] The very syntax of the sentence, ranging 'Muslim king' and 'Christian kingdom' antithetically, suggests that the writer perceived the conflict, if not as being inspired by differences of religion, then at least as being defined by them.

His chronicle is pervaded by the same dichotomy and the same acute hostility as are apparent in the charter. Its attribution, though it relies in the first instance on late and unreliable testimony, is justified not only by this consistency of tone but also by considerations of style, imagery

32 Ibid., pp. 50–53.
33 *Sampiro* (as n. 26), p. 476.
34 Ibid., p. 25.
35 Ibid., p. 449.

and vocabulary: even if the attribution were false, it would not materially affect the argument of these pages, for the values evinced by the chronicle remain the same, whoever wrote it. Of all the chronicles which have survived from the Spanish middle ages, there can be few which better deserve to be called 'chronicles of the *Reconquista*'. The writer does make brief mention of other matters: the deaths and marriages of royal persons; the itineraries of monarchs; the creation of sees; the building of monasteries; the resettlement of deserted towns; the suppression of rebellions and the fairly frequent dynastic conspiracies which blotted the record of the house Sampiro served, though his treatment of this last category is often oblique and always highly selective. None of these subjects, however, distracts the writer for long from the unifying theme of his narrative. The chronicle is, with brief asides, a catalogue of campaigns against the Moors.

This is not only an indication of commitment to a notion of *Reconquista* on the author's part but also a clue to the date and circumstances of the writing of the chronicle. The period between the initiation of Almanzor's campaigns in 977 and the death of 'Abd al-Malik in 1008 was one in which Cordovan hegemony throughout the peninsula was enforced with terrifying brutality and Christian arms had no success against Moorish adversaries. Of the predecessors of Vermudo II, both Ordoño IV 'the Bad' (958–60), and Sancho I 'the Fat' (956–58 and 960–65) had been clients of Cordova and, in the course of their struggles with one another, at different times supplicants at the caliph's court, while Ramiro III (966–81/85) had made valiant but bootless efforts to reverse the trend before his deposition in Vermudo's favour. Vermudo began his reign subject to the same thraldom and his attempts to escape from it were a failure. From the darkness of those years, Sampiro's chronicle looks back to the glories of the *Reconquista*. The work begins not with the creation of the world or the foundation of the dynasty or any other conventional starting-point but with the reign of Alfonso III, the epitype, if not the prototype, of the *Reconquista*-hero, whose dedication to the southward extension of the frontiers of his realm made him the perfect example to set before the eyes of a king whose morale needed reanimation.

Vermudo II and Alfonso V were just such kings. It was his predecessor's failures against Almanzor that made possible Vermudo's bid for the crown. Only by securing Almanzor's endorsement did Vermudo succeed in pressing his claims when Ramiro III died in 985. His first attempt at easing himself free of dependence on Cordova in 986 was an unmitigated disaster. A rebellion incited from Cordova and a punitive invasion in 987 forced him back into Galicia, from where he was unable to return until 990. In 992 he was free to act against some of the counts who had supported the Moorish invaders and in 993 gave his daughter to Almanzor in marriage. The Cordovan, however, seems only to have been biding his time, while Castile was punished to his satisfaction, before launching a further onslaught against León in 995. This may have exhausted Vermudo's willingness to continue the policy of appeasement. In 997, applauded by Sampiro, he attempted 'revenge' with as little success as previously.[36] In the same year, Almanzor launched his deepest raid ever, reaching Santiago de Compostela and returning to Cordova with the doors and bells of the cathedral of the apostle. The minority of Alfonso V lasted from Vermudo's death in 999 until the slackening of Cordovan hegemony throughout the peninsula in 1008. Although a clear chronology is impossible to work out satisfactorily, those years were characterised by the same alternation between timorous submission to Cordovan power and ill-judged efforts to throw off the yoke. It therefore makes the basis of a reasonable thesis to set the chronicle in the context of Sampiro's attempt, also demonstrated by the charter of 992, to encourage Vermudo II to resist Almanzor and to portray that resistance in the *Reconquista* tradition. A probable further or alternative purpose was to educate the young Alfonso V in the *Reconquista* traditions of his dynasty, especially if Sampiro can be identified with the king's preceptor – *Sampirus scola regis* – who signed a charter in 1012.[37]

If that was the author's purpose, it was well served by his selection and presentation of his material. The great hero of the chronicle, Alfonso III, 'exulted in glory' because 'he broke the audacity of the enemy'.[38] The 'tyranny' of his supposed brother Vermudo was deepened, like the treachery of the rebels of Sampiro's own day, by association with 'Arab' allies.[39] Muslim raids were not mere raids but designed – again in language identical to that used by Sampiro in describing the disasters of his times – 'ad destruendum Dei ecclesiae'.[40] Except for Fruela II (924–25), who 'won no victory owing to the paucity of his days',[41] and

---

[36] Ibid., p. 345.

[37] Ibid., p. 71.

[38] Ibid., pp. 283–84.

[39] Ibid., p. 280. This episode is particularly impressive as it does not appear in any of Sampiro's known sources.

[40] Ibid., p. 282.

[41] Ibid., p. 318.

the infamous Sancho the Fat, every other member of the dynasty until
Ramiro III is represented as beginning his reign with a campaign against
the Moors: 'Chaldaeans', 'Agarenes', 'Ishmaelites' or 'Saracens'. Ramiro
II (930/1–950/1), whose deeds are, in the chronicler's eyes, excelled only
by those of Alfonso III, is credited with a saintly death.[42] Even Ordoño
'the Bad', though distracted at the outset of his reign by his struggle with
Sancho, is made to lose as little time as possible in launching a campaign
against Lisbon.[43] The only member of the dynasty for whom Sampiro has
no good word is Sancho the Fat himself, who besmirched dynastic honour
by his personal desertion to the Moors. The disgust the chronicler felt for
him even inspired a rare burst of humour: 'cum esset crassus nimis, ipsi
Agareni herbam attulerunt et crassitudinem abstulerunt a ventro eius'.[44]

Of all the kings reviewed, only Vermudo's opponent, Ramiro III, fails to
receive just acknowledgement for his efforts against the Moors, which in
reality were staunch if unsuccessful. His first campaign, for the recovery
of Gormaz in 975, was made before the attainment of his formal majority.
Almanzor's first series of invasions from 977 he resisted until his defeat
near Rueda in 981. Sampiro omits all this, limiting himself to saying that
'habuit pacem cum Saracenis et corpus Sancti Pelagii ex eis recepit'.[45]
The other success of the reign – the defeat of pagan Norse invaders – is
attributed to a count of uncertain identification and Ramiro's attempted
deposition justified on the grounds of his *puericia et modica scientia*.[46]
These disabilities contrast directly with the author's portrait of the
intruded Vermudo II as a wise lawgiver.[47] He is depicted as *satis prudens*
and as a restorer of the laws of Wamba, whose reputation as a scourge
of traitors and rebels may have made him seem, to Sampiro, a suitable
model. The conventional terms of the eulogy – 'Dilexit misericordiam et
judicium; reprobare malum studuit et eligere bonum' – mask Vermudo's
crimes: his insurrection against his predecessor, his compromises with
Almanzor, his repudiation of his wife and irregular further marriage.
If the chronicle was indeed addressed to Vermudo or his son such

[42] 'Accepit confessionem ab episcopis et abbatibus valde eos exortatus et vespere
aparicionis Domini ipse ex proprio regno abstulit et dixit, "Nudus egressus sum de utero
matris mee; nudus revertar illuc. Dominus adiutor meus. Non timebo quid faciat michi
homo"'. Ibid., p. 331.
[43] Ibid., p. 333–34.
[44] Ibid., p. 336.
[45] Ibid., p. 340.
[46] Ibid., p. 342.
[47] Ibid., p. 344.

partisanship is perfectly intelligible. Sampiro's personal debt to both kings is recorded in his autobiographical retrospect of 1042. After his flight from Muslim raiders: 'perveni in ciudatem Legionensem sedis et a paucis namque diebus perveni in palatium domini mei et serenissimi regis domni Veremundi, cuius memoria eius sit in benedictione, quasi fecit mihi multum bonum ad plenius dum vidam duxit. Et postea devenit in palatio filii eius dominus meus rex domnus Adefonsus, vir pius, et dedit mihi multam rem'.[48]

The further, deeper purpose of Sampiro's treatment of Vermudo II is made apparent by his account of the king's Moorish wars. The increase of Almanzor's power is ascribed to the *peccata populi christiani* but the author, revealing his knowledge of Arabic, denies the aptness of the cognomen the 'conqueror' assumed, 'qualis non antea fuit nec futurus erit'. Even the devastating invasion of 997 is contrivedly shown as a Christian triumph from which, intending to desecrate the apostle's tomb, Almanzor 'withdrew in fright'. The year of disaster is represented as a divinely ordained turning-point. 'Rex celestis memorans misericordie sue ultionem fecit de inimicis suis morte quidem subitanea et gladio ipsa gens agarenorum cepit interire et ad nichilum cotidie pervenire'.[49]

Sampiro became mayor of the royal palace and continued to serve the kings, drafting and attesting documents and helping to dispense justice as *maiorinus* until at least 1019.[50] He was so closely involved, on such a regular basis, over so long a period, in the counsels of Vermudo II and Alfonso V that it is reasonable to suppose that those kings had access to his notion of *Reconquista*. His text seems to have continued to be influential in the reign of Fernando I. The final 'chapter' of two sentences appears to have been added then, for it says only that Alfonso V was the father of Fernando's wife and that the new king 'ad expelendos barbaros in posterum regnaturus emicuit.'[51]

Corroboration, in genuine charter evidence, of the wider prevalence of a *Reconquista* mentality is notoriously hard to find. The only possible area in which such corroboration has been detected in the early eleventh century is in the revival of 'imperial' formulae by Spanish kings.[52] In recent years no historian who has touched this evidence has been much

---

[48] Ibid., p. 476.
[49] Ibid., p. 345.
[50] Ibid., p. 83.
[51] Ibid., p. 346.
[52] R. Menéndez Pidal, *España y su historia* (Madrid, 1957), vol. 1, pp. 319–48.

impressed by it, mainly because of the difficulty of assigning any clear meaning to terms like *imperator, rex magnus* and *princeps magnus*, in which the 'imperial' aspirations are expressed.[53] It would certainly be rash to suppose that the title of *imperator*, by which Leonese kings were sporadically called, signified any specific pretensions. The title was freely conceded by Sancho the Great of Navarre to the boy-king Vermudo III of León as well as to Alfonso V, evidently without an implicit acknowledgement of the supremacy of either.[54] Sancho himself, perhaps adopting a Navarrese usage, seems to have understood the term *imperium* to mean no more than local or regional authority or command and may therefore have employed *imperator* with a correspondingly limited meaning. His own styles of *Rex Ibericus*[55] and *Gratia Dei Hispaniarum Rex*,[56] both of the early 1030s, do seem, however, to evoke claims to peninsular-wide authority, or at least to imply claims extending over more than one kingdom. Certainly Sancho encouraged conquests at Moorish expense along the frontier and intended, at one stage, to respect the unity of his legacy by passing supremacy in his divided realm to García of Nájera.[57]

The next revival of 'imperial' formulae, in the reign of Alfonso VI of Castile, was clearly systematic and explicitly related to pan-Spanish ambitions. In a diploma of 1072 and two documents of 1075 he called himself *rex Hispaniae*,[58] and thereafter used the style of *totius Hispaniae rex*.[59] It is not necessary to broach the elusive problem of what he meant by arrogating the additional title of *imperator* from 1079 onwards in order to accept that Alfonso's chancery was capable of conceiving the peninsula as a political whole. This does not of itself imply a strategy of *Reconquista*, as loose forms of subordination of Muslim rulers, short of

[53] M.M. Cullinan, '*Imperator Hispaniae*: the Genesis of Spain' (Ph. D. thesis, City University, New York, 1975), pp. 86–187.

[54] Menéndez Pidal, *España* (as n. 52), pp. 334–36.

[55] Ibid., p. 336. This suspect form, because addressed to the king in flattery, may be genuine.

[56] J. del Alamo (ed.), *Coleccíon diplomática de San Salvador de Oña*, (Madrid, 1950), vol. 1, pp. 41–44.

[57] A. Ubieto Arteta (ed.), *Cartulario de San Juan de la Peña* (Valencia, 1967), vol. 1, pp. 183–87.

[58] R. Menéndez Pidal, *Obras*, 8 vols. (Madrid, 1944–1953), vol. 7, p. 726; T. Muñoz y Romero, *Colección de fueros municipales y cartas pueblas* (Madrid, 1847), pp. 259–62; L. Serrano, *El obispado de Burgos y la Castilla primitiva* (Madrid, 1936), vol. 3, pp. 44–48.

[59] L. Serrano, *Cartulario de San Millán de Cogolla* (Madrid, 1930), pp. 239–40.

violent dispossession or subjugation by force, were sufficient to satisfy Alfonso's ambitions. The existence, however, of a long-term programme of recovery of Moorish territories is disclosed by a source difficult to impeach, the 'Memoirs' of 'Abd-Allah, ruler of Granada, who claimed to have heard of it from Alfonso's own emissary, Count Sisnando David, in 1074. 'It is to the Christians that al-Andalus belonged in the beginning, until the moment when they were conquered by the Arabs who drove them back to Galicia, the part of the country least favoured by nature. But now that it has become possible, they want to recover what was seized from them by force'.[60] By then, even the most cautious sceptic can agree with Richard Fletcher that 'a shift in the terms of Christian-Muslim relations was taking place'.[61]

However disappointing the charters, and however unsatisfactory the argument from 'imperial' usage, the amount of evidence in favour of the survival of a notion of *Reconquista* in the late tenth and early and mid eleventh centuries seems sufficient, in view of the overall scarcity of sources, if not to decide the question, at least to raise a further one: why has the scepticism of recent years been so strong? It is, of course, possible to mount a challenge purely on the merits of the case, or out of an honourable impatience with the commonly espoused doctrine that the *Reconquista* had a decisive part in moulding 'the Spanish character' or making 'the Spanish state'. No one could accuse Marcelino Menéndez y Pelayo, for instance, the great apologist of 'Hispanic' values, of arguing *à parti pris*, when he cast doubt on the traditional understanding of the *Reconquista* as long ago as 1891. His claim that medieval Christian Spaniards cannot have been motivated by any conscious *Reconquista* strategy because they were actuated by 'an instinct which derived all its force not from the vague hope of a remote aim, but from the continual battle for the possession of concrete realities' suggests a philosophical, not a political bias.[62] Nor can accusations of prejudice be levied against the many foreign historians of Spain who before the intervention of Américo Castro doubted the importance of the *Reconquista* from a conviction of the greater importance of the long periods of fruitful peace between Christians and Muslims in the middle ages.[63] Today's *Reconquista*-sceptics

---

[60] E. Lévi-Provençal, 'Les "Mémoires" du roi zirid 'Abd Allāh', *Al-Andalus* 4 (1936–39), p. 36.

[61] Fletcher, 'Reconquest' (as n. 6), p. 37.

[62] Menéndez Pidal, *España* (as n. 52), vol. 1, p. 319.

[63] See for example H.E. Watts, *Spain* (London, 1893), pp. 165–71; R.B. Merriman, *The Rise of the Spanish Empire in the Old World and the New*, 3 vols. (New York, 1918), vol. 1,

inside Spain, however, do seem to have a political profile which may help to explain their stance: leftist in some cases, 'Europeanist' in others, always anti-nationalist and anti-Francoist. The *Reconquista* myth has lost adherents not only because it is thought to be untrue but also because it is an icon of the Spanish right: an official dogma, it is not too much to say, of Francoist historiography and a passionately defended item in the historical creed of that great spokesman of the anti-Francoist right, Claudio Sánchez-Albornoz.[64] In the years of Franco's rule in Spain and Sánchez-Albornoz's exile in Argentina it became tainted by association with nationalist propaganda and right-wing rhetoric.

In the fifties and sixties, the two great exponents of the traditional view of the *Reconquista* were Sánchez-Albornoz and his sometime friend, Ramon Menéndez Pidal. They were men of similar background: illuminati of the pre-civil war Ateneo and members of the intellectuals' party, Acción Republicana, they sided under the republic with secularist politicians, despite personal commitment to the Catholic faith. Both were drawn to the Republican side in the civil war and both went into exile at the end of it. Menéndez Pidal, however, rapidly made his peace with the nationalists – realising, perhaps, that his conservative and patriotic instincts were better served by collaboration with the regime than by remaining in the company of leftists and anti-clericals in exile. He returned to Spain to become, in a sense, the court historiographer of Francoism, developing a version of Spanish history which identified 'Spanishness' with those virtues of austerity, sobriety, dogmatic Catholicism and loyalty to a unitary state which suited the regime's book.[65] The doctrine of the central importance of the *Reconquista* in Spain's historical experience had an obvious appeal to a dictatorship installed as a result of a 'crusade' against latter-day infidels for the restoration of the 'sacred unity' of Spain.

Meanwhile, from outside the fold of the regime, Sánchez-Albornoz sustained very much the same view of the *Reconquista*, although he fell out with Menéndez Pidal over such closely connected matters as the

pp. 87–89 (though this author continued to opine that 'the medieval history of Spain is first and foremost the history of a crusade'); B. Bevan, *History of Spanish Architecture*, (London, 1938), pp. xi–xiv; J.B. Trend, *The Civilization of Spain* (London, 1967), pp. 19–21, 31–32, in a work first published in 1944.

[64] C. Sánchez-Albornoz, *España y el Islam* (Buenos Aires, 1943), pp. 15, 42; *España; un enigma histórico* (as n. 3), vol. 2, pp. 9–11; *La España cristiana de los siglos VIII al XI* (Madrid, 1980), vol. 1, pp. xxi–xxii.

[65] See the just remarks of M. Bataillon, 'L'Espagne réligieuse dans son histoire: lettre ouverte a Américo Castro', *Bulletin hispanique*, 52 (1950), p. 16.

nature of human settlement in reconquered regions.[66] The impeccability of Sánchez-Albornoz's credentials as an anti-Francoist may be judged by the fact that he became president of the republican government in exile in 1970; yet his version of Spanish history was entirely acceptable to the regime – as, with double irony, was that of his great scholarly adversary and fellow-exile, Américo Castro, whose emphasis on the Moorish contribution bolstered Franco's Arab-oriented diplomacy. Sánchez-Albornoz was 'un homme de centre-droit'[67] in the great tradition of Spanish liberalism, which, while rejecting the dogmatism and authoritarianism of the nationalists, wholeheartedly embraced the notion of Spanish 'nationhood', over-arching regional identities, and the principle of administrative centralisation. The *Reconquista* myth was compatible with this tradition and for Sánchez-Albornoz it had a further value as the alleged historical foundation for Spanish freedoms. Owing to the *Reconquista* – in essential outline, the argument went – vast tracts of territory had to be colonised with meagre human resources; settlers had therefore to be induced by lavish immunities and exemptions; Castile, in consequence, became a land of free peasant communities, unsubjected to seigneurial control, 'peopled with a great majority of free men and small proprietors . . . an island of free men in medieval Spain'.[68] Clearly, if the materialists were right and the expansion of the Christian kingdoms, unmotivated by *Reconquista* 'spirit', were merely the result of the grinding *structures* of demographic and economic change, the basis of this whiggish interpretation would disappear.[69]

In partial consequence of the reaction against Sánchez-Albornoz's views, the challenge to the traditional historiography of the *Reconquista* has been mounted, by opponents of nationalism and of *albornocista* liberalism alike, as part of a more general attempt to dismantle the conviction – which was Sánchez-Albornoz's starting-point – that Spain's history has been unique. Scholars sceptical about the *Reconquista* have gone on to attempt to redepict medieval Spain, in terms of the handiest

[66] C. Sánchez-Albornoz, *Despoblación y repoblación del valle del Duero* (Buenos Aires, 1966), p. 5.
[67] H. Lapeyre, 'Deux inteprétations de l'histoire d'Espagne: Américo Castro et Claudio Sánchez-Albornoz', *Annales: Economies, Sociétés, Civilisations* 20 (1965), pp. 1021–22.
[68] This theory, broached in *España: un enigma histórico*, was repeated in C. Sánchez-Albornoz, *Nuevas páginas sobre el pasado de España* (Barcelona, 1979), p. 51.
[69] See A. Barbero and M. Vigil, *La formación del feudalismo en la península ibérica* (Barcelona, 1978) and the reply of C. Sánchez-Albornoz, 'Otra vez a la defensa, frente a Barbero y Vigil', *Estudios polémicos* (Madrid, 1979), pp. 322–28.

general category available, as a 'feudal' society, heedless of warnings from abroad of the futility of applying such a crude and anachronistic category.[70] Increasingly the historians who have dedicated what are often impressive feats of research to this sterile enterprise seem to talk only to each other. From their most recent conference – ironically sponsored by the Fundación Sánchez-Albornoz – dissident voices were conspicuously absent.[71] Yet in Spain the orthodoxy they have established is now almost as complete as the opposing orthodoxy which prevailed during the Franco era, and the well-meaning intervention of Pierre Bonnassie, by suggesting a possible explanation of the differences between the 'feudal' and 'non-feudal' versions of the Spanish high middle ages as merely terminological,[72] has been used to cloak its real ideological basis.[73]

Without subscribing either to the implicit traditionalism of Menéndez Pidal or the romantic liberalism of Sánchez-Albornoz, it is surely possible to acknowledge as a matter of fact that *Reconquista* notions are detectable in the work of Sampiro and perhaps in other Leonese texts of the relevant period. An 'idea' of *Reconquista* cannot, perhaps, be said to be fully expressed in those texts, as it can in others of the eighth, ninth, twelfth and thirteenth centuries. The notion, however, is a strong one, compounded of reminiscences of the reign of Alfonso III, of consciousness of the potential unity of Spain and of intensely perceived credal enmity for the Muslim adversary. At this level, the *Reconquista* does seem to have been a remarkably enduring force in the history of some parts of medieval Spain.

In uttering a warning against the premature elimination of the *Reconquista* from our picture of the late tenth and early and mid eleventh centuries, I do not mean to suggest that an inimical and bellicose spirit pervaded the whole culture of Christian Spain throughout the middle ages, or had any formative influence on such dubious metaphysical constructs as the 'Spanish character' or 'Spanish spirit', or that it affected the nature of the Spanish state when, many centuries later, such a state

[70] P.A. Linehan, 'La reconquista de Toledo y la supuesta feudalización de Castilla', *Estudios sobre Alfonso VI y la reconquista de Toledo: Actas del II Congreso de Estudios Mozárabes* (Toledo, 1988), vol. 2, pp. 27–42.

[71] *En torno al feudalismo hispánico: I Congreso de Estudios Medievales* (Avila, 1989).

[72] P. Bonnassie, 'Du Rhône á la Galice: Genèse et modalités du régime féodale', *Structures féodales et féodalisme dans l'occident méditerranéen* (Rome, 1980), p. 23.

[73] R. Pastor, 'Estudio preliminar', in P. Bonnassie *et al., Estructuras feudales y feudalismo en el mundo mediterraneo* (Barcelona, 1984 [a selection of papers in translation from the Toulouse conference at which Bonnassie's paper was originally given]), pp. 7–20.

can be said to have come into being. Nor do I mean to take sides between *albornocistas* and their critics with their rival but equally unhelpful visions of a 'free' and 'feudal' Castile, which convey such a strong sense of *déja vu* to historians whose undergraduate reading included Freeman and Round. In general, the revision of the historiography of 'different' Spain is welcome and has been long overdue. But if the traditional understanding of the nature of the *Reconquista* is discarded, we shall lose both part of the reality of the Spanish middle ages and a salutary example of the force of ideas.

9

The Rise and Fall of the Hereditary Steward in English Ecclesiastical Institutions, 1066–1300

Paul Brand

It is now generally accepted that by 1166 the practice of hereditary succession to lands held by military service was as well established on ecclesiastical baronies as it was on lay baronies.[1] There is, however, still disagreement as to whether this was simply a matter of practical convenience for the lords concerned or whether it was a consequence of its having been part of the initial understanding between lords and tenants that knight's fees would be heritable.[2] Just how large an inroad into the property of the church the granting of what were in practice hereditary military tenancies made varied from ecclesiastical corporation to ecclesiastical corporation.[3] But there could be little doubt that these inroads were justified by the practical requirements of the churches concerned. Each of the institutions which had made such grants had been required to provide a quota of knights for the king's army: these grants simply enabled them to meet that quota.

---

[1] For specific examples see E. Miller, *The Abbey and Bishopric of Ely* (Cambridge, 1951), p. 176; F.R.H. Du Boulay, *The Lordship of Canterbury* (London, 1966), p. 60; E. King, *Peterborough Abbey, 1086–1310* (Cambridge, 1973), p. 29.

[2] For a recent survey of the literature see J. Hudson, 'Life-Grants of Land and the Development of Inheritance in Anglo-Norman England' in *Anglo-Norman Studies* 12 (1990), pp. 67–90.

[3] King, *Peterborough*, pp. 12–15.

Further evidence of the strength of the pressures favouring lay inheritance in this period, even in circumstances where this was in apparent conflict with the longer-term interests of the ecclesiastical institutions concerned, is to be found in the way in which various lay ministerial posts in the service of such institutions also became hereditary or were granted on an hereditary basis during the same period. Ministerial tenures varied greatly in importance. In this essay I want to look at just one particular type of permanent hereditary official (though arguably the official with the largest and most important responsibilities): the steward. I will examine the evidence for the creation of hereditary stewardships in a number of English sees and abbeys during the century after the Norman Conquest, look at what functions these stewards performed and then trace what happened to the stewardships during the following century and a half.

The first direct evidence that the Amundeville family claimed to be hereditary stewards to the bishops of Lincoln comes from 1190 when Jollan de Amundeville accounted on the Pipe Roll for 'having the stewardship of the bishop of Lincoln'.[4] Such a proffer only makes sense in the context of a hereditary claim to the stewardship. This is confirmed by a further entry on the 1204 Pipe Roll of another proffer by Jollan this time for having an assize of *mort d'ancestor* at Westminster to assert his right to succeed to the 'stewardship of the lands and household of the bishop of Lincoln'. Moreover, the Amundeville family had in fact held the stewardship for most of the twelfth century and had passed it on from family member to family member in a way which clearly demonstrates that both they and the bishops had long regarded the stewardship as hereditary. The first Amundeville known to have held the stewardship is the Jocelin de Amundeville who is referred to simply as Goslin *dapifer* in the 1115 × 1118 Lindsey survey and who accounted in the 1130 Pipe Roll for the farm of the bishop's wapentake of Stow. He may have been preceded in the stewardship by the first Jocelin de Amundeville to hold lands in England, who is known to have been a tenant of the bishopric of Lincoln by 1086. His place of origin (Mondeville, dep. Calvados) suggests a connection with the first bishop of Lincoln, Remigius (1072–92), because Mondeville was held of Fécamp and Remigius had been a monk there. The son of

---

[4] The following discussion of the Amundeville family and its claim to be hereditary stewards to the bishops of Lincoln is heavily indebted to C.T. Clay, 'The Family of Amundeville', *Lincolnshire Architectural and Archaeological Society Reports and Papers* new series 3 (1948), pp. 109–36. Full references will be found in this article for otherwise unsupported assertions made in the text.

the second Jollan, Walter, certainly succeeded to the stewardship as is shown by his witnessing charters as steward, being addressed by the bishop as his steward in charters and making grants as such. Walter was succeeded in his lands and in the stewardship *c.* 1166 by his brother William. He was in turn succeeded in the family lands by a third brother Ellis, though there is no evidence that Ellis ever acted as steward. It was Ellis's son, Jollan, whom we have seen attempting to assert his right to the stewardship at the turn of the century. Although we cannot be absolutely certain that a hereditary grant of the stewardship was made to the first or the second Jollan de Amundeville, the apparently unbroken succession of at least three members of the Amundeville family in the stewardship and their claims to a hereditary stewardship at the end of the twelfth and beginning of the thirteenth century provide strong evidence pointing in that direction.

A second episcopal see which had hereditary stewards was Norwich. One Guy the steward occurs as a witness to charters of the first bishop of Norwich, Herbert de Losinga (1090–1119), in favour of the monks of his cathedral priory;[5] he is also found as witness to two royal mandates perhaps of 1110 relating to agreements between the abbot of Ramsey and his tenants.[6] He was succeeded in the stewardship by his son John, who occurs as a witness to deeds of Bishop Everard (1121–45) and who in one of them is specifically described as John son of Guy *dapifer*.[7] In a charter of the same bishop of 1139 × 1143 we hear of a settlement between the monks of the cathedral priory and the bishop's steward John and John's son Adam concerning land at Gnatingden in Ringstead in Norfolk.[8] An Adam the steward, presumably the son of the John mentioned in this charter, is then found as a witness to deeds of Bishop William (1146–74).[9] I have found no evidence to connect this Adam and the Geoffrey *dapifer* who occurs as witness to three deeds of the same bishop.[10] It seems clear, however, that Geoffrey also claimed to be steward by hereditary right and probable that he was related in some way to his predecessors in the stewardship. In the 1166 return of knights' fees made by the

[5] *The Charters of Norwich Cathedral Priory, part I*, ed. B. Dodwell (Pipe Roll Society, new series 40, London, 1974), nos. 107, 108.

[6] *Regesta Regum Anglo-Normannorum 1066–1154: volume II: Regesta Henrici Primi 1100–1135*, ed. C. Johnson and H.A. Cronne (Oxford, 1956), nos. 966, 967.

[7] *Norwich Charters*, nos. 119, 116 and (as John son of Guy *dapifer*) 117.

[8] Ibid., no. 119.

[9] Ibid., nos. 130, 134.

[10] Ibid., nos. 124, 133, 140.

bishop, Geoffrey *dapifer* is listed as tenant of five knights' fees of the old enfeoffment.[11] The bishop would hardly have referred to him in this way if he held the office only on a temporary rather than a permanent basis. What seems to be the same holding (but now described as four and a half knights' fees) is mentioned in another list of tenants of the bishopric of the period 1210 × 1212.[12] Its tenant is now said to be *senescallus de Bredistone*, the steward of Bradeston: an indication that the centre of the holding was Bradeston, Norfolk, but also that its holder was identified as 'the' steward, presumably because he was the bishop's hereditary steward.[13] He is probably to be identified with the Robert the steward who occurs as a witness to many of the deeds of John de Grey as bishop (1200–14).[14]

The first clear evidence of an hereditary stewardship of the see of Durham comes only from the second decade of the fourteenth century.[15] In 1311 Bishop Richard Kellaw made an agreement with Robert of Willoughby concerning the services owed by Robert for his Lincolnshire manor of Eresby.[16] Part of the service Robert owed was that of acting as the bishop's 'high steward', placing dishes before the bishop on the day of his enthronement and at Christmas and Whitsun and receiving certain perquisites in return. Robert and his heirs were also said to owe the duty of acting as the bishop's 'bailiff' in all his lands and fees in Lincolnshire, holding the bishop's courts there and executing their process and levying their profits for the bishop. In the light of other evidence it seems probable that these services are also to be associated with Robert's hereditary

[11] *The Red Book of the Exchequer*, ed. H. Hall (3 vols., Rolls Series, London, 1896), vol. 1, pp. 391–92.

[12] *Red Book*, vol. 2, p. 476.

[13] The bishops of Norwich also had an hereditary constable. In 1166 the bishop returned Peter the constable as tenant of 3 knights' fees (*Red Book*, vol. 1, p. 391) while in 1210 × 1212 *constabularius de Meutone* was returned as tenant of the same number of fees (ibid., vol. 2, p. 476).

[14] *Norwich Charters* (as n. 5), nos. 144, 149, 151–52, 154–58, 160, 164, 166, 167, 169, 171, 172, 176.

[15] For previous discussions of the Durham stewardship, to which I am heavily indebted, see H.H.E. Craster, 'Some Anglo-Saxon Records of the See of Durham', *Archaeologia Aeliana*, fourth series, 1 (1925), pp. 189–98, especially pp. 197–98; *Durham Episcopal Charters, 1071–1152*, ed. H.S. Offler (Surtees Society 179, Gateshead, 1968), pp. 2, 97–98, 137; C.M. Fraser, *A History of Anthony Bek, Bishop of Durham 1283–1311* (Oxford, 1957), pp. 5–9.

[16] *Registrum Palatinum Dunelmense*, ed. T.D. Hardy (4 vols., Rolls Series, London, 1873–78), vol. 2, pp. 1142–44. The same services are also mentioned in the inquisition post mortem held after Robert's death in 1317: *Calendar of Inquisitions Post Mortem*, vol. 6, no. 60, p. 48.

stewardship.[17] It seems improbable that the hereditary stewardship was a recent creation in 1311 and it has been suggested that it is no coincidence that Robert of Willoughby was an indirect descendant and heir of the first recorded steward of a bishop of Durham, Pinceon. Pinceon *dapifer* is mentioned as holding Lincolnshire lands of the bishop in the 1115 × 1118 Lindsey Survey.[18] Pinceon was succeeded both in his lands and in the stewardship by his son Hugh (Hugh son of Pinceon).[19] He describes himself as *senescaldus episcopi Dunelm'* in a grant to the cellarer of Bury St. Edmunds,[20] and in 1144 it was as steward of Bishop William de Sainte Barbe that he was left in charge of affairs within Durham while the bishop visited Northumberland. Hugh betrayed him and took up the cause of his rival, William Comyn.[21] When the bishop recaptured Durham later that year Hugh lost some of his lands but evidently retained the bulk of them.[22] He is to be found witnessing subsequent deeds of Bishop William though in neither is he described as the bishop's steward.[23] It is at this point that the trail of evidence for the Durham hereditary stewardship goes cold only to re-emerge in the early fourteenth century. Walter Bek married Agnes the daughter and sole heiress of Hugh son of Pinceon and successive heirs to the Pinceon lands were in the service of successive bishops. None, however, seems ever to have been given the title of steward.[24] It is possible that it was only the tenure of the see of Durham by a member of the Bek family (Anthony Bek, bishop 1284–1311) that led to the revival of a long dormant hereditary claim.

The one Welsh see where we have clear proof that an hereditary stewardship had been created by no later than 1176 (and probably before 1166) is St. David's.[25] The first known steward here was Henry FitzHenry, the bastard son of Henry I by Nesta, the daughter of Rhys ap Tewdr, who

---

[17] See below, pp. 154, 156.

[18] *The Lincolnshire Domesday and the Lindsey Survey*, ed. C.W. Foster and T. Longley (Lincoln Record Society 19, n.p., 1924), pp. 248, 253, 254–55, 257.

[19] *Sir Christopher Hatton's Book of Seals*, ed. L.C. Loyd and D.M. Stenton (Oxford, 1950), p. 41, no. 28 [= *Regesta* (as n. 6), no. 1465].

[20] *Feudal Documents from the Abbey of Bury St. Edmunds*, ed. D.C. Douglas (British Academy Records of Social and Economic History 8, London, 1932), no. 213, p. 177.

[21] *Symeonis Monachi Opera Omnia*, ed. T. Arnold (2 vols., Rolls Series, London, 1882–85), vol. 1, pp. 154, 156–57.

[22] *Durham Charters* (as n. 15), pp. 99, 135–37.

[23] Ibid., pp. 156, 159.

[24] Fraser, *Anthony Bek* (as n. 15), pp. 5–8.

[25] I must thank Dr. David Crouch for drawing my attention to the St. David's material in the Gormanston Register.

was granted the stewardship by Bishop Bernard (1115–48).[26] Although Henry had issue the stewardship did not pass to them but went instead to his half-brother, Maurice FitzGerald, one of Nesta's sons by Gerald of Windsor.[27] A copy of the charter of Bishop David FitzGerald (1148–76) shows the bishop granting his brother the 'stewardship of the whole land of St. David throughout our bishopric' to hold in fee and heredity to him and his heirs plus various lands which Henry FitzHenry had held with the stewardship and certain additional lands.[28] The charter must date before the deaths of Bishop David and of Maurice FitzGerald in 1176. It seems probable that it dates from shortly after the death of Henry FitzHenry in 1157. Maurice also obtained confirmations from the chapter of St. David's and from Henry II.[29] Maurice's eldest son William succeeded him in the stewardship and acquired a confirmation of the stewardship and associated lands from David's successor, Bishop Peter (1176–98).[30] His eldest son William likewise succeeded to the stewardship and obtained from Bishop Geoffrey (1199–1214) an *inspeximus* of all these charters in favour of his ancestors and a general confirmation of his hereditary right to the stewardship.[31]

No charter survives recording the initial grant of the stewardship of the abbey of St. Benet of Holme in Norfolk to Herman the steward though Herman is found witnessing charters of Abbot Richer (1101–25),[32] and when Abbot William granted the stewardship to Herman's son Adam in 1128–29 to hold 'to himself and his heir' in fee and inheritance this was to hold the stewardship 'as best his father had ever held it'. The grant was of rather more than just the stewardship. Adam was to be 'after the abbot, the representative of the whole abbey and steward' and he was also confirmed in the possession of various lands and a corrody. The charter also records the king as confirming the grant.[33] Adam did not

[26] This grant is mentioned in the charter granting the stewardship to Maurice FitzGerald: *Calendar of the Gormanston Register*, ed. J. Mills and M.J. McEnery (Royal Society of Antiquaries of Ireland, Dublin, 1916), pp. 202–3.
[27] The relevant relationships are shown in the genealogical table opposite p. 266 of *Giraldus Cambrensis: Expugnatio Hibernica*, ed. A.B. Scott and F.X. Martin (A New History of Ireland: Ancillary Publication 3, Dublin, 1978).
[28] *Gormanston Register*, pp. 202–3.
[29] Ibid., pp. 203–4.
[30] Ibid., p. 203.
[31] Ibid., pp. 202–4.
[32] *The Eleventh and Twelfth Century Sections of. . . the Register of the Abbey of St. Benet of Holme*, ed. J.R. West (Norfolk Record Society 2, n.p., 1932), pp. 68–69, 69, 70.
[33] *Register of St. Benet of Holme*, vol. 2, p. 73, no. 126.

hold the stewardship for long, for before 1135 a writ of Henry I ordered that the abbot have custody of his lands until the claims of his brothers Robert and William to them were determined. This suggests that Adam was already dead or had entered a religious order; and we may assume that the two brothers were also contending for the stewardship.[34] It is not, however, possible to show that any subsequent member of the family was in possession of the stewardship though, as will be seen, the hereditary stewardship of the abbey was among the property claimed by Adam's descendant, Peter of Hautbois, in the early thirteenth century.[35] Nor is there any surviving charter recording the grant of the hereditary stewardship at the abbey of Bury St. Edmunds to the first known steward of the abbey, Ralph.[36] There is a writ of King William II describing Ralph as the steward of the abbot and confirming his tenure of two manors held of the abbey[37] and also a charter recording an agreement relating to the church of Hoxne in Suffolk between Bishop Herbert de Losinga of Norwich and Ralph and his wife Edith in which he is again described as 'steward of St. Edmunds'.[38] A copy does, however, survive of two related charters of Abbot Albold of Bury (1114–19) in favour of the second steward, Maurice of Windsor, granting him both the stewardship and the lands which Ralph[39] had held in fee and inheritance together with various perquisites and rights attached to the stewardship and certain additional lands.[40] Subsequently, between 1135 and 1139, Maurice had his tenure of the lands and stewardship confirmed by King Stephen.[41] Maurice was succeeded in both by his nephew Ralph de Hastings, the

---

34 *Regesta* (as n. 6), no. 1714 [= *Register of St. Benet Holme*, vol. 1, p. 28, no. 51].

35 See below, p. 160.

36 Perhaps the Ralph FitzUrse who is sole witness to a charter of William II in favour of Bury and who occurs as witness in no other surviving writs of William I or William II: *Regesta Regum Anglo-Normannorum 1066–1154: volume I: Regesta Willelmi Conquestoris et Willelmi Rufi 1066–1100*, ed. H.W.C. Davis (Oxford, 1913), no. 393 (and no. lxiv at p. 135).

37 *Bury St. Edmunds Documents*, p. 60, no. 17 = *Regesta* (as n. 36), no. 395 (and no. xlii at p. 134).

38 B. Dodwell, 'Some Charters Relating to the Honour of Bacton' in *Early Medieval Miscellany for Doris Mary Stenton*, ed. P.M. Barnes and C.F. Slade (Pipe Roll Society, new series 36, London, 1960), pp. 160–61.

39 The surviving copies of the charter mistakenly call him Robert.

40 *Bury St. Edmunds Documents*, p. 110, no. 108 and p. 111, no. 109.

41 Ibid., p. 80, no. 57 = *Regesta Regum Anglo-Normannorum 1066–1154: volume III: Regesta Regis Stephani ac Mathildis Imperatricis ac Gaufridi et Henrici Ducum Normannorum 1135–1154*, ed. H.A. Cronne and R.H.C. Davis (Oxford, 1968), no. 764.

queen's steward, and obtained a royal confirmation of his title to both from Henry II in 1155.[42] The hereditary stewardship can then be traced in the hands of the Hastings family down to 1300 and indeed well beyond that date.[43]

The Evesham Abbey chronicle ascribes the creation of a hereditary stewardship at Evesham to the Abbot Walter who was head of the house from 1077 to 1086.[44] The first documentary evidence of a hereditary stewardship at the abbey seems to be a charter of Philip the steward by which he renounced all claim to a measure of ale from the abbey's brewery in return for a grant of property.[45] This renunciation belongs to the abbacy of Abbot Adam (1160–91). There is then no further evidence of this hereditary stewardship till the mid thirteenth century when William, steward of the abbey of Evesham, was suing the abbot to allow him to enjoy various of the profits associated with his hereditary office.[46]

There was also an hereditary stewardship at the abbey of Peterborough. The first indisputable evidence of this comes from the last decade of the twelfth century when we find enrolled on an early Bench plea roll an agreement between Hugh de Waterville and the abbot of Peterborough under which Hugh agreed to waive all right in the stewardship during the abbacy of the current abbot. The agreement makes clear that Hugh had been bringing litigation against the abbot to claim the stewardship as his right.[47] Edmund King has, however, suggested that the hereditary stewardship probably goes back in the Waterville family of Marholm to the early Norman period and has discussed the various pieces of evidence which would support such an hypothesis.[48]

An hereditary stewardship was created at Westminster Abbey by Abbot Gilbert Crispin (abbot *c.* 1085–1117 × 1118). Any charter he may have granted does not survive but there is a royal writ of William II

---

[42] Ibid., pp. 97–98, no. 87. The stewardship is here described as 'totum dapiferatum de tota terra et tenura et honore sancti Edmundi et abbatis monachorum sancti Edmundi'.

[43] L.J. Redstone, 'The Liberty of St. Edmund' in *Proceedings of the Suffolk Institute of Archaeology and Natural History* 15 (1915), pp. 200–11.

[44] *Chronicon Abbacie de Evesham*, ed. W.D. Macray (Rolls Series, London, 1863), p. 97.

[45] London, British Library, MS Cotton Vespasian B. XXIV, f. 41r. The ale is presumably to be associated with his position in the abbey's service.

[46] This litigation is discussed further below, p. 156.

[47] *Rotuli Curie Regis: Rolls and Records of the Court held before the King's Justiciars or Justices*, ed. F. Palgrave, 2 vols. (London, 1835), vol. 2, p. 24 (1194).

[48] King, *Peterborough*, pp. 32–33.

confirming the abbot's grant of the stewardship to Hugh of Colham and his heirs. The editor of volume 1 of *Regesta Regum Anglo-Normannorum* regarded this writ as spurious,[49] but more recently the editors of a volume of early Westminster Abbey charters have been inclined to give it the benefit of the doubt.[50] The wording is reminiscent of that of the hereditary stewardship of St. Benet's Holme to Adam FitzHerman. Hugh and his heirs are not just to be 'stewards of the whole abbey' but also to be the 'representative' of the abbey 'after the abbot'. There is then, however, no further evidence of the stewardship until the final decade of the twelfth century when Walter son of Thurstan of Colham can be found claiming the stewardship against the abbot and eventually quitclaiming it to him.[51]

One other hereditary stewardship which may have been created during the same period is that of the abbey of St. Augustine's, Canterbury. In the last decade of the twelfth century Reginald of Cornhill and his wife Maud quitclaimed all right in the 'stewardship of the abbey with appurtenances'.[52] In 1177 there had been an exchange of tenants in Canterbury between the monks of Christ Church and the monks of St. Augustine's. One of the tenants granted by St. Augustine's to Christ Church was Maud, daughter of Hamo the steward. In Archbishop Richard's confirmation of the same grant made in the same year what is evidently the same holding is described as that of Gervase of Cornhill. All is made clear by a further exchange between the monks of Christ Church and Gervase of Cornhill and his son Reginald and Reginald's wife Maud. By this they exchanged property in Canterbury for a quitclaim of rent due for a holding held by Gervase of Christ Church in London.[53] Maud must have inherited her claim to the stewardship from her father Hamo and brought her claim by marriage to her husband Reginald of Cornhill. In 1177 she was probably still in the wardship of Gervase and may not yet have been married to Reginald (hence the two references to Maud and Gervase as tenants of the property). Urry has pointed to evidence suggesting that Hamo was himself the son of Roger the cook.[54] This may mean that he

---

[49] *Regesta* (as n. 36), no. 437.

[50] *Westminster Abbey Charters, 1066–c. 1214*, ed. E. Mason, J. Bray and D.J. Murphy (London Record Society 25, London, 1988), p. 47, no. 40.

[51] See below, p. 159.

[52] *Feet of Fines, 9 Richard I* (Pipe Roll Society 23, London, 1898), pp. 35–36.

[53] The relevant deeds are printed by W. Urry, *Canterbury under the Angevin Kings* (London, 1967), pp. 405–11.

[54] Ibid., pp. 56–57.

was the first hereditary steward of the abbey; but it could also simply mean that he had inherited the stewardship from someone other than his father.

By origin the steward was an official of the lord's household.[55] Some of these hereditary stewards seem to have been expected to perform functions there. When Jollan de Amundeville proffered a fine of 20 marks in 1204 for an assize of *mort d'ancestor* his claim was to the 'stewardship of the lands and household of the bishop of Lincoln', which suggests that he claimed to exercise responsibilities within as well as outside the household.[56] The compiler of an account of the Bury St. Edmunds stewardship in the White register of Bury St. Edmunds[57] which perhaps belongs to the third quarter of the twelfth century[58] also seems to envisage the abbey's steward functioning as a member of the abbot's household, for it specifies that he is to receive an honourable allowance of candles at bed time and wine and beer when he travels round the manors in the liberty with the abbot. A similar view is taken in another account of the same office, more difficult to date but perhaps from the last quarter of the twelfth century, in the Pinchbeck register.[59] This says that the steward of Bury ought always to travel around with the abbot except when with the abbot's permission or by his order he is sent off elsewhere. There is also other indirect evidence for hereditary stewards playing (or having once played) a day to day role in the household of their lords. The grant to Adam FitzHerman of the stewardship of the abbey of St. Benet of Holme in 1128–29 includeda hospice (evidently some kind of house) which his father had constructed at the abbey and also a corrody (an allowance of food and drink probably on a daily basis)

[55] N. Denholm-Young, *Seignorial Administration in England* (Oxford, 1937), pp. 66–67.

[56] *The Great Roll of the Pipe for the Sixth Year of the Reign of King John, Michaelmas 1204*, ed. D.M. Stenton (Pipe Roll Society, new series 18, London, 1940), p. 78.

[57] London, British Library, MS Additional 14847, f. 26v.

[58] Its reference to Hugh le Bigod as earl of Norfolk would fit the period between 1153 and 1177 or the period between 1221 and 1225; its reference to Aubrey, earl of Oxford would fit any time between 1141 and 1214. This suggests it belongs to the period between 1153 and 1177. The mention of William de Hastings as the current steward limits it further to the period between 1164 (when William de Hastings succeeded to the stewardship) and 1177.

[59] *The Pinchbeck Register relating to the Abbey of Bury St. Edmunds*, ed. F. Harvey, 2 vols. (Brighton, 1925), vol. 1, pp. 137–38. It refers to Henry de Hastings as the current steward. This would fit the period 1182–95 but would also fit a thirteenth-century date.

there.[60] When in the mid thirteenth century the hereditary steward of Evesham sued the abbot for various perquisites attached to the post these were said to include a daily corrody at the abbey.[61] Some connection with the bishop of Durham's household, though only a residual one, is to be glimpsed in the details of the 1311 agreement between the bishop and Robert of Willoughby.[62] Among the services Robert was said to owe for the manor of Eresby was that of acting as the bishop's steward in placing dishes before him on the day of his consecration and at Christmas and Whitsun each year (for which he was to get various appropriate perquisites).[63]

The steward had, however, long ceased to be merely an officer within the lord's household. As we have already seen in at least two abbeys (St. Benet of Holme and Westminster) charters associated with the creation of a hereditary stewardship describe the steward in terms which suggest that he was intended to be a general representative of the house in all its dealings with the outside world and second in importance (in this role at least) only to the abbot of the house.[64] More specifically, we find evidence that a number of these hereditary stewards played a major role in the running of the seignorial courts of the ecclesiastical corporations with which they were associated. In the mid thirteenth century the Evesham hereditary steward claimed the right to hold the courts, halimotes and hundred courts of the abbey in the vale of Evesham and to receive various associated perquisites.[65] The hereditary steward of Bury St. Edmunds was responsible for holding the court of the honour

---

[60] *Register of St. Benet Holme*, vol. 2, p. 73, no. 126.

[61] London, Public Record Office, JUST 1/56, m. 32.

[62] *Registrum Palatinum Dunelmense* (as n. 16), vol. 2, pp. 1142–44.

[63] In the thirteenth century evidence also emerges of similar hereditary honorary 'high' stewardships at Exeter and Canterbury. In the 1281 Devon eyre Hugh de Curtenay was suing Peter bishop of Exeter for not allowing him to exercise the *seneschalcia hospicii* of the bishop on the day of his enthronement as he and his ancestors had exercised it in the past. The parties reached an agreement but its details do not seem to have been recorded: London, Public Record Office, JUST 1/185, m. 25d. The Canterbury high stewardship (as also a hereditary butlership) exercised only on the day of the archbishop's enthronement by the earl of Gloucester is mentioned in an agreement between archbishop and earl of 1258 (which also settles the perquisites appropriate to the exercise of these offices): *Fifth Report of the Royal Commission on Historical Manuscripts* (London, 1876), appendix, p. 458. Neither stewardship can be traced prior to this.

[64] *Register of St. Benet of Holme*, vol. 2, p. 73, no. 126; *Westminster Abbey Charters, 1066–c.1214*, p. 47, no. 40.

[65] London, Public Record Office, JUST 1/56, m. 32.

of Bury. This is clear from the later twelfth-century account in the White Book of Bury of the perquisites associated with the office,[66] which notes that by custom the abbot finds all necessary expenses for the steward when he holds the abbey's court, unless the abbot is in or near Bury and the steward is able to reach him afterwards to dine with him, and that he is in any case entitled to various perquisites for an overnight stay afterwards.[67] The steward's responsibility for the running of the honour court also emerges from the oath which he, his clerk and any under-steward he may appoint have to take, which includes a clause promising that they will not appropriate anything of the pleas or fines which belong to the abbot.[68] The pleadings in a dispute between the hereditary steward (John de Hastings) and the abbot over the stewardship in 1293–94 also make it clear that the steward executed the process of the abbey court.[69] As we have already seen, similar responsibilities were also exercised in the early fourteenth century by the hereditary steward of the bishop of Durham though only in the Lincolnshire lands of the see.[70] In the case of the hereditary stewardship of St. David's there is no direct evidence of responsibility for the courts of the bishopric until the later thirteenth-century agreement between William FitzDavid, baron of Naas, and Bishop Richard of St. David's (1256–80). By this date the bishop had his own steward and the baron of Naas was no longer described as 'steward' of the bishop but the services which the baron owed for his holding probably reflect the duties once associated with the hereditary stewardship. These included responsibility for holding the bishop's court of Pebidiog (though now in association with the bishop's own steward), and for holding his court of Llawhaden. The baron was also responsible for the custody of prisoners awaiting trial in the bishop's court.[71]

The hereditary stewards at Bury St. Edmunds can also be seen acting in another role: as representatives of the abbey in matters touching the abbey (and more especially its liberty) outside the liberty, especially in the king's courts and in the county court. This part of his functions is already to be glimpsed in one of the two charters of Abbot Albold to

[66] For this account and its date see above, notes 57 and 58.

[67] For an early fourteenth-century account of the steward's perquisites when he holds the court see *Calendar of Inquisitions Miscellaneous*, vol. 1, no. 1880.

[68] London, British Library, MS Additional 14847, f. 26v; *Pinchbeck Register* (as n. 59), vol. 1, pp. 137–38.

[69] London, British Library, MS Additional 14847, ff. 57v–59r.

[70] *Registrum Palatinum Dunelmense*, vol. 2, pp. 1142–44.

[71] *Gormanston Register* (as n. 26), pp. 204–6.

Maurice of Windsor of 1114 × 1119[72] which provides that if Maurice travels far or near in the abbot's service he is to travel at the abbot's cost.[73] The account of the stewardship given in the abbey's White Book starts by noting that the steward's holding is larger than those of the earls of Oxford or Norfolk because he 'ought to defend the rights of the church of St. Edmund and the said liberties. . .'. It mentions two particular journeys that the steward is expected to make on the abbey's business: to the Suffolk county court at Ipswich and to the king's exchequer.[74] This account makes clear that it is the steward who is immediately responsible to the king for executing royal writs within the liberty and that his responsibilities include the levying of moneys due to the king. The alternative account of the office incorporated in the Pinchbeck Register[75] also envisages the steward travelling outside the liberty on the abbey's business. The county court at Ipswich is again mentioned as one possible destination. So also is London: not just the Exchequer, but London generally, perhaps to cover the defence of the abbey's liberty in the Bench as well as answering for the liberty at the Exchequer. A third possible destination (again apparently outside the liberty) is the 'abbot's great pleas' which presumably means important litigation affecting the abbey held outside the liberty. Similar functions were still envisaged for the steward in the early fourteenth century:[76] attendance at the county court at Ipswich; attendance at the Exchequer twice yearly to make a proffer and to account there; and appearance elsewhere on the abbot's business. Although it seems probable that similar functions were performed by other hereditary stewards for their masters, this seems to have left no direct trace in the surviving documentation.

By the thirteenth century on most estates the primary function of the steward was to act as overall manager of those estates for his lord.[77] There is only indirect evidence to suggest that this may also have been one of the functions of our hereditary stewards in the twelfth century. It was certainly not the case at Bury St. Edmunds, where the account of the

[72] *Bury St. Edmunds Documents* (as n. 40), p. 111, no. 109.

[73] Note that Maurice occurs as witness to a number of royal charters and writs relating to Bury: *Regesta* (as n. 6), p. 71, no. 39; p. 74, no. 44; p. 74, no. 45.

[74] London, British Library, MS Additional 14847, f. 26v. For the date of this account see n. 58.

[75] *Pinchbeck Register* (as n. 59), vol. 1, pp. 137–38.

[76] *Calendar of Inquisitions Miscellaneous (Chancery) Preserved in the Public Record Office* (London, 1916), vol. 1, no. 1880.

[77] Denholm–Young, *Seignorial Administration* (as n. 55), pp. 67–68.

office in the Pinchbeck Register is careful to stipulate that the steward had no business meddling with the abbey's lands.[78] The very need to spell it out this clearly suggests that it was the normal understanding that this was part of the duties of the steward, hereditary or otherwise. It may also be the fact that stewards were in control of the estates which explains how at St. Benet of Holme Adam FitzHerman was in quite such a good position to accumulate not only lands held by knight service but also lands held of the abbey at farm for money rents and rents in kind,[79] and why at Peterborough we find Hugh de Waterville gaining control of three manors held of the abbey at farm in addition to the lands his family held of the abbey by knight service.[80]

The particular circumstances of particular ecclesiastical institutions help to explain some of the other functions performed by hereditary stewards. The extent and nature of the abbot's jurisdictional franchises at Bury St. Edmunds explains why we find evidence in the late thirteenth century that the hereditary steward was also coroner for the liberty.[81] The particular conditions of the Welsh lordships explain why holding meetings (*parliamenta*) on the borders of the bishop's lands with the bishop's adversaries was among the duties said in the later thirteenth century to be attached to the holding of the baron of Naas.[82]

The beginnings of a movement against the hereditary tenure of offices in ecclesiastical institutions can be seen as early as the reign of Henry I. Although Henry I's original foundation charter of Reading Abbey of 1125 survives only in an 'improved' version, it seems clear that it included a clause prohibiting the hereditary grant of any office in the abbey.[83] A similar prohibition also appears in the subsequent charters for Reading

---

[78] *Pinchbeck Register*, vol. 1, pp. 137–38.

[79] *Register of St. Benet of Holme*, vol. 2, p. 73, no. 126.

[80] King, *Peterborough*, pp. 32–33.

[81] London, British Library, MS Additional 14847, ff. 57v–59r. It is however clear that there were also under-coroners in the liberty: *Calendar of Inquisitions Miscellaneous*, vol. 1, no. 2382.

[82] *Gormanston Register*, p. 205.

[83] 'In abbatis et monachorum domo Radingensium et possessione nullus per hereditatem officium teneat sed in arbitrio abbatis et monachorum de transmutandis prepositis seu aliis quibuslibet officiariis causa consistat': *Reading Abbey Cartularies vol. I*, ed. B.R. Kemp (Camden Fourth Series 31, London, 1986), p. 34, no. 1. Honorius II's confirmation of 1125, which has not been 'improved', has a clause in exactly the same words: W. Holtzmann, *Papsturkunden in England* (3 vols., Berlin and Göttingen, 1930–52), vol. 3, pp. 136–37.

of Stephen, Henry II and Richard.[84] When Henry II refounded Waltham Abbey in 1178 one of the provisions he made was to prohibit any hereditary grant of office within the abbey.[85] Similar provisions are to be found in two confirmation charters of Richard I,[86] and also (though in somewhat different language) in Pope Celestine III's confirmation of 1191.[87]

Even in those ecclesiastical institutions where hereditary stewardships had been created, a significant proportion had disappeared by the mid thirteenth century. At St. Augustine's, Canterbury the hereditary stewardship was extinguished by a final concord of 1197 in return for a payment of 80 marks and a grant of 50 acres of land.[88] The following year the same procedure was followed for extinguishing the stewardship at Westminster Abbey[89] though here the claimant settled for an annual payment of five marks a year for life rather than a lump sum. In this instance, however, there is some evidence to suggest that there may have been genuine prior litigation between the claimant and the abbey before the final concord.[90] A third hereditary stewardship which appears to have been extinguished in the last years of the twelfth century or early years of the thirteenth was that at Peterborough. Here all we have is the agreement reached in 1194 under which Hugh de Waterville agreed not to press his claim to the stewardship during the current abbacy.[91] It is reasonable to assume that the Watervilles gave up their claim to the hereditary stewardship at Peterborough not long after this.

Three more hereditary stewardships disappeared during the first half of the thirteenth century. In each case this was after litigation between claimants to a hereditary stewardship and those whom they claimed

[84] *Regesta* (as n. 41), pp. 249–50, no. 675; *Reading Abbey Cartularies*, p. 48, no. 18; p. 51, no. 20; p. 62, no. 34; p. 74, no. 48.

[85] *Cartae Antiquae, Rolls 11–20*, ed. J. Conway Davies (Pipe Roll Society, new series 33, London, 1957), p. 40. The same provision was also contained in Henry's 1177 charter: ibid., p. 44.

[86] Ibid., pp. 47–48.

[87] 'nec administracionem quarumlibet exteriorum rerum aliquorum abbates qui pro tempore fuerint consanguineis vel cognatis largiri vel de quolibet ministerio quempiam infeudare': Holtzmann, *Papsturkunden* (as n. 83), vol. 2, pp. 583–84, no. 290.

[88] *Feet of Fines, 9 Richard I* (as n. 52), pp. 35–36.

[89] Ibid., p. 159.

[90] *Rotuli Curie Regis* (as n. 47), vol. 1, p. 138: adjournment in a case between the abbot of Westminster and Walter de Coleham *de placito senescalcie* made in 1194.

[91] *Rotuli Curie Regis* (as n. 47), vol. 1, p. 24.

to serve. We have already noted the payments made by Jollan de Amundeville which indicate that he was pursuing a claim to the steward-ship of the see of Lincoln.[92] It was his son Peter who finally surrendered the family claim through an undated deed now in the Duchy of Lancaster deeds in the Public Record Office.[93] A second deed in the same collection gives us a probable date and supplies more of the context for the surrender. It is a bond by which William of Ely, the king's treasurer (and a canon of Lincoln), and W(illiam) archdeacon of Huntingdon (and thus also a canon of Lincoln) acknowledge owing Peter forty marks for the quitclaim, of which they agree to pay him 10 marks directly and to pay the remainder on his behalf to discharge an existing debt at the Exchequer. They also agree to do their best to get the king to grant him a respite from the accumulation of further interest on his Jewish debts for so long as he is paying off his debts to the king, as from the Sunday after Sts. Peter and Paul in the king's eleventh year.[94] William of Ely was the king's treasurer from 1196 to 1215 but since Peter did not succeed his father until some time between 1206 and 1212 the king referred to must be John. This suggests that the agreement was probably made on 5 July 1209. Both deeds provide for Gerard de Camville to act as stake-holder, keeping both deeds till the money was paid in full.

Litigation between Peter of Hautbois and the abbey of St. Benet of Holme began in 1206. In this litigation Peter was claiming not only the hereditary stewardship of the abbey but also various other property.[95] In 1208 the litigation was adjourned *sine die* when the abbey was taken into the king's hands,[96] but in 1210 Peter paid the king twenty-five marks for seisin of all the property in dispute (including the stewardship).[97] When a new abbot was elected and given possession of the abbey's property he dispossessed Peter who brought an assize of novel disseisin against him for doing so in 1213.[98] Eventually Peter made a quitclaim of all of the

[92] Above, p. 146.

[93] London, Public Record Office, DL 25/3251.

[94] London, Public Record Office, DL 25/3250.

[95] *Curia Regis Rolls* (London, 1928), vol. 4, p. 243. For an earlier stage see ibid., p. 194. In 1205 Peter had been impleading one Eustace of Thurgerton for the manor of Thurgerton and the abbot had sought the case for his court: ibid., p. 49.

[96] *Curia Regis Rolls* (London, 1931), vol. 5, p. 271. For an intermediate stage in the litigation earlier in the same year see ibid., p. 201.

[97] *The Great Roll of the Pipe for the Twelfth Year of the Reign of King John, Michaelmas 1210*, ed. C.F. Slade (Pipe Roll Society, new series 64, London, 1951), p. 30.

[98] *Curia Regis Rolls* (London, 1935), vol. 7, pp. 3, 6, 24, 40.

property in dispute including the stewardship. There are two different versions of this quitclaim in the abbey's cartulary. One is dated 12 August 1239 and says nothing of any previous litigation or any consideration for the quitclaim.[99] The other, which is undated, refers to additional property and to there having been litigation over the stewardship and other property: it indicates that Peter is to get an annual payment of 17 pounds for life for this quitclaim to 'relieve his poverty in his old age'.[100]

Evesham's hereditary steward brought litigation in the 1247 Buckinghamshire eyre to enforce his right to hold the abbey's courts and to ensure that he received the perquisites of his office. The abbot offered to deny the steward's right and seisin through his champion. Eventually two years later an agreement was reached. This left the steward in possession of all his lands and of a daily corrody and various other perquisites, but he had to renounce all claim to the hereditary stewardship.[101]

Elsewhere hereditary stewardships survived till the end of the thirteenth century and beyond but at the cost of a redefinition of the duties attached to the post which reduced the steward's powers and responsibilities. The 1311 agreement confined the Durham steward to the performance of purely ceremonial duties at the bishop's enthronement and at two major festivals each year and to running the bishop's Lincolnshire courts: probably only a small part of the duties originally attached to the post. The later thirteenth-century agreement between Bishop Richard of St. David's and the baron of Naas shows that the baron no longer enjoyed the title of steward and suggests that he may have lost some of the duties once attached to the position to the steward appointed by the bishop. The most firmly entrenched of all the hereditary stewards was the steward of Bury St. Edmunds who certainly retained the title and important responsibilities in the running of the liberty. Even he, however, had long played no part in the management of the abbey's lands; by the later twelfth century he had probably ceased to be used by the abbot to represent the abbey in its litigation elsewhere.

The heyday of the hereditary steward in the bishoprics and abbeys of England was the first century of English feudalism. Hereditary stewards were by no means an invariable feature of such institutions even then though they are found in a significant number and may have once have been more common than the surviving evidence suggests.

---

99 London, British Library, MS Cotton Galba E. II, f. 95v.
100 Ibid., f. 95v.
101 London, Public Record Office, JUST 1/56, m. 32.

No hereditary stewardships were created after this period and by 1200 the process of buying out hereditary claims (even dormant hereditary claims) had already begun. This process continued during the first half of the thirteenth century. Some hereditary stewardships survived as late as 1300, though the price for this was a substantial reduction in the powers and responsibilities of the stewards concerned. The hereditary principle, so firmly established for land, was for office much weakened in practice through these developments. Our evidence sheds little light on the reasons for the changes, but it seems likely that they are to be connected with the rise of the professional administrator,[102] and reflect the wish of ecclesiastical institutions to exercise a much greater degree of control over the officials in their service than was possible in the case of hereditary officials. Hereditary officials, particularly officials as important as the steward, were probably by now seen as an anomaly if not an anachronism.

---

[102] See the discussion of S.L. Waugh, 'From Tenure to Contract: Lordship and Clientage in Thirteenth Century England', *EHR* 101 (1986), pp. 811–39.

10

Conquering Kings: Some Twelfth-Century Reflections on Henry II and Richard I

John Gillingham

'The writers of the twelfth century', Karl Leyser has reminded us, 'were interested in the individuality of rulers' and especially so in England where there was a 'close-meshed system of government under which they experienced their rulers more acutely and harshly than most, even when these rulers were absentees'.[1] In consequence there are few kings whose political personalities should be better known than Henry II and Richard I, particularly since they lived in 'a golden age of historiography in England'.[2] Certainly modern historians have had few qualms in discerning two radically different styles of kingship. Whereas Richard is seen as the archetypal warrior king, *rex bellicosus*, his father – who 'despised violence and hated war' – is regarded as a ruler devoted to the arts of peaceful government.[3] For more than two hundred years now Henry has enjoyed the reputation of being a great king, responsible for major developments in law and government. According to Stubbs he was

---

[1] 'Some Reflections on Twelfth-Century Kings and Kingship', in K.J. Leyser, *Medieval Germany and its Neighbours, 900–1250* (London, 1982), pp. 246–47, 266.

[2] A. Gransden, *Historical Writing in England, c. 550 to c. 1307* (London, 1974), p. 219.

[3] J.O. Prestwich, 'Richard Coeur de Lion: *rex bellicosus*' in *Riccardo Cuor di Leone nella storia e nella leggenda* (Accademia Nazionale dei Lincei, Problemi Attuali di Scienza e di Cultura 253, Rome, 1981); W.L. Warren, *Henry II* (London, 1973), p. 208.

'first and foremost a legislator and administrator', 'a most industrious, active and workmanlike king who bestowed vast benefits on the English nation'. For Warren, 'it was Henry's genius to make efficient management synonymous with sound government'. Indeed where Henry II is concerned the word 'genius' has become hard to resist. 'That man of genius – the word is not too strong – who was by instinct a lawyer' is how van Caenegem refers to him; and in a recent popular history of the monarchy we are told that Henry 'had a genius for government'.[4] Richard, on the other hand, has been seen as a ruler who preferred to leave the 'real business' of government to others while he himself went off in pursuit of wayward aims, above all the crusade. Since the eighteenth century few contrasts have been so deeply entrenched in the historiography of English kingship as that between father and son, lawyer-king and soldier-king.[5] Here I shall argue that Richard was probably quite as much interested in justice as his father had been, and that Henry was certainly a more bellicose and aggressive ruler than his son was ever to be. I shall argue, in other words, that the conventional modern contrast is an entirely false one.[6]

I begin with law and justice. I shall not, however, be arguing that Richard's reign was as important for the development of the Common Law as his father's much longer reign had been. Unquestionably Henry II's reign

[4] W. Stubbs, *Constitutional History of England* (Oxford, 4th edn., 1883), vol. 1, p. 484; Warren, *Henry II*, p. 237: R.C. van Caenegem, *The Birth of the English Common Law* (Cambridge, 2nd edn., 1988), p. 100; J. Cannon and R. Griffiths, *The Oxford Illustrated History of the British Monarchy* (Oxford, 1988), p. 151. 'Genius was at work' wrote D.M. Stenton, *English Justice between the Norman Conquest and the Great Charter* (London, 1965), p. 26; cf. pp. 39, 53. Even B. Lyon, 'Henry II: A Non-Victorian Interpretation', *Essays in Medieval History Presented to G.P. Cuttino*, ed. J.S. Hamilton and P. Bradley (Woodbridge, 1989) pp. 24, 30, refers to him (ironically?) as 'England's greatest king' and as 'that mighty builder of English institutions and father of the common law'.

[5] David Hume was the first to make explicit what has since become the standard interpretation of these two kings: *The History of England* (London, 1871; reprint of 1786 edn.), vol. 1, pp. 248–51, 256, 279. The beginnings of this anachronistic re-interpretation can be traced – as I hope to show elsewhere – in some seventeenth-century writers, but until Hume most chroniclers and historians remained fairly true to twelfth-century opinion.

[6] While not denying, of course, that in other ways they were very different individuals. Here I treat them almost exclusively as kings of England. Although this distorts their own priorities, it does reflect the relative abundance of contemporary historical writing in England.

witnessed immensely important developments in this field, notably in the forms of administration of justice, e.g. the systematic use of itinerant royal judges and the emergence of a central court at Westminster.[7] Here I am concerned only with 'the individuality of rulers' and thus with the question of how far we should give the credit for these developments to Henry II himself. Obviously there is a sense in which as the king who authorised them he can – must – take responsibility for them. But many historians, often specialist legal historians, go further than this: they see him as the driving force, the inspiration behind the changes. Indeed in van Caenegem's hands Henry's personality becomes a 'key element' in explaining the whole remarkable development of English law.[8]

When Stubbs considered this question his first thought had been to cite Ralph Niger's statement that Henry 'abolished the ancient laws and every year published new laws which he called assizes'.[9] But as a fierce critic of the king, Niger might be thought guilty of some exaggeration, and we would probably do well to look instead to a more detached, and better informed, observer, Roger of Howden. Indeed it is primarily thanks to Roger's remarkable chronicles that the texts of some of the assizes, the instructions given to the king's judges, survive.[10] Roger's words seem perfectly clear. Of the Assize of Clarendon (1166) he tells us that 'This is the assize which King Henry ordered'. Of Northampton (1176) he wrote that Henry 'made it and ordered that it be obeyed'. Similarly it was Henry who 'decided upon' the Assize of Arms (1180) and who 'made' the justices of the forest swear to observe the forest assizes, the first of which Roger calls 'prima assisa Henrici regis'. All well and good. Problems arise, however, when we turn to Roger's account of Richard I's reign. According to Howden the instructions given to the judges in 1194 'came from the king'. The 1195 set of instructions for keeping the peace were known as the 'royal edict'. The 1197 assize of weights and measures was 'facta per dominum Ricardum regem'. The revised forest

---

[7] P. Brand, 'Henry II and the Creation of the English Common Law', *Haskins Society Journal* 2 (1990). Paul Brand very kindly sent me a typescript of this important article.

[8] Van Caenegem, *Birth*, chapter 4; cf. Stenton, *English Justice*, p. 53: 'It was Henry II . . . through his own versatility and that of his great justiciar, Ranulf de Glanville, who started the wheel in perpetual motion'.

[9] Stubbs, *Constitutional History* (as n. 4), pp 530–31. *The Chronicles of Ralph Niger*, ed. R. Anstruther (London, 1851), p. 168.

[10] J.C. Holt, 'The Assizes of Henry II: The Texts' in *The Study of Medieval Records*, ed. D.A. Bullough and R.L. Storey (Oxford, 1971), p. 86.

assize issued in the same year is described as 'the assize of the lord king' and we are told that 'an order was sent out from the king' summoning people to hear 'the king's commands'.[11]

Howden, in other words, consistently attributes these measures to the reigning king, whether it is Henry or Richard. Historians, however, interpret his words inconsistently. They regard them as meaningless formulae when the king was Richard I, but take them at face value when it was Henry II. What justification can there be for this inconsistent treatment of Roger's consistent usage? One possible justification might be that Richard was rarely in England. In these circumstances, so the argument might run, responsibility for the administration of English law clearly lay with his ministers.[12] It is, however, striking that although routine administration continued unabated while Richard was on crusade and in prison, no new assizes seem to have been issued until after the king's return to his own dominions. Administrative innovation, it seems, required the king's authorisation. Once Richard was back the pace of judicial and legal development was resumed. In this context it is clearly a mistake to imagine that Richard's 'absences' in France meant that he neglected England. J.C. Holt has looked at Richard's management of financial business and patronage and concluded that from Normandy Richard 'intervened frequently and persistently in the control of English affairs', doing so even when the man left in charge of England was Hubert Walter, 'one of the greatest royal ministers of all time'.[13] Clearly Richard in Normandy, like Henry II in Normandy, could have involved himself

[11] Roger of Howden, *Gesta Henrici et Ricardi*, ed. W. Stubbs (Rolls Series, London, 1867) vol. 1, pp. 107, 269, 323; Roger of Howden, *Chronica*, ed. W. Stubbs (Rolls Series, London, 1868–71) vol. 3, pp. 262, 299; vol. 4, pp. 33, 46, 63–4. However, note some chapters introduced by words like *Vult, or Prohibet etiam dominus rex, Chronica*, 2, pp. 248–52. The nearest any of the assizes came to being officially published was probably Richard I's naval law, issued in 1190 in charter form: 'Sciatis nos de communi proborum virorum consilio has fecisse justitias subscriptas' and ending 'Teste me ipso', *Gesta* vol. 2, pp. 110–11. See J.C. Holt, 'Ricardus rex Anglorum et dux Normannorum', *Magna Carta and Medieval Government* (London, 1985), pp. 29–30, for the possible significance of 'teste me ipso'.

[12] Here the practice of historians can be traced back to Roger of Wendover who interpolates the words 'ad instantiam H. Cantuariensis archiepiscopi et Anglie justiciarii' into Howden's introduction to the Assize of Weights and Measures, Matthew Paris, *Chronica Majora*, ed. H.R. Luard (Rolls Series, London, 1872–73), vol. 2, p. 442.

[13] Holt, 'Ricardus rex', pp. 25–32. It is worth noting that those officials put in charge of administrative reforms in England, e.g. Hubert Walter, Hugh Bardolf and Hugh Nevill, are sometimes to be found on the continent with the king shortly before the date of issue of new assizes.

in the administration of the English judicial system – if he had been interested in doing so.[14] Historians have simply assumed that he wasn't interested and that he didn't. On the other hand they believe, in the light of other evidence, that Henry was exceptionally interested and so they take Howden's formal phrases entirely seriously.

Now the most vivid portrait of King Henry at work is that drawn by the unknown author of the Chronicle of Battle Abbey. Indeed it was precisely this author's handling of one episode in 1175 which led Maitland to write of Henry that 'he was at heart a lawyer', and which led Eleanor Searle, the modern editor of the chronicle, to conjure up an archetypal image of the lawyer-king, 'on the bench and among his councillors, not only presiding, but patiently explaining his legal and administrative innovations to great men, petty knights and monks alike'.[15] Clearly this episode must be looked at closely. The monks of Battle wanted one of their royal charters renewed and Henry, after taking advice, agreed. However instead of using the customary formulae of confirmation, 'he himself dictated a phrase never before employed . . . and then deigned to explain the point of the new clause'.[16] Since this chronicle breaks off before Richard came to the throne' – indeed the author probably died before 1189 – we cannot know how he might have shown Richard at work, though, as I shall show below, there is good reason to think that he was a harder working king than his father. It is also worth remembering that there were major developments in the formulae of royal charters in Richard's reign.[17] Probably most kings were interested in their rights as set out in charters issued in their name. After all there was a direct connection between charter formulae and the rents and profits of the

[14] For Richard and Norman law see *Le Tres Ancien Coutumier de Normandie*, ed. E-J. Tardif (Rouen, 1881), pp. 13, 68–69.

[15] F. Pollock and F.W. Maitland, *The History of English Law* (Cambridge, 1968), vol. 1, p. 159 on which see Lyon, 'A Non-Victorian Interpretation' (as n. 4), p. 25: *The Chronicle of Battle Abbey*, ed. and trans. E. Searle (Oxford, 1980), p. 11.

[16] *Chronicle of Battle*, pp. 310–12. Henry was not always so masterful in his handling of charters, *The Chronicle of Jocelin of Brakelond*, ed. H.E. Butler (London, 1949), pp. 50–52.

[17] L. Landon, *The Itinerary of Richard I* (Pipe Roll Society New Series 13, London, 1935), p. ix. This sort of innovation may have been due, as Landon suggested, to the chancellor, Longchamp. On the other hand both the royal we of majesty and the *teste me ipso* formula touch the person of the king closely and Richard, after all, was well-known for his verbal skills. Contemporaries attributed many witticisms to him and he was a poet of some distinction, P. Dronke, *The Medieval Lyric* (London, 2nd edn., 1978), pp. 212–13. He probably dictated some letters himself, Holt, 'Ricardus rex', pp. 17, 29–31.

crown – as Henry himself pointed out on another occasion recorded by the Battle Chronicle.[18] Undoubtedly the Battle Chronicle shows us a king taking a close, thoughtful and innovative interest in the precise wording of a royal charter; this is not, however, the same thing as showing him taking a deep personal interest in those innovations in judicial procedure which were at the heart of the emergence of the Common Law.

On the other hand many historians have found just the evidence they needed in Walter Map's famous description of Henry II as 'clever in devising new and undiscovered legal procedures'. This at any rate is the translation offered in *English Historical Documents*. The Latin is 'inusitati occultique iudicii subtilis inventor'.[19] Other recent translations include 'the subtle discoverer of unusual and hidden judicial procedure', 'a subtle deviser of novel judicial processes', and that 'subtle inventor of new judicial forms'.[20] It is, however, likely that the translation preferred by Karl Leyser is more accurate: 'the subtle inventor of obscure and unaccustomed judgement', reading *iudicium* as a decision, a judgement, not as a procedure, a process or a judicial form.[21] What Map had in mind was Henry's capacity as a judge, not as a procedural reformer.[22] In his

[18] When shown a confirmation issued by Henry I, he turned to one of the litigants and said, 'By God's eyes, Gilbert, if you could prove this charter false, you would make me a profit of a thousand pounds'. *Chronicle of Battle*, pp. 214–17. See also William of Newburgh, *Historia Rerum Anglicarum*, ed. R. Howlett, *Chronicles of the Reigns of Stephen, Henry II and Richard I* (Rolls Series, London, 1884), vol. 1, p. 103 on the relationship between charters, crown lands and royal revenues.

[19] Walter Map, *De Nugis Curialium*, ed. and trans. M.R. James, C.N.L. Brooke and R.A.B. Mynors (Oxford, 1983), p. 476; *English Historical Documents II: 1042–1189*, ed. D.C. Douglas and G.W. Greenaway (London, 2nd edn., 1981), p. 419.

[20] Warren, *Henry II* (as n. 3), p. 360; Van Caenegem, *The birth* (as n. 4), p. 100; M.T. Clanchy, *England and its Rulers* (London, 1983) p. 151. Both Warren and Van Caenegem explicitly use this phrase to support their view that the Common Law owed much to Henry's personal interest. Michael Clanchy, however, adopts a more sceptical approach, one to which I am much indebted.

[21] Leyser, 'Some Reflections' (as n. 1), p. 251, citing M.R. James. Cf. 'a clever deviser of decisions in unusual and dark cases' Map, *De Nugis*, p. 477 and also 'skilful to discover unusual and secret ways of judgement' in *Master Walter Map's Book De Nugis Curialium*, trans. F. Tupper and M.B. Ogle (London, 1924), p. 298.

[22] That this was the quality which concerned Map is clear from the anecdotes he told about Henry as a judge, *De Nugis*, pp. 486, 488–95, 509. Although later chroniclers knew nothing of the modern notion of Henry as founder of the common law, many of them, from Wendover onwards, *Chronica Majora* (as n. 12), vol. 2, p. 299, were to be as impressed as Map was by Henry's adjudication of the Castile-Navarre dispute.

view Henry was a clever judge, able to see what lay behind difficult cases. Presumably many twentieth-century historians have avoided what is after all the most obvious translation of the word *iudicium* because they think they know that Henry II was interested in legal procedure and they have therefore preferred a translation which brings out this supposedly crucial aspect of his character. But this is to read into Map's words something that is not there.

A well known passage in 'Bracton's' great treatise on English law has been interpreted in similar fashion. According to 'Bracton' the Assize of Novel Disseisin was 'contrived and thought out in many watches of the night'.[23] Modern historians sometimes assert that one of those who suffered sleepless nights was Henry himself.[24] In fact the Latin has nothing whatever to say on the subject of who did the thinking and contriving – indeed the phrase was borrowed from Justinian's Code. Admittedly there is good evidence that Novel Disseisin dates from Henry's reign, so it is reasonable to suppose that some of his advisers were thinking and contriving, yet it is striking that not even in the most general terms does 'Bracton' associate Novel Disseisin with Henry's reign. Even more striking is the fact that in the whole of this massive treatise on English law there is not a single reference to Henry II.[25] Surprising if lawyers active in the decades either side of 1200 really had regarded him as the Common Law's founding father – not so surprising if they hadn't.

If we translate more conservatively then there is no evidence which entitles us to see Henry as the inspiration behind the Common Law. On the whole, apart from Howden – himself one of the king's forest judges – contemporaries do not seem to have concerned themselves about procedural changes.[26] What they did care about was precisely the point on which, as we have seen, Walter Map put his finger. Was the king a

---

[23] *Bracton: On the Laws and Customs of England*, ed. G.E. Woodbine, trans. with revisions and notes by S.E. Thorne (Cambridge, 1977), vol. 3, p. 25.

[24] E.g. R.W. Southern, 'The Place of England in the Twelfth Century Renaissance' in *Medieval Humanism* (Oxford, 1970), p. 178; Warren, *Henry II* (as n. 3), p. 370; W.L. Warren, *The Governance of Norman and Angevin England* (London, 1987), p. 114. Cf. the clear implication in Stenton, *English Justice*, p. 39. On the other hand there is some evidence that Richard was capable of working through the night, *Histoire de Guillaume le Marechal*, ed P. Meyer (Paris, 1891–1901), vol. 1, lines 8248–49.

[25] As noted by Brand, 'Henry II' (as n. 7).

[26] Thus Roger of Wendover, in a section using Howden, notes that at this point he would have copied out the text of Henry II's laws 'si non lectorem offendere dubitarem', *Chronica Majora* (as n. 12), vol. 2, p. 346

good and just judge? They also cared about the natural extension of this: did he appoint good judges, and keep them up to the mark? These of course were very traditional ways of assessing the quality of kings. King Alfred was and did, or so Asser tells us. Hanging many of his judges was, according to the early fourteenth-century Andrew Horn, one of the ways Alfred showed what a fine king he was.[27] There is plenty of contemporary opinion about Henry II's performance in this area. Ralph of Diceto, for example, never gives us the texts of any of the assizes, but in a long and famous passage describes how Henry's difficulties in finding honest men eventually led him to appoint churchmen as judges.[28] Not surprisingly a much more favourable view of the king's judges is expressed in Glanvil. But most observers – including Howden – shared Diceto's opinion that most of Henry's judges had been oppressive; indeed in Map's view churchmen were worse than laymen. Even Ranulf Glanvil, most learned in the law though he may have been, was regarded by Howden as a nasty and corrupt judge.[29]

Despite these widespread criticisms of Henry II's judges, it is of course true that the restoration of political stability after Stephen's reign led many writers to see Henry as a champion of law and order. According to William of Newburgh, looking back from the 1190s, 'he was most diligent in defending and promoting the peace of the realm . . . in appointing judges and legal officials to curb the audacity of wicked men and do justice to litigants'. But having appointed judges, Newburgh continues, Henry was inclined to let them get on with it: 'In the meantime the king himself either indulged his pleasures or gave his attention to more important matters. Only when disturbed by the volume of complaints against his ministers did he take action himself'.[30] Here there is the clear implication that, in William's view, Henry had regarded judicial business as being of lesser importance. Indeed it is very easy to accumulate

[27] *Asser's Life of King Alfred*, ed. W.H. Stevenson, revised by D. Whitelock (Oxford, 1959), pp. 92–93. Horn's view is cited by James Campbell in a statement of the importance of continuity of English government, J. Campbell, *The Anglo-Saxons* (Oxford, 1982), p. 241.

[28] *Radulfi de Diceto Opera Historica* ed. W. Stubbs (Rolls Series, London, 1876), vol. 1, pp. 434–35. Wendover chose to omit this passage too.

[29] *Tractatus de Legibus et Consuetudinibus Anglie qui Glanvilla Vocatur*, ed. G.D.G. Hall (London, 1965), p. 2; Howden, *Gesta*, vol. 1, pp. 207, 314–16; vol. 2, pp. 74–6; Map, *De Nugis*, pp. 10–14; John of Salisbury, *Policraticus* V 11, ed. C.C.J. Webb (Oxford, 1929), vol. 2, pp. 340–44. For a useful survey of contemporary opinion see R.V. Turner, *The English Judiciary in the Age of Glanvill and Bracton* (Cambridge, 1985), pp. 3–11.

[30] Newburgh, *Historia* (as n. 18), vol. 1, p. 102.

evidence suggesting that Henry was dilatory in settling lawsuits and devoted little of his own time to judicial business.[31] Of his pleasures the most time-consuming was probably hunting. To this he was notoriously addicted and in consequence was on horseback from dawn until nightfall. According to Map, Henry's judges used to encourage him to go hunting so that while he was out playing they could fleece a few victims of their own.[32] In the well-recorded dispute between Canterbury and Battle, the abbot came to court 'but he could get nothing that day since the king had gone hunting'. This seems to have been the common experience of frustrated litigants. Henry's restlessness made him almost impossible to pin down. At times it seems that the only way his subjects could find him still for long enough to listen to their troubles was to interrupt him at mass; only prayer mattered less to Henry than judicial business.[33] As Map suggests, Henry was intelligent enough to be a very shrewd judge, and doubtless in politically significant cases he was prepared to get involved, but there is no evidence that he was either so diligent or so fascinated by the king's role as fount of justice that he was willing to give much time to it. Those who had dealings with Henry were constantly frustrated as postponement followed postponement, 'as was his custom' as both Roger of Howden and Gervase of Canterbury noted.[34] According to Walter Map, 'he wastes time in dealing with the affairs of his people; and so it comes about that many die before they get their matters settled, or leave court depressed and thwarted, driven away by hunger'.[35]

---

[31] Giraldus Cambrensis, *Expugnatio Hibernica*, ed. A.B. Scott and F.X. Martin (Dublin, 1978), p. 130: *Chronicles of Niger*, p. 169.

[32] According to Giraldus only war was allowed to interrupt Henry's hunting, *Expugnatio*, pp. 126–28. According to Newburgh, *Historia*, vol. 2, p. 280, 'He loved the delights of the chase more than was proper'. In Walter Map's opinion, *De Nugis* (as n. 19), pp. 476, 510–13, he was 'most greedy of that vain sport'. Bryce Lyon argues that so much hunting would have left Henry with neither time nor energy for thinking and planning about government and law, 'A Non-Victorian Interpretation' (as n. 4), p. 31. By contrast the silence of the sources suggests that Richard's attitude to hunting was unremarkable.

[33] *Chronicle of Battle* (as n. 15), p. 156; Gerald, *Expugnatio*, p. 130.

[34] Howden, *Gesta* (as n. 11), vol. 1, p. 346; *The Historical Works of Gervase of Canterbury*, ed. W. Stubbs (Rolls Series, London, 1879), vol. 1, p. 382.

[35] To be fair, in one passage Map says that Henry kept a keen eye on the exchequer court, but usually he emphasises the king's dilatoriness, stating indeed that Henry, on his mother's advice, elevated delay into a principle of government: Map, *De Nugis*, pp. 478, 484, 508. According to Ralf Niger this was so that he could sell law, *Chronica*, p. 169. Karl Leyser, more kindly, describes it as 'a recognisable form of man management', 'Some Reflections' (as n. 1), p. 252.

Fortunately the long drawn-out quarrel between the monks of Christ Church, Canterbury and their archbishop enables us to make a direct comparison between Henry II and Richard. Since Stubbs edited the great body of material bearing on this dispute, his comments on the two kings who had to cope with it make interesting reading. Having noted that 'Richard soon showed himself even more determined than his father that his rights and dignity should not be infringed' (a view of the two kings which was shared by the early thirteenth-century Adam of Eynsham[36]) he went on to observe that Richard 'stands in pleasant contrast with his father in respect both of his openness and his firmness', concluding that Richard achieved the desired result without descending to either 'chicanery or bullying'.[37] 'He condescended to none of what St. Thomas called his father's mousetraps: the tricks by which that astute king managed to put his adversaries in the wrong without committing himself to a decided course'. In order to bring this strikingly favourable assessment of Richard into line with his overall view of him as 'a bad ruler', Stubbs introduced it with the comment that the dispute illustrated the character of Richard 'in some minor respects'.[38] Whether contemporaries regarded these as minor respects is another matter. According to Howden, after the Canterbury council of December 1189, when a settlement was – at least temporarily – achieved, 'everyone went home, magnifying and praising the king's great deeds' (*magnalia regis*).[39] This is not quite the

[36] *Magna Vita Sancti Hugonis*, ed. D.L. Douie and H. Farmer (Oxford, 1985), vol. 2, p. 40. See K.J. Leyser, 'The Angevin Kings and the Holy Man', in *St. Hugh of Lincoln*, ed. H. Mayr-Harting (Oxford, 1987), pp. 49–73.

[37] Karl Leyser has suggested that 'the most common characteristic of twelfth-century rulers seems to have been chicanery', 'Some Reflections' (as n. 1), p. 253. Unquestionably Gervase, the chronicler of the Canterbury dispute, thought it one of Henry II's chief characteristics, and a most objectionable one. Richard by contrast Gervase clearly admired as a business-like king, though he too could be described *cupidus et dolosus*, Gervase, *Historical Works*, vol. 1, pp. 318–19, 323, 327, 372, 382, 392, 418, 420, 435, 439, 465–81. For Richard's ability to outwit as astute a politician as Philip Augustus see J. Gillingham, 'Richard I and Berengaria of Navarre', *Bulletin of the Institute of Historical Research* 53 (1980), pp. 157–73. Richard is seen as an example of *perfidia anglica* by the German chronicler Otto of St. Blasien, ed. A. Hofmeister (MGH SRG, Hanover, 1912), p. 55.

[38] *Chronicles and Memorials of the Reign of Richard I*, ed. W. Stubbs (Rolls Series, London, 1864–65), vol. 1, p. xxvii; vol. 2, p. cxiv. In the opinion of David Knowles, Stubbs' 'fairness of judgement on the characters involved' in the Canterbury dispute was 'excellent'. His own judgement was that Henry's death removed an obstacle to peace, *The Monastic Order in England*, 2nd edn. (Cambridge, 1963), vol. 1, pp. 321–22.

[39] Howden, *Gesta* (as n. 11), vol. 2, pp. 97–99. It is clear from Gervase's account that the settlement of 1190 owed much to Richard's personal intervention. At the same council

language to be used of competence 'in some minor respects'; but Stubbs, of course, believed that he judged men 'by a better standard' than twelfth-century writers.[40] Another contemporary to praise Richard's justice was Richard of Devizes. Whereas Richard at Messina appointed judges who dealt impartially and severely with thieves and looters, no matter whether male or female, foreigners or natives, Philip Augustus kept quiet about the wrongs his own men did or suffered. Richard considered every man his subject and left no offence unpunished. For this reason the Greek population of Sicily called Philip the lamb and Richard the lion.[41]

Clearly both Henry and Richard were intelligent men capable of taking a keen interest in some aspects of law and government. Moreover the entourages of both of them contained acknowledged experts: men like Glanvil and FitzNigel in Henry's, Hubert Walter and Geoffrey FitzPeter in Richard's. Richard's record as a judge and as an appointer of judges at least matches his father's – indeed the Canterbury dispute suggests that it surpasses it. Admittedly it was not so easy to interrupt Richard at mass, for he took religious services seriously and was praised for doing so. Nor did he spend all day hunting. He was pre-eminently a business-like king, not one who indulged his pleasures.[42] The difference between the two kings can be seen in the contrasting reactions to the news of their deaths. When Henry II died we are told – by Howden – that only a few men were saddened and that Richard's accession was greeted with joy and the hope of reform. Thus Richard found it politic to begin with a series of gestures, all of which were related to the perception of Henry II as an unjust and oppressive ruler.[43] However when John came to the

Richard also settled the question of the English king's claim to lordship over Scotland. It was in the context of their account of this council that Roger of Wendover and Matthew Paris called Richard *rex sapientissimus: Chronica Majora* (as n. 12), vol. 2, p. 354.

[40] *Chronicles and Memorials*, vol. 2, p. xxxiv.

[41] *The Chronicle of Richard of Devizes*, ed. J.T. Appleby (London, 1963), pp. 16–17.

[42] Unless, like Stubbs, we believe that war was his pleasure, engaged in 'not for the sake of glory or acquisition of territory, but as other men love science or poetry', *Chronicles and Memorials*, vol. 1, p. xix.

[43] *Richard of Devizes*, pp. 4–5; Howden, *Gesta*, vol. 2, pp. 74–76. Contrast Howden's reaction to Richard's death, *Chronica*, vol. 4, pp. 84–85: the Vitellius MS of Howden's *Gesta* ends with Vinsauf's lament on Richard's death, vol. 2, pp. 251–52. Wendover's praise of Richard's justice 'he did right to all and would not allow justice to be perverted' (*Chronica Majora*, vol. 3, p. 215) had been expressed at much greater length in Radulfus Presbiter's letter on Richard's death, printed by C. Köhler in *Revue de l'Orient Latin* 5 (1897).

throne ten years later he felt no need to begin his reign with this sort of comment on his predecessor's rule.[44]

As Warren has observed, none of the chroniclers seemed to like Henry. 'Only time has rescued Henry II from the calumny of contemporaries.'[45] Ironically the calumny of contemporaries has come to serve Henry well. The vivid pen portrait, warts and all, drawn by Giraldus has formed the basis of every subsequent characterisation.[46] This has meant that Henry appears before us as a living human being. By contrast, precisely because he was so much admired by contemporaries, Richard was portrayed more as a bloodless ideal than as a real person. When in *De Principis Instructione* Giraldus set out to be vitriolic about all the Angevins, the only insult he could hurl at Richard was to assert that he was an arrogant man since he did not sufficently thank God for all his achievements.[47] The trouble with Richard, as Disraeli said of Gladstone, was that he had no redeeming defect.

The process of rescuing Henry's reputation from the calumny of contemporaries got under way soon after his death. Writing in the late 1190s, Newburgh wrote that 'the experience of present evils has revived the memory of his good deeds, and the man who in his time was hated by all men, is now declared to have been an excellent and beneficent prince'. He goes on to put into Richard's mouth the remark made by Rehoboam: 'My father chastised you with whips but I shall chastise you with scorpions'. Newburgh's next sentence, however, suggests that there were many people who did not share his opinion of present evils. 'This foolish people makes less complaint now when it is chastised with scorpions than it did when it was chastised with whips.'[48] Undoubtedly Richard was taxing his subjects harder than his father had done, so why did they complain less? My impression is that contemporaries accepted that his policies, though expensive, were reasonable and honourable. They would have agreed with Coggeshall's comment that though there had never been

---

[44] On John's one gesture, the lowering of chancery fees, see S. Painter's comment, 'the brand new royal broom erased a fly-speck', *The Reign of King John* (Baltimore, 1949), p. 95.

[45] Warren, *Henry II* (as n. 3), p. 215.

[46] Giraldus, *Expugnatio*, pp. 124–33. Note however that years later in his *De Principis Instructione* he observed that what in 1189 he had claimed as a warts and all description of Henry 'verbis excusatoriis temperavimus': *Giraldi Cambrensis Opera*, ed. G.F. Warner (Rolls Series, London, 1891), vol. 8, p. 213.

[47] *Giraldi Opera*, vol. 8, p. 249.

[48] Newburgh (as n. 18), vol. 1, p. 280

a king who had raised so much money as Richard had, yet he could to some extent be excused since he had used the money to win allies, to make his nephew emperor, to defend his own land and to subjugate the provinces of others to his rule.[49] By contrast, although contemporaries were undeniably impressed by Henry II, it was generally either by his energy or because, as Newburgh put it, he enjoyed the renown of a king who ruled over a wider empire than all of his predecessors. In the words of Guernes de Pont-Sainte-Maxence he was 'the rich king who owned so much of the world'.[50] Yet they also felt that in three ways he fell short of their expectations: he oppressed the church;[51] he failed to manage his family, with consequent civil war in 1173–74, 1183 and 1188–89;[52] and he failed to go on crusade.[53]

I suppose that most modern historians accept that Henry mishandled both the Becket affair and his own family. On the other hand they tend to sympathise with his reluctance to go on crusade. This is of a piece with the widespread modern view that Henry's interests were so much focused upon internal government that he hardly had a foreign policy at all. He

---

[49] *Radulphi de Coggeshall Chronicon Anglicanum*, ed. J. Stevenson (Rolls Series, London, 1875), p. 93. See below, n. 66. By contrast it is clear that the first historian to take a decidedly critical view of Richard did so because he regarded him as a king who wasted the huge sums he raised in taxation. This was Samuel Daniel in *The Collection of the History of England* (London, 1621), pp. 96–107. In an extraordinary passage, p. 101, Daniel shows that he was aware of being both original and anachronistic in taking this view. 'Pardon us Antiquity, if we miscensure your actions, which are ever (as those of men) according to the vogue and sway of times, and have only their upholding by the opinion of the present: we deal with you but as posterity will with us (which ever thinks itself the wiser) that will judge likewise of our errors according to the cast of their imaginations.' As M. McKisack noted, 'Samuel Daniel as Historian', *Review of English Studies* 23 (1947), p. 239, Daniel's judgement on Richard 'accords very closely with that of Stubbs', but whereas she saw this as the moment when historians at last began to get Richard right, I take exactly the opposite view.

[50] Newburgh, p. 106; Coggeshall, p. 26; Guernes de Pont-Sainte-Maxence, *La Vie de Saint Thomas le Martyr*, ed. E. Walberg (Lund, 1922), p. 14. For most chroniclers in subsequent centuries Henry's greatness lay 'in the extent of his dominions'.

[51] E.g. Coggeshall, p. 26. After the Reformation, of course, this was to tell in Henry's favour. Protestant writers had the great advantage of being able to dismiss contemporary opinion as being, in John Foxe's phrase, 'blinded and tainted with superstition', *Acts and Monuments* (London, 1854), vol. 2, part 1, p. 247.

[52] Giraldus, *Expugnatio*, pp. 120–25, 130–33; Guernes, *Vie de Saint Thomas*, pp. 206–8.

[53] K. Schnith, 'Betrachtungen zum Spätwerk des Giraldus Cambrensis: *De Principis Instructione*', in *Festiva Lanx*, ed. K. Schnith (Munich, 1966), pp. 59–61; R. Bartlett, *Gerald of Wales* (Oxford, 1982), pp. 77–86.

was not, so we have been told, an expansionist, either in the British Isles or on the continent.[54] This may be a fair assessment of the Old King's foreign policy, but it can hardly be applied to the first two-thirds of his reign. He may have been reluctant to go on crusade, but in every other direction Henry had been an aggressive and expansionist ruler, as any of his neighbours, the kings of France and Scotland, the kings and princes in Ireland and Wales, the counts of Brittany and Toulouse, could have testified. Usually, of course, Henry claimed to be pursuing his rights, but in some cases his claim was a very tenuous one – as when he tried to seize Bourges in 1170 and again in 1177, or the French Vexin (also in 1177). Sometimes his territorial acquisitiveness involved breaking his word, as when he forced Malcolm of Scotland to hand over Northumbria in 1157.[55] On occasion Henry could be accused of invading without declaring war, as when he attacked Brittany in 1167.[56] He even invaded where he had no hereditary claim at all, as in the attack on Ireland in 1171–72.[57] Towards the end of his life Henry may have been 'sick to death of war', as Newburgh put it, but for most of his reign he was anything but a king who stayed quietly at home. Diceto's epitaphs on Henry, though trite, are certainly appropriate, and probably on both accounts are rarely quoted: that a man who had never been content with what he possessed now had to be content with just a few feet of soil.[58]

How did Henry want men to see him? There may be indirect evidence of this in the way he was represented in works composed during his lifetime and either intended for, or likely to come to, his ears. Jordan Fantosme, for example, proclaiming his desire to compose verses about the best king who ever lived, wrote that there was 'never any king who was his equal in bravery and might'; he was 'the most honourable king and the greatest conqueror who ever was anywhere on earth since Moses, save

[54] This is the argument of Warren, *Henry II* (as n. 3), pp. 220–237.

[55] For a very brief summary see J. Gillingham, *The Angevin Empire* (London, 1984), pp. 20–28.

[56] Etienne de Rouen, *Draco Normannicus*, in *Chronicles* (as n. 18), vol. 2, p. 697.

[57] Thus the invasion of Ireland had to be justified in extraordinary terms, appealing either to *Laudabiliter* or to the legends of King Arthur. But these justifications did not altogether still critical voices, as is clear from the way Gerald protests too much, *Expugnatio*, p. 148. See also Niger, *Chronica* (as n. 9), p. 92 (where Henry's force is contrasted with Strongbow's right 'ex successione uxoris sue'), and William of Canterbury in *Materials for the History of Thomas Becket*, ed. J.C. Robertson (Rolls Series, London, 1875–85), vol. 2, p. 364.

[58] Newburgh (as n. 18), vol. 1, p. 249; Diceto (as n. 28), vol. 2, p. 65.

only Charlemagne whose might was immense'.[59] In 1188 Giraldus wrote 'The Topography of Ireland' and dedicated it to Henry. 'Your victories challenge the boundaries of the world. You, our Alexander of the West, have extended your hand from the Pyrenees to the westernmost limits of the Ocean. Even Ireland, for long untouched by the incursions of foreign nations, has now at last been subjugated by you, most invincible king, and by your intrepid courage. The terror of your name and the threats of your attacks have sent your renown blazing through the world.'[60] Even the author of 'Glanvil' praises the vigour and cunning with which 'our most excellent king has practised warfare . . . as a result of which his praise has gone out to all the world and his mighty deeds to the ends of the earth'.[61]

Yet, when it came to it, the greatest conqueror since Charlemagne, the Alexander of the West, would not go to Jerusalem. This was a serious failure to live up to men's expectations at a time when the crusade was virtually universally perceived as a just and holy war.[62] In this war Richard did remarkably well. Against the odds he recovered the Palestinian coastal plain and in 1192 negotiated the Treaty of Jaffa, 'an almost incredible success which prolonged the life of the crusader states for another century'.[63] Moreover, since the kingdom of Jerusalem was held by a junior branch of the Plantagenet family, the crusade was, as J.O. Prestwich has pointed out, family as well as religious duty.[64] Unlike Henry, Richard did his family and his followers proud. He was able to bestow the vacant throne of Jerusalem on one of his nephews,

---

[59] *Jordan Fantosme's Chronicle*, ed. and trans. R.C. Johnston (Oxford, 1981), pp. 2–3, 10–11.

[60] *Giraldi Opera*, vol. 5, pp. 189–90. Gerald later admitted that this was *blande aliquantulum* (ibid., vol. 8, p. 198) but presumably he thought that this is what Henry wanted to hear. Intriguingly in his first edition of the *Topographia* Gerald said nothing about Henry's learning.

[61] *Glanvil*, p. 1. Passages rarely quoted from Peter of Blois' otherwise much quoted letter ('with the king of England it is school every day', etc.) tell how Henry both enormously extended his inheritance and inspired terror in other princes – all in the cause of peace, of course, *Materials* (as n. 57), vol. 7, p. 574.

[62] Just as, in our time, the war against Hitler was so regarded. Note the title of Eisenhower's book *Crusade in Europe*. Henry's excuse was that he had to defend his own lands against barbarian attacks, Diceto, vol. 2, p. 34.

[63] H.E. Mayer, 'Henry II of England and the Holy Land', *EHR 97* (1982), p. 739.

[64] Prestwich (as n. 3), pp. 7–8. See also J. Gillingham, 'Roger of Howden on Crusade' in *Medieval Historical Writing in the Christian and Islamic Worlds*, ed. D.O. Morgan (London, 1982).

Henry of Champagne, just as later, in 1197–98, he provided for another nephew, Otto of Brunswick, by helping him to the throne of Germany. He conquered Cyprus and gave it to Guy of Lusignan. To Stubbs this seemed a nonsense. How could anyone in his right mind conquer Cyprus and then give it away? It was this act which led him to write that Richard must have been 'the veriest tyro in politics' and to comment, disparagingly, that Richard 'had no scheme of territorial aggrandisement such as gave a unity to the whole life of his father and of his competitor Philip'.[65] That at least is right. Richard may be the supreme example of a warrior king of England but, as Prestwich emphasised, all his wars were fought to defend or recover his undoubted rights, for the crusade too was regarded as a defensive war, fought to save and then, after 1187, to rescue the Patrimony of Christ.[66] In this Richard was very different from his father, for Henry – as Map observed – had no compunction about disturbing the peace of half of Christendom.[67]

In their different ways both kings attained the stature of heroes. Richard achieved this in his own lifetime; was seen in this light by men who had met him. And he was to retain this heroic stature for centuries. Nowadays he tends to be the hero of children's books, Ladybird Books and the like – as well, of course, as of my *Richard the Lionheart*.[68] Henry, by contrast, is the hero of serious and substantial works of scholarship. Consider the language of the last sentence of Warren's great biography. 'He was no god-like Achilles, either in valour or in wrath; but in cunning and ingenuity, in fortitude and courage, he stands not far below the subtle-souled Odysseus.'[69] Henry, however, only came to be seen in this heroic light as the result of misconceptions formulated during the Enlightenment and sustained by the values, as well as by the scholarship, of the Victorians. As Henry's reputation rose so that of his son sank. Yet for about 600 years, from the twelfth century to the eighteenth, most chroniclers and historians got it about right. It is time that we returned to those old-fashioned and unenlightened views.

[65] *Chronicles and Memorials* (as n. 38), vol. 2, p. xxv.

[66] The requirements of the crusade, as well as rescuing his followers, presumably justified the invasion of Cyprus.

[67] 'fere dimidium Christianismi vexare non miseretur', Map, *De Nugis*, p. 484.

[68] J. Gillingham, *Richard the Lionheart* (London, 2nd edn. 1989).

[69] Warren, *Henry II* (as n. 3), p. 630.

11

Gilbert de Middleton and the Attack on the Cardinals, 1317

Michael Prestwich

On 1 September 1317, near Rushyford on the road between Darlington and Durham, a notorious outrage took place. Gilbert de Middleton with an armed band attacked and robbed the party bringing the bishop-elect of Durham, Louis de Beaumont, for consecration and enthronement in his cathedral. Accompanying Beaumont and his brother Henry were two cardinals, Gaucelme de Jean and Luca Fieschi: their presence made the outrage all the more appalling. The Beaumonts were led off to captivity in Mitford castle: the cardinals were allowed to proceed to Durham, but most of their possessions were seized from them. Such armed interference in the affairs of the church was startling. It was the most serious attack on papal envoys to take place in medieval England, and while it may not compare in gravity with, say, Frederick II's treatment of the cardinals and other clerics after their capture at sea in 1241, Middleton's attack deserves re-examination.

The incident has been frequently discussed: there were such complex cross-currents involved in it that it can bear very different interpretations.[1] The various strands need to be disentangled carefully if the robbery is to be understood in its full context. Was this an isolated incident, or was it

---

[1] The fullest analysis remains that by A.E. Middleton, *Sir Gilbert de Middleton and the Part he Took in the Rebellion in the North of England in 1317* (Newcastle-upon-Tyne, 1918). There is a useful account in *Northumberland County History*, ed. H.H.E. Craster (Newcastle and London, 1909), vol. 9, pp. 106–12.

inspired by the earl of Lancaster's hostility to the crown? The question of the relationship of the attack to the Scottish wars needs to be discussed: was it a gesture born of disenchantment at government failure to deal with Scottish invasions, or was it undertaken with the active assistance of the Scots? The role of the church can also be interpreted in various ways.

The disputed election to the see of Durham created rivalries which may have contributed to Middleton's action. The previous bishop, Richard Kellaw, himself a Durham monk, had been elected to the see in 1311 by the chapter. On his death in October 1316, powerful pressures were brought to bear to influence the new election, for this was a most important see, of great strategic significance in the Anglo-Scottish conflict. According to Robert Greystanes, the Durham chronicler, the earl of Lancaster pressed the case of his clerk John Kinnersley, who he promised would provide an effective defence against the Scots. The king put forward the case of the keeper of the privy seal, Thomas Charlton, but the queen then interceded, asking that the bishopric should go to her relation Louis de Beaumont. The earl of Hereford pressed the case of John Walwyn, his clerk. The monks stood out and selected Henry de Stanford, prior of Finchale, an elderly man, who, argued Greystanes, in contrast to the other candidates led a proper life and was sufficiently well lettered. The chronicler suggested that had it not been for Isabella's intervention, Edward would have accepted Stanford as bishop. As it was, Edward wrote to the pope, asking for Louis de Beaumont to be appointed to the see. Henry de Stanford and three of the monks set out to put their case at the papal curia, but they were too late. John XXII had already provided to the see Louis de Beaumont, a man who, it was to be claimed, did not even know Latin.[2]

Any of the disappointed parties could have had a hand in organising the attack on Louis de Beaumont and the party escorting him to Durham, but it has been argued that Lancaster in particular was incensed at the rejection of his candidate, and angered at the selection of Louis, whose brother Henry de Beaumont and sister Isabella de Vescy were court

---

[2] *Historiae Dunelmensis Scriptores Tres*, ed. J. Raine (Surtees Society 9, Durham, 1839), pp. 98–99, 118. K. Edwards, 'Bishops and Learning in the Reign of Edward II', *Church Quarterly Review* 138 (1944), pp. 62–64, doubts Beaumont's alleged illiteracy. It should be noted that the *Vita Edwardi Secundi*, ed. N. Denholm-Young (London, 1957), makes no reference to Walwyn's candidature, a fact which weakens the argument that he was in fact the author of this chronicle. This was not the only case where the king and queen disagreed in this way: they backed rival candidates at Rochester, where the king's candidate, Hamo de Hethe, was successful after appeals to the papal Curia.

favourites whose exile had been demanded by the Ordainers in 1311.[3] It is, however, difficult to see what the attack could have been expected to achieve if this was why it took place. Capturing Louis de Beaumont and his brother and leading them off to Mitford castle would not persuade the pope to reverse his decision. By 1 September 1317 it was too late to do anything about the election: in this context, the attack could have been no more than an unintelligent act of pique.

Another possible motive for the attack was the desire of Robert de Sapy, keeper of the temporalities during the vacancy, to hold on to his office for as long as possible. Sapy's appointment on 20 November 1316 had been a temporary one: Henry de Beaumont, Louis' brother, was granted 'superior custody' of the temporalities, but Sapy was to receive the revenues of the bishopric until a new appointment of a receiver was made.[4] In fact no such appointment took place, and Sapy was anxious to continue in office at least until the revenues of the see were paid in at Michaelmas. This is strongly suggested by a well-known indenture preserved in the muniments at Durham. It was made on 25 April 1317 between Sapy, and John de Eure, then keeper of Mitford castle, a knight with property in Yorkshire and Northumberland. It provided that if Beaumont was consecrated, or received the temporalities of the bishopric, before Michaelmas, then Eure would pay Sapy the value of all the costs of running the episcopal estates between the date of the agreement and Michaelmas. If Eure refused, then a sum of a hundred marks was to be levied from him, in accordance with a bond placed in the custody of the prior of Durham.[5] The intention was not, it seems, to prevent Beaumont's installation altogether, but that Eure should find a means of delaying it until after Michaelmas. This might seem to provide a good explanation for the attack and robbery, but by 1 September circumstances had changed since the indenture was drafted. A writ delivering the temporalities of the bishopric to Louis de Beaumont was issued on 4 May 1317.[6] Once that was done, Robert de Sapy had no real interest in delaying the installation.

The pipe roll account for the vacancy shows that Sapy accounted for the period from 10 October 1316 to 4 May 1317. It reveals the very considerable sums of money involved. The total receipts for the seven-

[3] J.R. Maddicott, *Thomas of Lancaster 1307–1322* (Oxford, 1970), pp. 204–7.

[4] *Calendar of Patent Rolls, 1313–17* (London, 1898), p. 563.

[5] Durham, Dean and Chapter muniments, MC 4238, MC 4022; Middleton, *Middleton*, pp. 25–26, provides a translation of the indenture.

[6] *Calendar of Patent Rolls, 1313–17*, p. 664.

181

month period of Sapy's tenure of office came to £2,146 19s. ½d., while expenses totalled only £66 9s. In addition, however, Sapy was allowed 200 marks for his personal expenses, far more than normal, because of the condition of the north, affected as it was both by Scottish raids and by the severe famine of the period. He had, it was stated in the account, spent much because he could not see to the custody of the bishopric without a force of men-at-arms. An additional worry was perhaps the sum of £138 12s. 4d. which Sapy spent on sowing 486 acres with wheat, on which he would naturally want to see a return. In the event, this sum was charged to Beaumont.[7]

Robert de Sapy, therefore, may well have prompted the idea for the assault, but by the time that it took place he no longer had the direct interest in Durham that had led him to make the arrangement with Eure. Is it possible that a further motive was provided by the presence of the cardinals in the party? According to Greystanes' account, the attack was directed at the Beaumonts, not at the cardinals. Louis and Henry de Beaumont were taken captive and led off to Mitford, while the cardinals were allowed to proceed to Durham. The author of the *Vita Edwardi Secundi*, on the other hand, interpreted the attack solely in terms of the robbery of the cardinals.[8]

The two cardinals had been sent to England with a wide ranging brief. Both men were already closely connected with the court: Luca Fieschi was addressed by both Edward II and his father as *consanguineus*, and was granted pensions. Gaucelme de Jean had been a member of the council in Gascony in 1313, and was both king's clerk and royal pensioner. One reason for the possible unpopularity of the cardinals was the growth in papal provisions at this period. Pope John XXII, in a letter to the two men, set out a strong defence of papal authority, stressing the papacy's right to make provisions to church benefices. Clement V had already extended papal claims in the bull *Etsi in temporalium* of 1305, providing a very general list of the types of benefice involved.[9]

The Durham election itself provided an example of the operation of the system of papal provision; during Edward's reign the papacy used

---

[7] E 372/164 (unless otherwise stated all references to manuscripts are to documents in the Public Record Office, London). Beaumont was much later to request pardon for the amount due for the sowing of the episcopal lands: *Ancient Petitions relating to Northumberland*, ed. C.M. Fraser (Surtees Society 176, Durham, 1961), pp. 153–54.

[8] *Historiae Dunelmensis Tres*, p. 100; *Vita Edwardi Secundi*, pp. 82–83.

[9] J.R. Wright, *The Church and the English Crown, 1305–1334* (Toronto, 1980), pp. 8–11, 293–94.

its right to nominate candidates in addition to the sees of Canterbury, Hereford, Coventry and Lichfield, Norwich, Winchester and Worcester. Beaumont's nomination to Durham forms part of a more general pattern. The heavy procurations, set at the rate of 4*d*. in the mark, levied by the cardinals, were another cause of their unpopularity.[10] Yet although many might have welcomed an assault on the representatives of a papacy whose interventions in the affairs of the English church were seen as increasingly aggressive, there is no evidence that this was in fact a motive for the attack at Rushyford.

Possibly more relevant was the role of the cardinals in the Anglo-Scottish conflict. John XXII was anxious to bring this war to an end, or at the least to impose a truce, and the cardinals were fully empowered to issue excommunications against Robert Bruce and the Scots in support of this aim.[11] There was no question of the cardinals mediating between the two countries: their support for the English position was abundantly clear. The two men were intending to go on northwards, after Beaumont's installation at Durham, to try to compel Bruce to cease his struggle. Bruce's decision, given to messengers, was not to meet the cardinals while they refused to write to him as king, until he had had the opportunity to discuss the matter in detail with his full council and his barons.[12] It is conceivable that Bruce decided to try to block the northwards progress of the cardinals and, if so, it could have made sense for him to have made use of Gilbert de Middleton, so as to prevent any direct criticism of himself or his compatriots. Some evidence points to Scottish involvement with Middleton. The official indictment states that he had Scots with him, and the chronicle of Meaux Abbey even charged him with promising them land in the marches.[13] It was not until the 1340s, however, that mention was made of the involvement of the earl of Moray and James Douglas in the affair. This came in an allegation against Walter of Selby by Thomas Surtays and his wife. Selby had brought an action of novel disseisin

---

[10] W.E. Lunt, *Financial Relations of the Papacy with England to 1327* (Cambridge, Mass., 1939), pp. 564–67.

[11] Ibid., p. 201; *Foedera, conventiones, litterae et cujuscunque generis acta publica . . .*, ed. T. Rymer (London, 1818) vol. 2, part 1, pp. 317–18, 327–28. See also 'Gesta Edwardi de Carnarvan', in *Chronicles of the Reigns of Edward I and Edward II*, ed. W. Stubbs (Rolls Series, London, 1882–83), vol. 2, pp. 52–53.

[12] *The Acts of Robert I King of Scots, 1306–1329*, ed. A.A.M. Duncan (Regesta Regum Scottorum 5, Edinburgh, 1989), pp. 141–42.

[13] *Chronica Monasterii de Melsa*, ed. E.A. Bond (Rolls Series, London, 1867), vol. 2, p. 333.

against them, and this was their counter-accusation: in the absence of supporting evidence, such biased testimony is clearly not to be trusted.[14] Selby certainly did join the Scots at about the time of the Rushyford attack: his Durham lands were later confiscated by the bishop because he was 'of the fealty of Robert Bruce in Scotland, where he stayed as an enemy'.[15] What seems most probable is that Selby turned to the Scots in the aftermath of Middleton's rebellion.

Plausible as is the hypothesis that Middleton was acting in collusion with the Scots, the evidence to support it lacks solidity. Scottish involvement in the robbery was not mentioned by Greystanes, whose account is the fullest. The pattern of Scottish incursions into northern England does not mesh easily with Middleton's activities. The English defeat at Bannockburn in 1314 was inevitably followed by an increase in Scottish raids. These were so frequent that it is not always possible to reconstruct a clear chronology.[16] It does not seem, however, that the Scots invaded in 1317 on a scale to have enabled them to take a significant part in Middleton's activities.

There was a major raid into County Durham in the summer of 1315, when the prior, Geoffrey Burdon, was surprised by the Scots under Douglas and Moray when he was staying at his manor of Bearpark.[17] A two-year truce was then purchased by the community of the county; in the next year the Scots probably travelled through Durham when they invaded Yorkshire.[18] There is no evidence of a major Scottish raid in the Durham region in 1317, and none to support the late story of Moray and Douglas's presence at Rushyford. The local community paid the Scots large sums to stay away: 1,000 marks was promised for a truce agreed in September, and surviving receipts reveal payment of £659 in November and December alone.[19] At, or soon after, the time of the robbery of the cardinals, the Scots were engaged in an unsuccessful siege of Berwick:

[14] *Calendar of Close Rolls, 1341–43* (London, 1902), p. 98.

[15] *Calendar of Documents relating to Scotland*, ed. J. Bain (Edinburgh, 1887), vol. 3, no. 1335; *Northern Petitions*, ed. C.M. Fraser (Surtees Society 194, Durham, 1981), p. 249.

[16] C. McNamee, 'The Effects of the Scottish Wars on Northern England, 1296–1328' (Oxford D.Phil thesis, 1988), pp. 71–85, provides a very useful and important analysis of the raids of this period.

[17] *Historiae Dunelmensis Tres*, p. 96.

[18] *Chronica Monasterii de Melsa*, vol. 2, p. 333.

[19] J. Scammell, 'Robert I and the North of England', *EHR* 73 (1958), pp. 393, 401; Middleton, *Middleton*, p. 49. Middleton did not note that Durham Dean and Chapter Muniments, MC 4022, mentioned payment of £47 as well as 800 marks.

on 1 October John de Wysham was sent from York with ten men to relieve the town.[20] It was in the next two years that major incursions into the north of England took place, notably with the raid that culminated in the battle of Myton in 1319.

Even if the Scots did not invade in large numbers in 1317, by the time of Gilbert de Middleton's action there must have been a sense of acute frustration at the failure of Edward II's government to take effective steps to deal with the Scottish raids. Much damage had been done, notably in Northumberland, and the only remedy that seemed effective was to pay off the Scots. Thomas de Grey, in his *Scalacronica*, set Gilbert de Middleton's rebellion in this context. It resulted, he stated, from the arrest of Gilbert's cousin, Adam Swinburne, who had spoken harshly to the king about the state of the northern marches.[21] The story does not fully meet the facts, for Swinburne was not closely related to Middleton, but on the other hand he was indeed arrested, and held in custody in Nottingham from 9 August until 25 October 1317. He had been serving under contract with a force of eighty cavalry, defending Northumberland against the Scots and had also been commissioned to negotiate with Robert Bruce. It is very likely that a man in his position might have made the kind of criticism which Thomas Grey credited him with. He was, interestingly, appointed together with John de Eure early in 1317 to hear a complaint regarding the release of Scots who had been taken prisoner.[22]

It has been suggested that Middleton's action provides an early parallel to Andrew Harcla's decision to come to terms with the Scots in 1323.[23] There is no evidence, however, to show that Middleton saw peace with the Scots as the solution to the problems of the north. Unlike Walter of Selby, he did not take refuge with the Scots. It was Walter de Selby who changed sides in the war and was therefore more of a traitor than Middleton ever was.

The earl of Lancaster, who was undoubtedly responsible for much of the disorder which characterised Edward II's reign, has inevitably been seen as the *eminence grise* behind Gilbert de Middleton's activities. No direct link existed between Gilbert and the earl, but the involvement of

---

[20] *The Acts of Robert I*, p. 142; London, Society of Antiquaries, MS 121, f. 19.

[21] *Scalacronica*, ed. J. Stevenson (Maitland Club, Edinburgh, 1836), p. 144.

[22] Middleton, *Middleton*, pp. 36, 78–79; London, Society of Antiquaries, MS 121, f. 12v.; *Calendar of Patent Rolls, 1313–17*, p. 687.

[23] J.A. Tuck, 'Northumbrian Society in the Fourteenth Century', *Northern History* 6 (1971), p. 31.

John de Eure, John Lilburn and John de Lasceles with Middleton has been seen as indicating that Lancaster provided the inspiration for the Rushyford robbery. Yet John de Eure became a retainer of Lancaster's only on 29 December 1317, in the aftermath of the affair. John Lilburn received a pardon in 1318 as a follower of Lancaster but does not appear to have been associated with him before the autumn of 1317, when he and his men seized Knaresborough and claimed that this was done in the earl's name. He was to fight against Lancaster at Boroughbridge. John de Lasceles is not known to have been in Lancaster's service before he was appointed constable of Conisborough castle early in 1318. Adam de Swinburne was handed over to Lancaster when he was released from custody in October 1317, but he was not an associate of the earl and was probably no more than part of the earl's attempt to pacify the situation.[24]

If long-standing retainers of the earl had been involved in the attack at Rushyford, there would be good grounds for accusing him of complicity. There is, however, no evidence to connect any of those involved in the attack with Lancaster prior to the event: that attempts should have been made later to try to link the earl with the outrage was hardly surprising and should not be given much credence. In 1318, 188 of Lancaster's followers received pardons for all offences save for the robbery of the cardinals, but it is not evident that these men were members of the earl's following at the time of the attack, nor does this list include any of Lancaster's major retainers. The pardons certainly cannot be taken as evidence that the attack was instigated by the earl.[25] Had Lancaster been behind the attack, it is surely likely that he would have made use of his main supporter in County Durham, Richard FitzMarmaduke, steward of the late bishop, and his followers, rather than recruit men linked to the king's own household.[26]

More convincing connections between some of those involved in the robbery lie in their membership of the royal household. Although it has been noted that Gilbert de Middleton was a household knight – this was made clear in the indictment against him – the full extent of household involvement in the affair of the attack on the Beaumonts and the cardinals

[24] Maddicott, *Thomas of Lancaster*, pp. 41, 205–7; *Calendar of Patent Rolls, 1317–21* (London, 1903), p. 231; *Calendar of Close Rolls, 1313–18* (London, 1893), p. 575; *Calendar of Inquisitions Miscellaneous* (London, 1916), vol. 2, p. 131.

[25] *Calendar of Patent Rolls, 1317–21*, pp. 233–35.

[26] For FitzMarmaduke, see H.S. Offler, 'Murder on Framwellgate Bridge', *Archaeologia Aeliana*, fifth series 16 (1988), pp. 193–211.

has not been set out.[27] Gilbert de Middleton himself was the grandson of Richard de Middleton, chancellor at the end of Henry III's reign. His father, Gilbert, a younger son, went on crusade with the future Edward I in 1270. He acquired lands in Northumberland by inheritance and by marriage, worth some £20 a year. He died in 1291; wardship of his son Gilbert was granted to William de Felton, at the time a royal squire, and later to become a household knight.[28] It was scarcely surprising that a man with such a background, of no great landed wealth, but strong connections with the court, should himself find a career in the royal household. The first reference to him in this context is when he was accused in 1313 of refusing to account to the officials at Berwick for livestock which he and others seized; he was described as being of the king's household and livery.[29] His household career seems to have been somewhat peripheral: he appears only on one list, that for Christmas 1315, as a household knight. There is no doubt, however, that at the time of the robbery he was in receipt of royal fees and robes. The same list also includes John Lilburn, who had been constable of Mitford in 1316, and who took part alongside Middleton in the attack on the cardinals.[30] Robert de Sapy was also a household knight, appearing on the lists in the wardrobe books for 1316–18, and for 1322–23; his brother John had been admitted to the household earlier, in 1310.[31] John de Eure was not retained as a household knight, but he was retained by the crown to hold Mitford castle, between 15 November 1316 and 24 June 1317, and was therefore a temporary member of the royal military establishment.[32]

---

[27] Tout, curiously, had not noted Gilbert de Middleton's presence in the household until he read Middleton's book: he wrote to Middleton, 'That Gilbert was *valettus regis* had quite escaped my notice, and the fact interests me a good deal, as he was one of the few instances of a household servant of those days who got tired of his master and ended by taking the law into his own hands.' (Copy of letter from Tout to A.E. Middleton, pasted into the Durham University Library copy of Middleton's book).

[28] Middleton, *Middleton*, pp. 1–3.

[29] C47/22/10/11, cited by Middleton, *Middleton*, p. 10, and briefly calendared in *Calendar of Documents Relating to Scotland*, vol. 3, no. 337.

[30] E 101/377/1, noted by Middleton, *Middleton*, p. 13; *Calendar of Patent Rolls, 1313–1317* (London, 1898), 396. Middleton's absence from the lists of household knights in receipt in fees and robes is perhaps to be explained by the fact that by the time the relevant wardrobe account books were written up, no payments were due to him as he had been executed for treason.

[31] London, Society of Antiquaries, MS 120, ff. 59, 61; MS 121, ff. 37, 38v.; London, British Library, MS Stowe 553, f. 65; MS Cotton Nero C. VIII, f. 90v.

[32] London, Society of Antiquaries, MS 120, f. 45.

Adam de Swinburne was an important figure in the household, a banneret
who had been admitted as a knight in 1311.[33] His friends in the household
are likely to have been those from his own part of the country, and his
arrest is very likely to have spurred Middleton, Eure, Lilburn and others
to take action against the Beaumonts. The fact that no charges were later
brought against Swinburne proves nothing: as he was in custody, there
was no way in which he could have been involved in the outrage. John
de Sapy, equally, was likely to have tried to use his connection in the
household as well as locally to try to extend his profitable tenure of the
temporalities of the bishopric.

It may seem surprising that such a lawless act as the robbery of the cardinals could have been inspired by household knights of the king. Yet this
was not a unique case. The best known example of a ruffian in the king's
service is perhaps that of Robert Lewer, a man-at-arms whose expulsion
was demanded by the Ordainers in 1311, but who received the custody
of Odiham castle. He was arrested in 1320 for trespass and contempt and
retaliated by threatening to cut up those responsible limb by limb. He was
restored to favour in 1321, but rebelled against the Despensers in 1323,
suffering an unpleasant death by *peine forte et dure*.[34] Jack the Irishman
was notorious for his exploits in the north, such as the rape and abduction
of Lady Clifford: he was employed as a valet of the king's chamber. Roger
Swinnerton, admitted to the household as a knight in 1317, was a notorious criminal. John and Philip de la Beche rebelled against the king in
1322, and Nicholas de la Beche was arrested in 1323.[35] Edmund Darel was
accused by the author of the *Flores Historiarum* of attempting to betray
Queen Isabella to the Scots in 1318: he had been admitted as a household
knight in November 1315.[36] The atmosphere in the household at a lower
level was indicated by the well-known case of the messenger who slan-
dered the king, revealing that he spent his time digging and ditching.[37]

[33] London, British Library, MS Cotton Nero C. VIII, f. 91.
[34] *Chronicles of the Reigns of Edward I and II*, vol. 1, p. 199; *Calendar of Close Rolls, 1318–23* (London, 1895), p. 260; *Vita Edwardi Secundi*, pp. 127–29; H.R.T. Summerson, 'The Early Development of Peine Forte et Dure', *Law, Litigants and the Legal Profession*, ed. E.W. Ives and A.H. Manchester (London, 1983), pp. 116–25.
[35] M.C. Prestwich, *The Three Edwards: War and State in England, 1272–1377* (London, 1980), pp. 75, 103; *Northern Petitions*, pp. 26–27; London, Society of Antiquaries, MS 120, f. 17v.
[36] *Flores Historiarum*, ed. H.R. Luard (Rolls Series, London, 1890), vol. 3, pp. 188–89; E 101/376/7.
[37] H. Johnstone, 'The Eccentricities of Edward II', *EHR* 48 (1933), pp. 264–67.

In the aftermath of the attack the two Beaumonts were taken to Mitford castle. One account has it that Middleton had seized the castle by means of a ruse, but it is possible that he had been appointed its custodian. The cardinals were released and proceeded to Durham. The sheriff of York, ironically accompanied by Robert de Sapy, took them twelve horses to replace those stolen at Rushyford. A week after the outrage had taken place, the earl of Lancaster arrived at Durham to escort the cardinals south. Middleton himself also came to Durham, and the two men met in the cathedral. Presumably as a result of their conversation, some goods were restored to the cardinals, though the Beaumonts were not yet released.[38] Lancaster's role looks like that of a mediator rather than of an instigator of the robbery. If, however, he tried to persuade Middleton to abandon what was turning into a rebellion, he failed. It was probably not until mid October that the Beaumonts were released, after ransoms had been paid and hostages handed over. Middleton and his men extended their lawless activities. Surviving receipts show that Middleton began to take what amounted to protection money from the Durham community. One testifies to his receipt of 200 marks on 12 October 1317 from William de Denum, to ensure 'that no evil or damage should come from me, my men, or by anyone else according to my power'. A second, dated 14 December 1317, shows that Gilbert received 250 marks in part payment of what he described as a fine of 500 marks imposed because of certain transgressions against him.[39] He was, no doubt, imitating Robert Bruce in levying money in this way.

Middleton and his men also used force directly. They attempted to seize the fortified monastery at Tynemouth, but were repulsed by Robert Delaval.[40] In another action Gilbert's brother John captured John de Felton, constable of Alnwick castle. He was released, leaving three hostages, when he promised to hand over Alnwick by a set date.[41] Some of Middleton's associates took action on their own behalf. In October 1317 John Lilburn seized Knaresborough castle. Though this was said to be in Lancaster's name, the inquisition into Lilburn's occupation of the castle made no mention of Lancaster's role in the affair.[42] Walter de Selby seized the peel at Horton in Northumberland, where he held out for some time,

---

[38] London, Society of Antiquaries, MS 121, f. 7; *Historiae Dunelmensis Tres*, p. 101.

[39] Durham, Dean and Chapter muniments, MC 4049, 5033.

[40] *Ancient Petitions Relating to Northumberland*, p. 148.

[41] Middleton, *Middleton*, p. 51.

[42] Maddicott, *Thomas of Lancaster*, pp. 207–8; *Calendar of Close Rolls, 1313–18* (as n. 24), p. 575; *Calendar of Inquisitions Miscellaneous* (as n. 24), vol. 2, no. 392.

subsequently joining the Scots.[43] Jocelin d'Eyville was another involved in what must have increasingly appeared to be a major rising. He ravaged some of the Durham estates with a troop of men disguised as lay brothers from Rievaulx and seized the peel in Northallerton.[44] The capture of Aydon in Northumberland in December 1317 was part of a private feud, but may well have been inspired by, and connected to, the other attacks on castles at this time.[45] The seizure in October 1317 of the manor at Haslewood, Yorkshire, which belonged to a royal squire, may have been a further copy-cat offence.[46]

The rising was uncoordinated, and there is no indication that those participating in it had any clear programme. It did not prove hard to put down. Gilbert de Middleton himself was captured in December 1317 at Mitford castle. Prime responsibility was claimed by William de Felton and Thomas de Heton. Felton was no doubt incensed by the treatment his relation John de Felton had received from the Middletons. It may well be that there was a family feud resulting from Gilbert de Middleton's having been a ward of William de Felton's father.[47] The others involved in the rising remained longer at liberty than Middleton. On 8 January 1318 the earl of Angus, Robert de Umfraville, was commissioned with others to receive rebels in Northumberland and neighbouring parts into the king's peace. By April the disturbances were largely over.[48]

The two cardinals were, hardly surprisingly, furious at the way they had been treated by Gilbert de Middleton and his associates. They are said to have demanded in recompense a riding horse, or a load of wheat worth £10, from every cathedral church.[49] According to the *Vita Edwardi Secundi*, they suspended part of their mission, until they could obtain proper satisfaction in parliament. Meanwhile they launched excommunications against Middleton and his accomplices.[50]

The excommunications had some effect: in September 1318 sixty-two of those involved received licences to go to the papal curia, in effect on pilgrimage.[51] Royal gifts, totalling about £346 to Luca de Fieschi, and

---

43 Middleton, *Middleton*, pp. 63–66.

44 Offler, 'Murder on Framwellgate Bridge', p. 193; Middleton, *Middleton*, p. 73.

45 Ibid., pp. 70–74.

46 *Calendar of Patent Rolls, 1317–21* (as n. 24), pp. 287, 308.

47 Middleton, *Middleton*, pp. 3, 51.

48 Ibid., pp. 63–65; *Calendar of Patent Rolls, 1317–21* (as n. 24), pp. 71, 141.

49 *Chronica Monasterii de Melsa*, vol. 3, p. 334.

50 *Vita Edwardi Secundi*, p. 83.

51 *Calendar of Patent Rolls, 1317–21* (as n. 24), pp. 211–12.

about £360 to Gaucelme de Jean, may have helped somewhat to calm their fury.[52] On 27 November the cardinals published the papal truce in London: an attempt to do the same in Scotland, undertaken by a foolhardy friar, met with little success. The peace mission foundered on Scottish resistance: it may, indeed, have been counter-productive and have spurred Bruce on to the capture of Berwick.[53] It was presumably at the insistence of the cardinals that pardons issued by Edward II explicitly did not extend to the attack at Rushyford: thus when John de Lilburn received a pardon in March 1318, this was in return for his surrendering Knaresborough castle; the robbery from the cardinals was carefully excepted, 'if he shall be found guilty thereof'.[54]

The fact that Gilbert de Middleton was a household knight helps to explain why he took the action he did. It also helps to explain his final end: the fact that he had accepted the king's fees and robes made his actions all the more treasonable. After his capture, he was taken to London and tried. He was then hanged, drawn and quartered, suffering the full penalties for treason. The scale of the penalties had increased since the treason execution of the household knight Thomas Turberville in 1295: he had merely been dragged to the gallows on an ox hide, and hanged.[55] Similar treatment to Middleton's had, of course, been accorded to various Scots in the last years of Edward I's reign: among them, Simon Fraser and Herbert de Morham, both former royal household knights.[56] The technique used in the trial was that of conviction on the king's record, the method used by Edward I in 1306 when those taken at the battle of Methven were tried. The accusation stressed Middleton's status as a household knight in receipt of fees and robes, as well as the fact that he had ridden in warlike fashion with banners unfurled when he had ambushed the Beaumonts and the cardinals.[57]

After Middleton's death there were considerable arguments about the goods taken when he was captured. Felton and Heton argued that these

---

[52] London, Society of Antiquaries, MS 121, f. 33v.

[53] *Acts of Robert I*, p. 143.

[54] *Calendar of Patent Rolls, 1317–21* (as n. 24), p. 123.

[55] J.G. Edwards, 'The Treason of Thomas Turberville, 1295', *Studies in Medieval History Presented to F.M. Powicke*, ed. R.W. Hunt, W.A. Pantin, R.W. Southern (Oxford, 1948), pp. 296–309.

[56] M.C. Prestwich, *Edward I* (London, 1988), p. 508.

[57] J.G. Bellamy, *The Law of Treason in England in the Middle Ages* (Cambridge, 1970), pp. 46–49; *Select Cases in the Court of King's Bench under Edward II*, ed. G.O. Sayles (Selden Society, 74, 1957) vol. 4, p. 78.

totalled in value a mere 9 marks to each of them, and that they had divided them equally. A very different story was produced by a jury empanelled by the sheriff of Northumberland in 1319. In this it was claimed that Middleton had £1020 in cash and silver in Mitford castle, along with jewels to a value of £1000. There were two war-horses, valued at £70 each, substantial quantities of foodstuffs, five furred robes and four pieces of cloth. All of this, it was claimed, was taken by Felton and Heton. In addition, Gilbert had placed foodstuffs in Newminster Abbey. Other property was shared out: Richard de Huntercombe, for example, had beds, robes, arms and money worth in all £100. The total valuation came to £2840.[58] Felton and Heton claimed that the jury had been packed with Middleton's adherents. The truth of the matter is impossible to determine, but it is likely that Gilbert had accumulated very appreciable sums of money and quantities of treasure as a result of his activities. What is clear is that his captors were not substantially rewarded by the crown. In 1328 Heton was still petitioning for payment of arrears of the pension of 50 marks granted to him by Edward II. Neither Stapledon nor Melton as treasurers had, he argued, been prepared to accept royal writs relating to this matter, or to pay him a penny. This was symptomatic of the miserliness which was one aspect of the careful exchequer housekeeping of the 1320s. Not until 1330 was the exchequer ordered to issue Heton with a tally for the arrears owed to him.[59]

It is striking that Middleton, and his brother John, were the only men involved in the attack on the Beaumonts and the cardinals to suffer the penalties for treason of hanging, drawing and quartering. The only other man who suffered death was John de Cleseby, who refused to plead and died as a result of the horrors of *peine forte et dure.*[60] Walter of Selby, who was so clearly in league with the Scots and more obviously guilty of treason than Middleton, merely suffered imprisonment. He probably did not surrender until 1321, when he gave himself up to the earl of Angus, Ralph de Greystoke and John de Eure. They promised to obtain an amnesty for him from the king: he was in fact imprisoned in the Tower of London, but not executed. He was pardoned by Edward III in 1327,

[58] E 368/89, m. 172; E 159/97, m. 50d.

[59] M. Buck, *Politics, Finance and the Church in the Reign of Edward II* (Cambridge, 1983), 178–79; *Calendar of Patent Rolls, 1317–21* (as n. 24), p. 75; *Ancient Petitions relating to Northumberland*, p. 151; SC 8/337/15922–7.

[60] Middleton, *Middleton*, p. 101; *Chronicles of the Reigns of Edward I and II*, vol. 1, pp. 281–82; *Chronicon de Lanercost*, ed. J. Stevenson (Maitland Club, Edinburgh, 1839), p. 234.

only eventually to suffer execution as a traitor at the hands of the Scots in 1346.[61]

A commission was set up a month after the robbery took place to arrest John de Eure. The writ put the incident in the wrong place, at Acle in Northumberland, a clear error for Aycliffe in Durham (Aycliffe is close to Rushyford). No arrest took place, and Eure was evidently able to clear his name, obtaining Lancaster's backing by becoming his retainer.[62] Roger Mauduit, who had been with Walter of Selby at Horton and had probably been present at Rushyford, received a royal pardon in May 1318.[63] John Lilburn was pardoned for his deeds at Knaresborough in March 1318, with an exception made for the robbery of the cardinals.[64]

Most remarkably, it was not until 1358 that a major attempt was made to exact penalties for treason from the full range of those who had supported Gilbert de Middleton. In that year the escheator for the northern counties, William de Nessfield, began a process of seizure of the lands of alleged traitors and their descendants. It is questionable as to whether much credence should be given to these charges. The most outrageous case was that of six Yorkshire families whose lands were seized and then granted by Edward III to Nessfield in return for £200. Members of these families had, it was claimed, been adherents of Simon de Montfort, John Comyn of Badenoch, Andrew Harcla, John de Lilburn, Gilbert de Middleton, Jocelin d'Eyville, the Scots and other enemies of kings from Henry III to the present.[65] In many cases those accused by Nessfield were able to repurchase their lands in return for a fine. In the case of John de Eure, son of the man who made the indenture with Robert de Sapy, this was a substantial £400, but in other instances the sums involved were small.[66] Nessfield's extraordinary campaign demonstrates that, in one region at least, Edward III's reign was not characterised by

[61] Middleton, *Middleton*, pp. 65–66; *Ancient Petitions relating to Northumberland*, p. 150; M.H. Keen, *The Laws of War* (London, 1965), pp. 45–48, is incorrect in thinking that the Scots executed Selby for treachery towards the English: they were recalling his abandonment of their cause in Edward II's reign.

[62] Maddicott, *Thomas of Lancaster*, p. 41. Middleton's suggestion (*Middleton*, p. 34) that the mistake in the writ was deliberate, designed to provide Eure with an alibi, seems far-fetched.

[63] *Calendar of Patent Rolls, 1317–21* (as n. 24), p. 141.

[64] Ibid., p. 123.

[65] *Calendar of Patent Rolls, 1358–61* (London, 1911), pp. 288–89.

[66] Ibid., p. 361. Middleton, *Middleton*, pp. 86–105, provides a convenient tabulation of those alleged to have been involved in Middleton's rebellion.

the reconciliation of the quarrels of his father's reign with which it is often credited.

It is tempting to read too much into Gilbert de Middleton's ambush of the Beaumonts and the cardinals at Rushyford. The evidence for the involvement of the earl of Lancaster and the Scots is not convincing and there is no case for seeing the incident as indicative of the unpopularity of the two papal envoys. Yet it should not be dismissed as no more than an act of brigandage by an obscure north-country knight, one example among many of lawlessness in early fourteenth-century England. In a different context the author of the *Vita Edwardi Secundi* wrote that 'the whole evil originally proceeds from the court'.[67] The Rushyford robbery was in part the result of the confused and lawless state of the north of England, ravaged by Scottish raids and afflicted by poor harvests followed by famine. It also had its roots in the disaffection of a group of northern knights in the king's service. The atmosphere in Edward's household was embittered and overheated, and the events at Rushyford illustrate the consequences of factional disputes in an unhappy court.

[67] *Vita Edwardi Secundi*, p. 74.

12

Administrative Buildings and Prisons in the Earldom of Cornwall

Andrew Saunders

The administration of justice, the collection and accounting of the king's revenues, and the development of estate management in English medieval baronial households or honours, great and small, has received much attention from historians.[1] Such organisation required a range of officials with specific responsibilities and these bureaucracies tended to grow. While the details of administrative practice and the careers of some of the officials have been studied, the buildings within castles or great houses where these activities took place have been given less attention. To Jolliffe: 'It is probable that many royal residences had only one chamber designed and equipped for writing and living.' 'It would almost seem that any apartment where he may be in privacy, away from public access, becomes *camera regis*, whether in one of his own palaces, or in the house of a friend.'[2]

The authors of *The History of the King's Works* have, however, shown how the physical structures necessary for a permanent administrative

[1] T.F. Tout, *Chapters in Medieval Administrative History* (Manchester, 1933); N. Denholm-Young, *Seignorial Administration in England* (Oxford, 1937). – I am most grateful to Professor Norman Pounds and Dr. Robert Higham for their very helpful comments on an earlier draft and to Amanda Patton for her work on the illustrations.

[2] J.E.A. Jolliffe, 'The *Camera Regis* under Henry II', *EHR* 58 (1953), pp. 1, 337.

base for the king grew up at Westminster early in the twelfth century around the ceremonial centre of the Great Hall, and that the Exchequer was the first department of state to detach itself from the itinerant court with its own building.[3] This was the first purely administrative building to be built at Westminster. The development of courts of justice could more easily take place in the Great Hall, and any arrangement of benches and tables removed for its occasional ceremonial use. For other royal castles and houses, the position was summed up as follows: 'Within the walls stood those various buildings which were necessary for the castle's military, domestic and administrative functions. These are the 'houses in the castle (*domus Regis in castello*)' to which the records so constantly refer.[4] Similar arrangements may be expected in the castles of the baronage, albeit on a lesser scale, and by the end of the thirteenth century private administration was at its height.[5] The assumption has been fostered that most business was carried on in the hall, occasionally in the chapel, and indeed the multi-purpose nature of the medieval hall lives on in the various uses to which Oxford and Cambridge halls are still applied. 'Halls provided the centre both of social life and administrative activity.'[6] Other parts of the complex, such as towers, could provide for that familiar and frequent use of castles as prisons, extending the dual military and domestic function of a castle still wider.

The holding of courts, the receipt of fines and rents, the auditing of officials' returns, as well as the holding of felons awaiting trial, debtors, sureties for breach of forest law and the like, seem to have been accommodated in castles as a matter of course and must imply the provision of special buildings. This was particularly so for the sheriffs, who acted as the king's agents for revenue collection in the counties and presided over the shire courts and its hundreds in both civil and criminal matters. By the thirteenth century, the sheriff's various duties involved much 'paperwork', and his court was one of record requiring the maintenance of an archive. All this implied 'a permanent, efficient and fairly numerous clerical staff at the sheriff's office, the standard of whose work did not fall below that of the central government'.[7]

[3] R. Allen Brown, H.M. Colvin, A.J. Taylor, *The History of the King's Works*, 2 vols. (London, 1963), vol. 2, p. 538.

[4] Ibid., vol. 1, p. 79.

[5] Denholm-Young, *Administration*, p. 5.

[6] *King's Works*, vol. 1, p. 79.

[7] C.H. Jenkinson and M.H. Mills, 'Rolls from a Sheriff's Office of the Fourteenth Century', *EHR* 43 (1928), pp. 21–32.

To what extent were purpose-built and designed buildings provided? The Exchequer and the undercroft of the lesser hall which became the court of requests at Westminster were among the earliest. At a local level a shire house was normally sited in the castle of the county town. The shire house of Norwich needed repair in 1240 and that at Northampton castle in 1392–93 contained two *abaci* with rails round them, benches, eighteen chests and tables.[8] Contemporary descriptions and building accounts indeed show that castles and great houses, royal and seignorial, did have specific administrative buildings and gaols. Within the outer bailey of Hereford castle in the thirteenth century were three halls: the king's great hall, the king's small hall and the shire hall (*aula comitatus*), a counting-house (*domus scaccarii*), two gaols, a building in which siege-engines were kept, and a chamber for the clerks.[9] In 1282 at Hope castle there was a chamber for the pay clerks 'camera ubi compota scribebantur et pacaciones fiebant' during the building works.[10] At Carisbrooke castle, there was an 'exchequer house' in 1352, and there were also chambers and wardrobes for the king's private clerks and for keeping his robes and his records.[11]

Few such buildings have survived. In some instances they have been replaced by more recent assize courts and county gaols. Elsewhere, the evidence has disappeared as castles and other medieval buildings have fallen into ruin or have been adapted to more congenial residential use. Frequently only the hall, chamber and kitchen have survived among the internal buildings by virtue of being better built and more prestigious; the lesser buildings more often than not have disappeared. The physical evidence for specialised buildings of an administrative nature is more likely to be obtained archaeologically from buried foundations and surviving fabric incorporated in later structures. Yet those studying castles have tended to concentrate their attentions on the military and defensive attributes, the architectural development, or the organisation of domestic planning.

Recently, however, two examples of administrative complexes have been described. The raised quadrangular building of the early twelfth century on the north-west side of the inner bailey of Old Sarum castle has

---

[8] M.H. Mills, 'The Medieval Shire House (Domus vicecomitis)', *Studies Presented to Sir Hilary Jenkinson* (London, 1957), pp. 254–71.

[9] *King's Works*, vol. 2, p. 675.

[10] Ibid., vol. 1, p. 332.

[11] Ibid., vol. 2, p. 593.

been identified as an administrative centre for the shire, which included, from an early date, a dwelling house of considerable dignity to accommodate the sheriff and his officials, and continued in use throughout the middle ages. The structure was interpreted as a 'keep' by its first excavators early in the present century, and by later scholars as Bishop Roger's palace.[12] The other example, a reassessment of the outer gatehouse (D'Ireby's tower) of Carlisle castle, shows how the rebuilding begun in 1378 had to combine defence with the important existing administrative functions performed in the gatehouse, which contained the sheriff's offices, his exchequer and the county gaol. As rebuilt, and in its surviving form, it contained a residence for the sheriff on the upper floor and accommodation for a gaoler and a gatekeeper or steward with a prison below.[13]

During the 1960s and 1970s archaeological excavations at castles of the earldom of Cornwall, at Launceston (Cornwall)[14] and Lydford (Devon),[15] produced evidence for the survival of two forms of specialised administrative building: a court-room or 'office', and a combined courtroom and prison. Both were built initially at the end of the twelfth century and were modified during the course of the thirteenth. Together with the late thirteenth-century duchy palace at Lostwithiel (Cornwall), they provide a visible, structural counterpart to the well documented administrative organisation of the duchy, created in 1337, and by implication for many of the customs and practices of the preceding earldom.[16]

Launceston castle, originally the castle of Dunheved, was one of two castles referred to in the Domesday survey for Cornwall.[17] Both were held by Robert, count of Mortain. It is likely that both Launceston and Trematon castles had their origins as campaign castles in the unsettled period following the siege and surrender of Exeter early in

[12] *Ancient and Historical Monuments in the City of Salisbury* (Royal Commission on the Historic Monuments of England 1, London, 1980), pp. 1–15.

[13] M.R. McCarthy, H.R.T. Summerson, and R.C. Annis, *Carlisle Castle: A Survey and Documentary History* (London, 1990), pp. 31–50.

[14] A.D. Saunders, interim reports on excavations at Launceston Castle, *Cornish Archaeology* 3 (1964), pp. 63–69; 9 (1970), pp. 83–92; 16 (1977), pp. 129–37.

[15] Idem, 'Lydford Castle, Devon', *Medieval Archaeology* 24 (1980), pp. 123–86.

[16] *The Caption of Seisin of the Duchy of Cornwall, 1337*, ed. P.L. Hull (Devon and Cornwall Record Society, new series 17, Torquay, 1971); *Ministers' Accounts of the Earldom of Cornwall 1296–1297*, ed. L.M. Midgley (Camden Third Series 66, London, 1942).

[17] *A History of the County of Cornwall*, ed. William Page (Victoria History of the Counties of England 8: 'The Domesday Survey for Cornwall', London, 1924).

1068, after which Brian of Brittany seems to have assumed the title of 'earl of Cornwall'.[18] This hypothesis receives some support from the archaeological evidence at Launceston castle. It may be this period which provided the basis for the extensive territorial holdings which Robert of Mortain received in 1076 after the forfeiture of Brian's fief, and which placed the count of Mortain in a similar position to that of the marcher lords in terms of concentration of economic and political power.[19]

There followed for Cornwall a period of consolidation. The castle at Dunheved was strengthened and probably extended in area, perhaps as a result of the exchange of lands with the bishop of Exeter recorded in 1086.[20] This provided space for a new town in an outer bailey necessitated by the count's action in removing the flourishing market from the canons of St. Stephen's established on the hilltop a mile away across the valley of the River Kensey. The physical shift in the economic centre of gravity was also reflected in the later transference of the place-name Lan-Stephen-tun to the present Launceston. For two hundred years or so Launceston castle was the administrative centre of what was to become in 1140 the earldom of Cornwall.

Archaeological excavation within the castle has provided detailed knowledge of a large area within the bailey. It included the site of the mid thirteenth-century great hall and its associated kitchen.[21] This was a hall intended for courts as well as ceremonial from the outset and which continued to be used for assizes until the beginning of the seventeenth century, when a new assize hall was built in the town. It had been built over the remains of a complex and extensive sequence of earlier structures.

In the period prior to the construction of the great hall, towards the end of the twelfth century, a long narrow, hall-like building, 62 ft. by 18 ft. internally, with a door towards the centre of its long, north wall, was set gable-end to the roadway leading from the South Gate. It would have been the first building to be met upon entering the castle from this direction. This 'lesser hall' was by no means an isolated structure. Another late twelfth-century building was sited alongside to the north, and it was close and at right angles to the immediate predecessor of the

---

[18] J. Tait, 'The First Earl of Cornwall', *EHR* 44 (1929), p. 86.

[19] I.N. Soulsby, 'Richard FitzTurold, Lord of Penhallam, Cornwall', *Medieval Archaeology* 20 (1976), pp. 146–48; also 'The Fiefs in England of the Counts of Mortain' (M.A. thesis, University of Wales, 1974).

[20] H.P.R. Finberg, 'The Castle of Cornwall', *Devon and Cornwall Notes and Queries* 23 (1949), p. 123.

[21] A.D. Saunders, *Launceston Castle, Cornwall* (London, 1984).

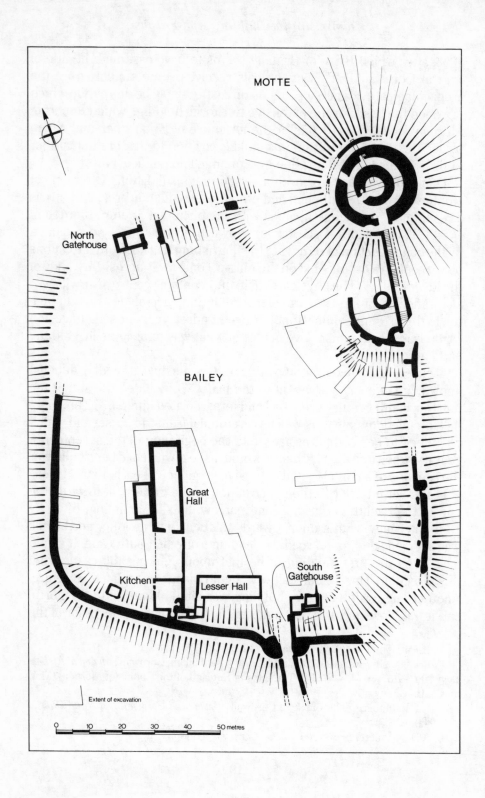

MOTTE

North
Gatehouse

BAILEY

Great
Hall

Kitchen

Lesser Hall

South
Gatehouse

Extent of excavation

0   10   20   30   40   50 metres

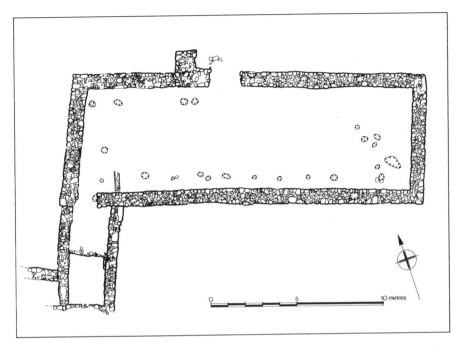

Fig. 3 (*left*) Launceston Castle: plan of the surviving thirteenth-century buildings in the excavated area of the bailey.

Fig. 4 (*above*) Launceston Castle: plan of the final phase of the Lesser Hall.

thirteenth-century great hall, which was itself a hall-like structure, 48 ft. by 22 ft., with an attached chamber block.

The lesser hall, inside the South Gate, was well built and its walls still stand up to 4 ft. high. It was a single-storey, free-standing structure, roofed in six bays, with the sockets for the uprights of the principal roof trusses, probably of cruck construction, set into the long walls. As well as having no attached chamber, it had no conventional provision for the service of food. It had been constructed on and over the remains of a substantial, twelfth-century building which had a hall, at least 40 ft. long and 17 ft. wide, and an end-chamber which may have been two-storeyed. This in turn had a timber-built predecessor.

The long, late twelfth-century lesser hall was a building which had at least three main periods of use until its demolition at the end of the thirteenth century. In its final phase during the mid thirteenth century, the hall was refurbished. The timber roof trusses were reset, the interior was replastered, and a line of ten postholes, close to and parallel with the south wall, were cut through the new floor surface as supports for benching. Seating was fixed round much of the long sides as well as at the upper end. At the lower (west) end of the hall there was a timber screen the impression of which still remained in the wall plaster and in a beam slot in the floor. This separated the entrance to a garderobe passage from the rest of the room. A doorway cut into the south wall gave on to a stone-built extension which contained a latrine pit. This pit was subsequently filled and floored over and replaced by another behind the back wall of the kitchen serving the great hall.

This large, distinctive and unusual building had a high level of use requiring the provision of a garderobe. Its plan and central hearth are not the characteristics of a domestic chamber. Its function seems to lie outside the normal residential and ceremonial attributes of the medieval hall. The high quality of the objects lost or broken within it and its immediate vicinity – a purse mount, buckles and other bronze fittings, fine glass-ware and dice – suggest that, for most of its life its social status was high. Its final form with benching round the walls, suggests a court-room or an administrative office. While the evidence for this interpretation is not as good for its earlier phase, it may have had a similar function. During most of the thirteenth century the lesser hall functioned alongside Richard of Cornwall's great hall and that of its predecessor on the same site. The lesser hall had, however, been deliberately demolished and its interior filled in by the end of the century. Its construction and period of use coincided with a general movement towards greater seignorial bureaucracy alongside an expansion of royal justice and its more effective organisation following the assize of Clarendon in 1166. The end of the building's life may have resulted from the transference of the earldom's administration, and that of the shire, to the purpose-built 'offices' at Lostwithiel by Edmund, earl of Cornwall in *c.* 1290. Presumably it then became superfluous. Launceston castle, or rather the honour of Launceston, remained thereafter the feudal capital of the county, including all lesser honours, and head of the Mortain fief. The feudal obligations were still owed to the castle in 1650 at the time of the parliamentary survey.[22] Launceston remained the place where the assizes were held until 1838, and the castle housed the county gaol.

The *Caption of Seisin of the Duchy of Cornwall* of 1337 mentions the court of wayternesse at the gate of the castle. A similar term *waite-fe* was a payment applied to Norwich castle and related to watchmen as was the case at Launceston.[23] This was otherwise known as the 'Court of the Gate' of the castle of Launceston. In his introduction to the 1971 edition, P.L. Hull quotes a case in Chancery of 1337 in respect of a dispute about the jurisdiction of the court of *Gayt* of the castle of Launceston which was formerly held, and 'ad quam quidem curiam homines residentes et terras et catalla habentes in feodis que sunt de tenura feodi de Gayt et non alij ad respondendos in eadem curia ad querelam alicuius venire consueuerint temporibus retractis'. The court of *Gayt* had been held at the gate of the castle of Launceston every three weeks 'a tempore a quo non extat memoria'.[24]

If the court of *Gayt* was associated with a particular gate at the castle there is a choice of two. That to the north was the gate to the town and was later to be the official residence of the constable. The South Gate gave access to the park and to the outside world and was perhaps more suitable for the feudal tenants. It is this gatehouse which was remodelled under Richard of Cornwall to provide the twin-towered frontispiece which is still the castle's grandest survival, apart from the keep itself. It may be no accident that the thirteenth-century lesser hall just described was sited where it is, immediately inside the south gate, and calls into question the function of its twelfth-century predecessor. There are other documentary references to courts held at castle gates. Excavations at Hen Domen

---

22 *The Parliamentary Survey of the Duchy of Cornwall*, ed. N.J.C. Pounds (Devon and Cornwall Record Society new series 25, Torquay, 1982).

23 J.H. Round, 'Castle Watchmen', *EHR* 35 (1920), pp. 400–1.

24 *The Caption of Seisin* (as n. 16), pp. xxiii–xxvi.

(Powys) have revealed the site of a subordinate hall just inside and with direct access from the bailey entrance which might have just such an association.[25]

Some twelve miles to the east of Launceston is Lydford castle on the western edge of Dartmoor. Lydford was the westernmost of the fortified *burhs* of the Saxon kingdom of Wessex, and at the time of the Norman Conquest it was one of the four boroughs of Devon and the site of a mint. An earth and timber castle was subsequently erected within the borough defences but its occupation was short-lived, not extending beyond the middle of the twelfth century.[26] The present 'castle' is to all appearances a small tower set on an earth mound, away from the Norman earthwork and closer to the centre of the village. It seems from the start to have been built as a prison and was to belong to the earldom of Cornwall, and the duchy thereafter, providing both courtroom and prison throughout the later middle ages and more fitfully into the eighteenth century.[27] Lydford had a key role in the administration of the royal forest of Dartmoor. It was also, from an early date, the administrative centre for the stannaries (tin industry) of Devon whose profits had come under closer royal control by the end of the twelfth century.[28] In 1195 £32 from the revenues of the Devon stannaries and £42 from those of Cornwall were spent 'in operatione unius domus firme ad custodiendos prisones R. in villa de Lideford'.[29]

The present castle is not all it seems. Excavations have established two distinct building phases. The first structure was substantial, 52 ft. square, with walls more than 10 ft. thick. It was more than one storey high for there was no ground level entrance. The ground floor, which is all that remains of this phase, was very secure. It was lit only by narrow, splayed loops and was divided into two unequal parts by a cross wall with the larger of the two rooms containing a well.

This initial structure was drastically rebuilt fifty or sixty years later, during the thirteenth century, perhaps having gone into serious ruin in

[25] P. Barker and R. Higham, *Hen Domen, Montgomery: A Timber Castle on the English–Welsh Border*, vol. 1 (n.p., 1982).

[26] P.V. Addyman, note on excavations within Norman fort, *Medieval Archaeology* 10 (1966), pp. 196–97.

[27] Saunders, 'Lydford Castle' (as n. 15).

[28] C.R. Lewis, *The Stannaries* (Cambridge, Mass., 1908) R.L. Pennington, *Stannary Law: A History of the Mining Law of Cornwall and Devon* (Newton Abbot, 1973).

[29] *The Great Roll of the Pipe for the Seventh Year of the Reigh of King Richard the First, Michaelmas 1195* (Pipe Roll Society New Series 6, London, 1924), pp. 125 and 132.

the meantime. Its walls were crudely levelled off at about first-floor level and a new building, two storeys high, with much thinner walls was added on top of the earlier masonry. A deep circular ditch was dug outside, and the spoil mounded up around the earlier building completely masking it, creating the illusion that the new tower was built on top of a mound or motte. Perhaps to maintain this illusion, the original ground floor was then filled up and floored over, except for a small 'cellar' contrived in the northern corner. By the time this reconstruction took place, the correlation between Lydford castle and the stannary prison was well established. There is a strong presumption that the earlier structure concealed within the later 'castle' is the remains of the *firme domus* of 1195.

The well-preserved shell of its successor demonstrates the operation of a purpose-built medieval prison and judicial centre whose discrete functions are documentarily attested and whose character is graphically described by some of its inmates. The principal room on the second floor was certainly the hall or court room with its own access by stairs from an entrance lobby. It was heated by a fireplace in the cross-wall and had its own garderobe. The smaller room on the other side of the cross-wall, perhaps divided by wooden partitions, could have provided accommodation for the resident keeper or gaoler. It too had a garderobe. The rooms below would have been used for various grades of prisoner according to medieval practice.[30] The large room below the hall was probably the general prison and was entered by a door from the entrance lobby. It was poorly lit but did possess a privy beneath that of the courtroom, using the same shaft. The two smaller rooms on the other side of the cross-wall did not possess such conveniences, and the smaller of the two had nothing more than a ventilation opening rather than a narrow window. Finally, below the smaller of these rooms, was the cellar or 'pit', which had remained unfilled in the northern corner of the twelfth-century building, and was presumably reserved for the worst category of prisoner. It was surely this 'pit' which was so hatefully described by Sir Richard Strode in 1510.[31]

There remains the puzzle of the manner in which the prison was rebuilt. The archaeological evidence from the filling of the lower storey points to this taking place during the thirteenth century and perhaps

---

[30] R.B. Pugh, *Imprisonment in Medieval England* (Cambridge, 1968), pp. 347–73.

[31] R.N. Worth, 'Lydford and its Castle', *Transactions of the Devonshire Association* 11 (1879), p. 244.

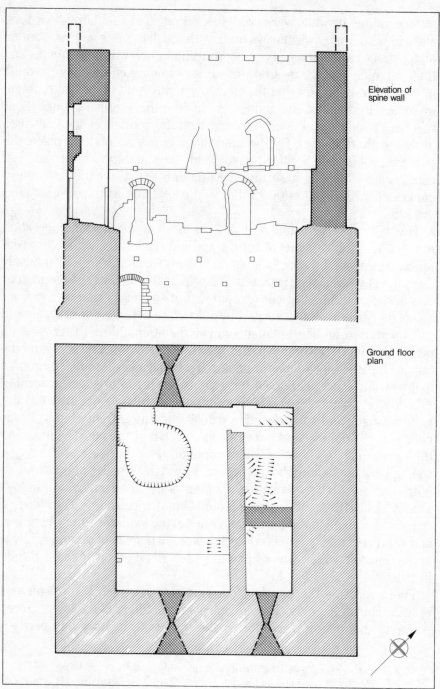

Elevation of spine wall

Ground floor plan

Fig. 5 Lydford Castle: the three floor plans together with a cross-section of the tower and elevation of the spine wall.

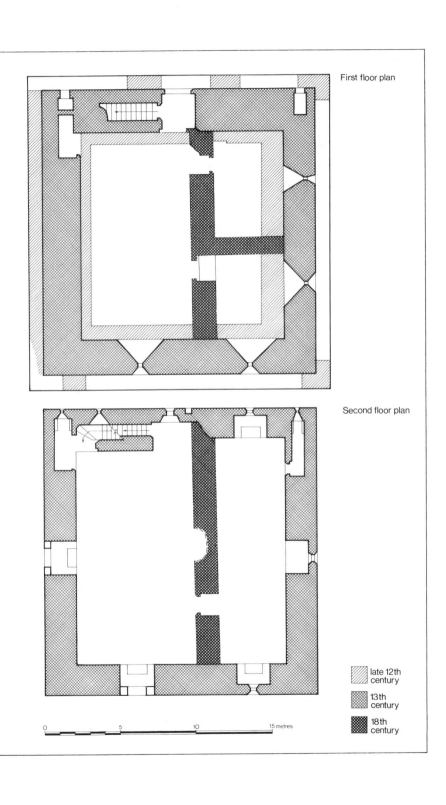

First floor plan

Second floor plan

late 12th
century

13th
century

18th
century

0   5   10   15 metres

during the lengthy period of the earldom of Richard of Cornwall. In 1267 Henry III granted Richard a Wednesday market at Lydford and a fair, and this attempt to revive the faltering economy of Lydford may well have coincided with the rebuilding of the prison.[32] Yet although it continued to be called 'castle' it was used solely as a prison and court house. The creation of a motte and miniature bailey was perhaps a deliberate anachronistic conceit to give visual confirmation of the title of Lydford castle, while at the same time, manifesting the lordship and authority of the earl of Cornwall and his control of the stannaries and the forest or chase of Dartmoor.

The other purpose-built administrative building of the earldom is the remarkable but, since the seventeenth century, ruinous Duchy Palace at Lostwithiel.[33] It was built around 1290 at the instigation of Earl Richard's son, Edmund. It was he who also refurbished neighbouring Restormel castle to a standard appropriate, after due repair, for the Black Prince to stay there in 1354. The main range of this administrative complex extended north-south beside the river and consisted of the great hall, 110 ft. in length and 24 ft. wide, and two storeys high. It was comparable in size with the great hall of Winchester castle, and was only a little smaller than that at Eltham Palace and Westminster Hall itself. Attached to it was a smaller hall, known in recent times as the 'convocation' hall, a structure of three storeys. To the west of this range and towards the town were other buildings for which there is now no evidence: a 'blowing house' for the assaying and smelting of tin and a 'weighing house'. Also in this area was the gaol for the Cornish stannaries. Besides this there was limited living accommodation for officials.

The move towards establishing Lostwithiel as the centre of the earldom's administration and chief seat of its authority within the county was begun by Richard of Cornwall, despite his expensive remodelling of Launceston castle. He had already moved the county court from the castle to Bodmin.[34] In 1268–69 he acquired part of the manor of Bodardle together with Restormel castle from Isolda de Cardinham. This process of consolidation of the earldom's land holdings in the vicinity was continued by his son Edmund.[35] Father and son were, no doubt, influenced by

[32] Ibid.

[33] N.J.C. Pounds, 'The Duchy Palace at Lostwithiel, Cornwall', *The Archaeological Journal* 136 (1979), pp. 203–17.

[34] *Caption of Seisin* (as n. 15), p. xliv.

[35] C. Henderson, 'Lostwithiel', *Essays in Cornish History* (Oxford, 1935), pp. 44–48.

Fig. 6 The Duchy Palace, Lostwithiel: the south-east view engraved by Samuel and Nathaniel Buck, 1734.

Lostwithiel's central location in the county, its close relationship to the then richest tin-bearing areas and its position at the navigable head of the River Fowey.

The administrative functions of the duchy, upon its creation in 1337, have been extensively examined.[36] Thus defined they probably differed little from those operating in the earldom during the previous century, much of it, if not all, carried out from Launceston castle before the move to Lostwithiel.[37] The latter was now the base for the administration of the duchy lands in the south-west which were 'governed more or less as an English shire'.[38] Here the steward exercised the functions of sheriff on the duke's behalf; the receiver acted as collector of the ducal revenues; the feodary supervised the duke's feudal rights and perquisites and was normally the constable of Launceston castle as well; the havenor, while based on Fowey, sent much of the duke's prise of wine to the Lostwithiel cellars and also acted as the weigher of tin at the duchy coinages and keeper of the tinners' gaol; and then there were the auditors who kept the duchy accounts. These officials were supported by assistants and other staff. The palace also served as the county court whose perquisites belonged to the duke.[39] The knights of the shire were elected here until the Reform Act of 1832. Lostwithiel was also the earliest coinage town in Cornwall, where much of the tin extracted in the county was assayed, stamped and weighed for export. The coinage usually took place twice a year under the supervision of the controller of the stannary.[40] There was a long history of fitful maintenance of the Duchy Palace which Leland was to describe as the 'ruines of auncyent buyldinges' beside the shire hall.[41] The Buck engraving of 1734 shows the great hall in ruins and, to

[36] M. Coate, 'The Duchy of Cornwall: Its History and Administration', *Transactions of the Royal Historical Society*, fourth series 10 (1927), pp. 135–69; M. Sharp, 'The Administrative Chancery of the Black Prince before 1362', *Essays in Medieval History Presented to Thomas Frederick Tout*, eds. A.C. Little and F.M. Powicke (Manchester, 1925), pp. 321–33 and 'The Central Administrative System of Edward the Black Prince', *Chapters in the Administrative History of Medieval England*, ed. T.F. Tout (Manchester, 1930), vol. 5, p. 321; S.M. Campbell, 'The Haveners of the Medieval Dukes of Cornwall and the Organization of the Duchy Ports', *Journal of the Royal Institution of Cornwall*, New Series 4/2 (1962), pp 113–43; *The Caption of Seisin* (as n. 15).

[37] *Ministers' Accounts* (as n. 16).

[38] Pounds, 'Lostwithiel' (as n. 33), p. 206.

[39] *Register of Edward the Black Prince* (London, 1931), pt. 2, p. 18.

[40] Lewis, *Stanneries* (as n. 28).

[41] L. Toulmin Smith (ed.), *Leland's Itinerary in England and Wales* (London, 1909), p. 323.

the north of it, the smaller hall, where the convocation of tinners met and courts were held.

These three buildings of the earldom of Cornwall are, in their respective ways, remarkable survivals; not least because they were all constructed within a century of each other by a single authority. Surviving examples of medieval administrative buildings of this nature in England are rare or not yet identified, although other honours and large estates must have required similar facilities.

Purpose-built prison buildings are the most distinctive. Pugh has observed that 'imprisonment in England has no connected history before the end of the twelfth century'.[42] There were, however, prisons before that. Penal imprisonment existed as part of ecclesiastical discipline and it was also a statutory element in forest law. The assize of Clarendon of 1166 set out general instructions on gaol provision, and in the next year sheriffs were told that they must site their gaols in one of the king's boroughs or castles. The Pipe Rolls provide evidence for widespread gaol construction in 1166, resulting in sixteen counties each having one gaol, and a further three having at least two apiece. There was another spurt in construction in the 1180s.[43] The sheriff of Cornwall planted a gaol at Helston in 1184–85,[44] and another in the castle at Launceston in 1186–87.[45] The county gaol for Devon was in Exeter castle, built in 1181–82.[46] When the forest laws were strenuously enforced, efforts were made in some regions to construct special forest prisons such as the gaol in Kinver forest, Staffordshire (1195–96), and for Galtre forest, Yorkshire (1216).[47]

The construction of the strong house at Lydford fits this pattern of prison building, serving as it did both the Forest of Dartmoor and the stannary for Devon, and perhaps for Cornwall as well in the first instance. Most prisons of the time, however, seem to have been timber-built, and

[42] Pugh, *Imprisonment* (as n. 30), p. 1.

[43] R.B. Pugh, 'The King's Prisons before 1250', *Transactions of the Royal Historical Society*, fifth series 5 (1955), p. 2.

[44] *The Great Roll of the Pipe for the Thirty-First Year of the Reign of King Henry the Second, AD 1184–1185* (Pipe Roll Society 33, London, 1913), p. 200.

[45] *The Great Roll of the Pipe for the Thirty-Third Year of the Reign of King Henry the Second AD 1186–1187* (Pipe Roll Society 36, London, 1915), p. 154, 'Et in operatione gaiole in castello de Lanzauenton'.

[46] Pugh, *Imprisonment* (as n. 30), p. 130–31.

[47] *The Great Roll of the Pipe for the Twenty-Eighth Year of the Reign of King Henry the Second, AD 1181–1182* (Pipe Roll Society 30, London, 1910).

on the evidence of the Pipe Rolls could cost as little as £2 to £5.[48] The expensive (£74) stone-built gaol at Lydford is something of an exception, perhaps because it was also a court house, and this may explain its survival. In its thirteenth-century reconstructed form it is still the earliest purpose built prison in England.

There are indeed very few medieval prisons surviving in England, as distinct from those elements of castles which were used as prisons. Pugh identified three: the Manor Office at Hexham: the former gaol of the liberty of Ely at Ely, and Lydford.[49] Dalton castle can be added to this list. Both the Manor Office, Hexham, and Dalton castle are, however, of fourteenth-century or later construction. Yet they do have similarities in scale and internal planning with Lydford castle. Dalton castle is the closest parallel. Although it has the appearance of a pele it is thought to have been built and maintained as a prison by the abbots of Furness Abbey.[50] A charter of 1127 conferred on the abbot the power to hold court and administer justice, and an earlier prison was referred to at Dalton in 1257. At the Dissolution, the castle became crown property. It was referred to in 1545: 'Heretofore has always been used as a prison and common gaol for the whole lordship and dominion of Fourneux (Furness) and the liberties there.'[51] It is a rectangular tower, 45 ft. by 30 ft. and 40 ft. high. The basement was sub-divided, as was the unlit first floor. The two upper floors were open, and that on the top floor was the court room.

The Manor Office at Hexham is more elongated in plan, about 80 ft. long by 33 ft. broad with walls 9 ft. thick. It has its origins in an instruction from Archbishop Melton of York to the receiver of Hexham in 1330 to build a gaol; followed in the next year by an order to the steward to furnish the gaol with chains, manacles and all things necessary for the repair of the building and the safeguarding of prisoners. The ground floor is divided by a cross-wall into two unlit, equal parts, with a vaulted 'pit' below the north room.[52] The upper floors had a single room each but these have been much altered. There is, however, a garderobe. Of the other possible prison buildings, Pugh reported of the Ely liberty

[48] *King's Works* (as n. 3), vol. 2, pp. 977–78.
[49] Pugh, 'King's Prisons' (as n. 43), pp. 13–14.
[50] Pugh, *Imprisonment* (as n. 30), p. 364.
[51] J. Melville, 'Dalton Castle', *Archaeological Journal* 127 (1970), p. 266–67.
[52] *Pleadings and Depositions, Duchy Court of Lancaster II* (Lancashire and Cheshire Record Society 35, n.p., 1897), p. 204.

that it had some medieval walling remaining and that its plan may have medieval origins; but much of the present fabric is of the eighteenth and nineteenth centuries.[53]

The closest functional analogy with Lydford castle is St. Briavel's castle in the Forest of Dean.[54] This castle acted as administrative and judicial centre for the laws and customs of the forest and for the iron miners who enjoyed a special status. It also was the centre for the manufacture of cross-bow quarrels. The much altered hall and solar range to the south of the 'Edwardian' gatehouse is on two floors, and the ground floor, with its several doorways from the courtyard, may well have served some administrative purpose. The courts themselves would be held in the hall above. The projecting chapel, in later centuries, contained a court and jury room below and there are traces of a prison in the gatehouse.

Surviving buildings constructed for administrative functions other than those of a gaol are more difficult to identify. There are, however, some parallels with the lesser hall at Launceston which perhaps support the claim for its special purpose, and provide the beginnings of a corpus of buildings which do not fit the conventional residential hall and chamber mode. Their distinguishing characteristics are hall-like plans having much greater length relative to breadth, no attached chamber, no ready access to a kitchen or for the provision of food but sufficiently intensive use to require heating and an attached garderobe or latrine. They are also buildings which may exhibit a degree of architectural refinement. There is also a tendency for these halls to be close or attached to the ceremonial great hall, or beside an entrance to the castle or house.

Faulkner, having defined the basic requirements for a medieval household as a hall and chamber block, goes on to stress that the domestic planning of castles may involve individual accommodation for several households, perhaps up to six or seven within a single establishment, for which a multiplication of halls is a natural corollary.[55] There are, nevertheless, instances where hall-like buildings may not be residential if they have no immediately connected chamber block. Just such a case occurs among Faulkner's examples. At Goodrich castle, four halls are identified and he acknowledges that the East Hall 'departs somewhat from the

[53] *A History of Northumberland* (Newcastle-upon-Tyne, 1896), vol. 3, pp. 225–26, 232–33.

[54] Pugh, *Imprisonment* (as n. 30), p. 365.

[55] P.E. Curnow and E.A. Johnson, 'St. Briavels Castle', *Chateau Gaillard* 12 (1985), pp. 91–114.

pattern so far noted in that it has an entrance at either end and is separated from its chambers in the South–East tower by a lobby'. It is, however, explicable as communal accommodation for guests of noble rank in the train of a principal guest or owner. An alternative interpretation is the more mundane administrative one, particularly as the hall in question lies immediately beside the gatehouse and has ready accessibility. It is not closely related to the more private and ceremonial elements of the castle. While it is separated from sets of residential chambers, it does have direct access to a garderobe. At Ludlow castle, which as the centre for the administration of the marches might be expected to have accommodation for clerks, courts and auditors. The early fourteenth-century great hall serves three chamber blocks.[56] This complex architectural conception may have been wholly residential but there is a particular room west of and on the same level as the hall which seems to have a more public dimension. It is at the low end of the hall and has two entrances, one from the hall itself, and significantly, a doorway from the porch before the main entrance to the hall. There is a fireplace and the room has its own garderobe as well as access to a fighting gallery in a projecting tower. It is unconnected with the chamber above, which is approached separately from the hall. This room is therefore distinct from the rest of the block, with public access either from the hall or direct from the courtyard. It is unlike the residential chambers elsewhere in the range, and well placed to fulfil an official role.

At Okehampton castle (Devon), a door from the gatehouse allows access to a small awkwardly shaped room in the angle between the gatehouse and the hall. It is believed to have served as an ante-room for those attending business in the hall, with a chamber for an official above.[57]

We are on stronger ground at establishments such as Clarendon palace and Old Sarum where administrative functions are well attested. At Clarendon a chancery is mentioned in the mid thirteenth century. In a survey of 1315 are listed among many buildings: the chamber for the chancellor and the clerks of the chancery; the chamber of the chaplain and of the clerks of the king and queen; and a further two chambers for clerks.[58] Administrative buildings are thought to have occupied the

---

[56] P.A. Faulkner, 'Castle Planning in the Fourteenth Century', *Archaeological Journal* 120 (1963), pp. 215–35.

[57] P.A. Faulkner, 'Domestic Planning from the Twelfth to the Fourteenth Centuries', *Archaeological Journal* 115 (1958), pp. 177–79.

[58] R.A. Higham, *Okehampton Castle* (London, 1984).

north-west range of the great courtyard of the palace. The long, narrow range is divided into two rooms (3a and 3b) with a small lobby between them. Room 3a has an attached garderobe. Architectural refinements indicate that these were not humdrum stores, workshops or stables. The report also suggests that the long structure (6a) on the southern side of the great courtyard may have been stables but this too has an architectural style suggesting use by persons of some, if not grand, status. There is a garderobe (6c) between it and a building with a fine fireplace which has been labelled 'The Old Hall' (6b) and which, it has been suggested, may have been the treasurer's chamber. All three buildings interconnect with a common lobby. An administrative function seems a reasonable hypothesis.

The great courtyard building at Old Sarum castle has been interpreted as the sheriff's residence and administrative centre for the shire.[59] His hall and great chamber were at first floor level. Below, and entered directly from the courtyard, are long narrow rooms on the south and east. The south-eastern angle is occupied by a chapel with another chapel on the floor above. On either side are rooms which are not domestic, although that to the east interconnects with both the chapel and a kitchen. The south range is divided into two rooms with benching along the north wall. There is a later hearth in the north-east corner and windows in the south wall. This suggests nothing so much as an office range on the south side with a further office or clerks' 'mess room' on the east.

At Hadleigh castle (Essex), it is tempting to see the 'nova longa domus juxta posternam castri' of *c.* 1312–13 as the long room, 41 ft. by 11 ft.,[60] built across the low end of the Phase III hall and solar.[61] Only the barest plan of the building had survived in the ground record, and it has been tentatively interpreted as the buttery, but its size, its position alongside the postern, and the fact that it has an associated garderobe suggest that it was a room more associated with the business functions of the great hall.

Hexham Moot Hall may be the only other substantially surviving parallel to the great office block at Lostwithiel. The present building was erected between 1355 and 1439 for the archbishop of York. There were two halls above and beside the gate passage. The lower one was for courts

---

59 T.B. James and A.M. Robinson, *Clarendon Palace: The History and Archaeology of a Medieval Palace and Hunting Lodge near Salisbury, Wiltshire* (Society of Antiquaries Research Report 45, London, 1988).

60 *City of Salisbury* (as n. 12), pp. 8–14.

61 Public Record Office, Exchequer Ministers' accounts SC 6/843/4.

and the upper hall, together with a solar, was for the archbishop's official. The building had a long history of use for court leats and the three week court.[62]

Another example of an office or business centre combined with a gate-house is that at Thornton Abbey, Humberside. It is 'the new house over and about the gate' for which there was a licence to crenellate in 1382.[63] This has a large apartment with an oriel window over the gate passage; Clapham believed it to be the abbot's lodging, a theory which Baillie-Reynolds dismissed because of the lack of kitchen or domestic offices.[64] A court room might be a better explanation. It and the room on the floor above are connected to an elaborate system of wall passages serving small chambers with occasional fireplaces and garderobes, in which there are the impressions in the wall plaster of shelving and partitions. There are wall chambers above these at second-floor level which can have been accessible only by ladder and were perhaps intended for the storing of records.

Buildings which appear to have been designed for some special administrative purpose, whether for courts or offices for clerks, deserve greater attention from archaeologists and architectural historians. Some, such as the lesser hall at Launceston castle, may serve as an archaeological model for future comparison. When their characteristics are more widely recognised it is probable that the few examples discussed here will be seen to represent only a small sample of those surviving.

---

[62] P.L. Drewett, 'Excavations at Hadleigh Castle, Essex, 1971–72', *Journal of the British Archaeological Association*, series 3 35 (1975), pp. 90–154.

[63] *History of Northumberland* (as n. 52), vol. 3, p. 226, 232–36.

[64] Sir Alfred Clapham, *Thornton Abbey, Lincolnshire* (London, 1956).

Index

Index

Ryarsh 14

Saint-Amand, monastery 30
Saint-Bénigne, monastery 48
Saint-Dié, monastery 49, 50, 57
Saint-Evre, monastery 44, 45, 46, 47, 52,
    53, 55, 56, 59
    as burial-place for bishops of Toul 54
Saint-Gengoul, monastery 46, 57
Saint-Mansuy, monastery 44, 45, 47, 48,
    52, 54, 55
Saint-Martin, petty monastery on the
    Meuse 46
Saint-Mihiel, monastery 48
saints, Anglo-Saxon
    late medieval cult of 108
    Norman attitudes to 95–99, 108
    revival of interest in by Normans 107
    veneration of 95
Saladin, capture of Jerusalem by 110
Salzburg,
    annals of xiii
    archbishop of 75–77
        military following of 83
        military service by 86
    St. Peter's, abbot of 82
Sampiro, bishop of Astorga,
    as royal servant 131
    chronicle, account of tenth-century
        Leonese kings 136
        account of Vermudo II 136, 137
        autobiographical passages in 137
        depiction of Christian-Muslim
            conflicts in 133, 134, 136
        and *Reconquista* 131, 137
Sánchez-Albornoz, Claudio,
    views on *Reconquista* 140
    views on Spanish history 141,
        142, 143
Sancho García I of Navarre, campaign
    of 920 by 128
Sancho I, 'the Fat' king of León, 134
    deserts to Muslims 136
Sancho the Great, king of Navarre,
    imperial titles of 138
Sarum, Use of 106
Saucourt, battle at 38
Saxons, invasion of Britain by 23
Sayn castle 92
Scotland, kings of 24
Scots 24
    Edward II's failure in wars with 180,
        185
    raiding by 184, 185, 194
scutage 84, 86, 87

Severin, St., Life of 75
Shipbourne 14
Shorne 14
Siegburg, monastery 71, 72
Siegfried, archbishop of Mainz 65
Sigebert of Gemgloux, historian 61
Simeon of Durham, historian 38
Snodland 5, 6
Soissons, translation of relics of Gregory
    the Great to 104
Southfleet 15
Spain,
    history of,
        as 'feudal' 142, 143
        determined by Christian, Muslim
            and Jewish influences 126
        European characteristics 128
        Moorish influences on 127
        peculiarities of 123, 124, 141
        Roman 124
        Visigothic 124
    idea of unity of 131
    see also Reconquista
Speyer, bishop,
    involved in feud 86
    military service by 87
St. Benet of Holme, monastery 151
    hereditary stewards of 150
        duties of 154, 155, 158
        elimination of 160, 161
St. Briavel's castle, as administrative
    centre 213
St David's, bishopric,
    hereditary stewards of 149, 161
    duties of 156, 158
St. Neots, monastery, calendar of 104
St. Veit, military following of abbot of 82
stannaries of Devon and Cornwall,
    administration 204
    prisons 207, 210, 211
Stansted 14
Stephen, bishop of Toul 51
Stephen, king 151
Stephen of Valence, priest, vision of 113
stewards, ecclesiastical,
    and seignorial courts 155–57
    as estate managers 157
    as representatives of their churches
        155–57
    hereditary 146–54
        elimination of 159, 160, 162
        functions of 154
        prohibition of 158, 159
        reaction against 158
        survival of 161

227

List of Subscribers

Prof. Richard Abels
Eric Michael Ainley
Anthony J. Anderson
Dr. Benjamin Arnold
David Ashcroft
C. J. Aubrey
C. P. Baird
The Rt. Hon. Kenneth Baker
Dr. Julia Barrow
D. G. F. Barry
Neil Beckett
The Hon. Michael Beloff
Matthew Bennett
Robert L. Benson
Prof. M. Biddle
P. J. W. Black
Charles Boase
Christopher Bobinski
A. R. Bonner
Prof. Dr. Hartmut Boockmann
David D. C. Braine
Dr. Paul Brand
Prof. C. and Dr. R. Brooke
Prof. N. P. Brooks
Prof. Dr. C. Brühl
G. J. M. Buckley
Prof. D. A. Bullough
Prof. Dr. Neithard Bulst
C. Butcher
Ronald J. Caffrey
Angus Campbell
James Campbell
R. Carmichael
M. D. Chataway
Giles Constable
Kate Cooper
H. E. J. Cowdrey
Richard Crewdson
Dr. J. C. Crick
David Croom
Dr. Katy Cubitt
D. Curley
A. S. Dalton
Prof. J. Denton
Richard Eales
Prof. Dr. Imme Eberl
Jasper Evans
Lucy Fergusson
Dr. Felipe Fernández–Armesto
R. A. Fletcher
Dr. Sarah R. I. Foot

J. Fox
S. J. Fraser
David Ganz
George Garnett
Dr. John Gillingham
A. N. Golding
Dr. S. J. D. Green
Prof. P. Grierson
D. C. R. Grieve
Dr. Gerald Harriss
Miss Barbara F. Harvey
R. A. Hathaway
Francis Haydon
John Hayward
Lord Henderson
Nigel Higgins
Dr. J. R. L. Highfield
Prof. Christopher Holdsworth
Prof. N. Housley
Michael Hurst
Paul R. Hyams
George Ireland
Miles Jebb
The Rev. Canon Roger Job
Prof. Michael Jones
Dr D. J. Keene
Bernand Kelly
Michael A. Kenny
Graham Kent
Dr. Sigrid Krämer
Keith Kyle
Robin Leanse
W. J. Leedham
Andrew Lewis
Peter Lewis
Conrad Leyser
E. W. Lister
The Rev. Canon J. R. Little
Dr. B. B. Lloyd
Prof. Derek W. Lomax
Dr. G. A. Loud
J. R. Lowen
J. D. Lynn
Dr. Peter Mandler
The Rev. J. W. Masding
A. Maycock
Dr. R. McKitterick
W. H. Mealing
Tim Miller
T. E. Mills
R. I. Moore

D. A. L. Morgan
C. P. Mould
Dr. M. E. Mullett
S. J. Munro
Janet L. Nelson
Michael Nelson
Rosalind Nicholson
Dr John Nightingale
Prof. Thomas F. X. Noble
Prof. N. I. Orme
Eva Osborne
Dr. John Palmer
Dr. Peter Partner
Prof. Richard W. Pfaff
Mark Philpott
Charles E. P. Plowden
A. J. Presswell
Prof. Michael Prestwich
N. L. Ramsay
Dr. Timothy Reuter
James Rivington
Irfon Roberts
Andrew Robinson
The Rt. Hon. Lord Rodgers
Prof. Randall Rogers
Andrew Saunders
M. B. Sayers
N. D. Sayers
Andrew Scarborough
The Earl of Scarborough
Prof. Dr. P. G. Schmidt
Prof. Dr. B. Schneidmuller
Prof. Dr. Josef Semmler
Dr. Richard Sharpe

David Schonfield
A. A. W. Sich
Andrew M. Smith
J. M. Smith
Dr. Julia M. H. Smith
David G. F. A. X. Soskin
Margaret Sparks
N. E. Stacy
John Steane
Charles G. T. Stonehill
J. W. Stoye
John Sturgess
J. J. Suich
Roderick C. Thomas
Michael Tidy
David S. Tomlinson
David Treffry
Dr. C. J. Tyerman
Richard Walker
Roger Watkins
Dr. Teresa Webber
Robin Webster
Prof. Dr. S. Weinfurter
M. A. J. Wheeler-Booth
Dr. Mark Whittow
Dr. C. J. Wickham
W. Wigglesworth
R. P. Wilkinson
Eric Wolf
Robert G. E. Wood
Dr. I. N. Wood
The Rev. Eric Woods
Adrian Wright
Prof. Dr. H. Zimmerman